Stanley

From Arkwright Village to Commuter Suburb: 1784–2003

Anthony Cooke

ISBN 0 905452 38 0

Published by
Perth & Kinross Libraries
AK Bell Library
York Place
Perth
PH2 8EP

PERTH &
KINROSS
COUNCIL

Printed by
Cordfall Ltd
0141 572 0878

For Judith, with love

And in memory of my Grandmother, Annie Hughes

Contents

	List of Illustrations	6
	Acknowledgements	7
1.	**Houses and Offices in a Tasty Stile**	11
	Land Ownership and Agricultural Change	
2.	**An Erect and Outlooking Spirit Abroad**	21
	Factory Villages and the Scottish Cotton Industry	
3.	**Several Gentlemen in the Mercantile Line in Perth**	39
	The Foundation of Stanley Mills and the Arkwright Connection, 1784–1800	
4.	**A Positive Greedy Fellow**	72
	James Craig, David Dale, Robert Owen, and the Dale Trustees, 1800–1823	
5.	**The Spirited Proprietors**	99
	The Buchanans of Glasgow, 1823–1852	
6.	**The Memory of the Just is Blessed**	107
	Samuel Howard and his Trustees, 1852–1876	
7.	**The Secret Room**	110
	The Sandemans and Diversification, 1876–1921	
8.	**Stanley Mills has a Way With Women**	116
	From Jute Industries to Stanley Mills (Scotland) and Closure, 1921–1989	
9.	**Sober, Virtuous and Industrious**	120
	The Stanley Workforce	
10.	**Rational and Praiseworthy Amusements**	130
	Education, Religion and Social History	
11.	**Postscript**	135
	Commuter Suburb and Heritage Site—Stanley Today	
	Appendix 1: Valuations of Stanley Mills	140
	Bibliography	142
	Index	152

List of Illustrations

Old Mill, Stanley (Anthony Cooke)   cover

James Stobie's Map of Perthshire, 1805 (Perth and Kinross Libraries)   10

Stanley House, c.1880 (Perth Museum)   12

John Murray, 4ᵗʰ Duke of Atholl (1755–1830)   17
  (Sir Thomas Lawrence, Perth Museum)

Richard Arkwright (1732–1793) (Joseph Wright of Derby)   32

George Dempster of Dunnichen, MP (1732–1818) (George Willison)   52

James Stobie's Plan of Stanley Mill Lade, 1785 (Atholl Mss.)   55

Contract of Co-Partnery, Stanley Mills, 1 January 1787   56
  (National Archives of Scotland)

William Sandeman of Luncarty (1722–1790) (artist unknown)   60

Duchess Street, Stanley, c.1900 (National Monuments Record of Scotland)   62

Summons, Royal Bank of Scotland against   90
  the Stanley Company, 1816(National Archives of Scotland)

Patrick MacNaughton's Plan of the Lands of Stanley, 1823 (Atholl Mss.)   94/95

Store Street, Stanley, 1968 (NMRS)   100

Colonel Frank Stewart Sandeman, mill owner,   110
  outside Beech House, Stanley, c.1890 (Mrs. Amess, Perth)

'Jeek' Gunn, village bellman, Stanley, c.1890 (Perth Museum)   113

Insurance Plan of Stanley Mills by Allen Mellor,   114
  Valuers, Oldham, June 1911 (NMRS)

Construction of Turbine House at Stanley Mills, 1921   117
  (the late John Culbert, Stanley)

All-female trade union committee, Stanley Mills, 1915 (Anthony Cooke)   126

Curling on the frozen Tay, Stanley, 1895 or 1897 (Mrs. Sim, Stanley)   134

East Mill, Stanley during renovation by Phoenix Trust, 2000 (Anthony Cooke) 136

Water Wheel Pits by Old Mill, Stanley, 2002 (Anthony Cooke)   138

Acknowledgements

This book has its origins in my thirty year interest in industrial history in general and the history of Stanley Mills in particular. I first became aware of the existence of Stanley when I took up an academic post at Dundee University in 1969. As a Lancastrian, I was intrigued by the survival of a cotton mill so far north, and one with such an extraordinary history, involving Richard Arkwright, David Dale and Robert Owen, amongst others.

Anyone who writes a book of this kind, owes a great debt to other people. My first contact with Stanley was through the affable James Mair, then Public Relations Officer with Jute Industries, now of Mair Wilkes Books. He provided access to the records held by Jute Industries and arranged my first visit to Stanley. At Stanley Mills, the manager, the late Bert Stott, and his assistant, John Shaw, were models of hospitality and very patient in answering my elementary questions about the practicalities of textile production. Their successor at Stanley, Colin Dracup, was also very supportive of the Mills' heritage.

My access to the rich archives at Blair Castle was smoothed by the factor of the Atholl Estates, Major Munro, and by three archivists—Margaret Stephen of Aberdeen University, the late Joan Auld, then Archivist of the Eastern Survey of the National Register of Archives, later of Dundee University, and Jane Anderson, of Blair Castle Archives. I am grateful to librarians and archivists at Dundee and Edinburgh Universities, the National Archives of Scotland, the National Library of Scotland, the General Register Office for Scotland, the National Monuments Record, and the Guildhall Library, London. Jeremy Duncan and Steven Connolly, of Perth and Kinross Libraries, have been particularly helpful over the years.

Ann Thompson of Abernyte, who chose Stanley for her Open University dissertation, shared her enthusiasm with me. Another enthusiast for Stanley was John Hume, formerly of Historic Scotland, whose deep knowledge of industrial history and interest in Stanley Mills led eventually to the Heritage Lottery Fund grant for their conservation.

I was privileged to lead an extra-mural class in Stanley for two years from 1975 to 1977. This was a rewarding and enjoyable experience, as anyone who has ever taught adults will know. Like most adult classes, it contained an enormous depth of life experience and expertise, including textile manufacturing, farming, religion, education and health. All the class members contributed a great deal to the booklet that we eventually published but two made special contributions—Leslie Fraser and the late John Culbert. Leslie was the owner of Perth Bookshop and still actively promotes the history of the locality. John had spent a lifetime in Stanley Mills and was an encyclopedia of knowledge about the place. I have taught adult classes for most of my working life and have found teaching history to highly motivated students to be a continuing pleasure and stimulus.

I have benefited a great deal from contact with two English historians of the cotton industry—Professor Stanley Chapman of Nottingham University and the late Dr. R. S. (Bob) Fitton of Manchester Metropolitan University. I met Bob at a Pasold Conference at Cambridge and we corresponded over the years about Arkwright matters, until his untimely death. Professor Chris Whatley of Dundee University and Dr. Ian Donnachie of the Open University have been stimulating colleagues on a pioneering Distance Learning Course in Modern Scottish History and offered encouragement in my researches. I owe a particular debt to Ian, who has shared his deep knowledge of Robert Owen and New Lanark with me and has read a draft of the book. Professor Chris Smout of St Andrews University has also been kind enough to read a draft and make helpful comments. To all of these people, I am most grateful.

Amongst my colleagues at Dundee University, I would like to mention Dr. Bob Harris, Dr. Laurence Williams and the late Dr. Bill Walker of the History Department. My colleague and friend of many years standing, Professor Antony Black, has been a tower of support and a model of academic creativity. Another long standing friend, Dr. Roy Partington, has provided much needed hill walking companionship and argument.

I would like to thank Historic Scotland, particularly Chris MacGregor and Mark Watson, for commissioning a historical study of Stanley from me, in 1996, which formed part of a successful bid for Heritage Lottery Funds and indirectly kick started this book, after a hiatus of many years. Perth and Kinross Library Service, in particular the Chief Librarian, Mike Moir, have been very supportive in publishing the book.

Within my own immediate family, I am grateful to my sons, Alistair and Michael, and their partners, Louise and Gill, for tolerating my oddities and broadening my musical tastes over the years. My greatest debts are to my wife Judith, who has put up with me for thirty three years of married life, my parents, who passed on to me their love of history, and my grandmother, Annie Hughes, a tiny but indomitable Blackburn cotton weaver, who believed her grandchildren were capable of anything they put their minds to.

Anthony Cooke
Dundee
January 2003

Cultrennie
Newbigging
ny wight
New.
Cairnachill
Charlestown
STO
Myretown
Souterhill
Brownpark
Knockshinnan
ur wright
Barns of
Mi
Auchtergaven
Coldham
Ma
PH
Bellock
Ardonachie
Airntully
Dam
Drun
Loanhead
Terminan
Pitsindry
Birkhead
Mill of
Airntully
Newlands
Bride
Loanhead
Burnhead
Neth: Bellock
Hilltown
Newbigging
Los of Ca
Wood
of Nairn
Safebanding
West tots
Campsie
Thrashylee
Jackstown
Low
court hill
Stanley
inchru ers
Westport
Byres
Bla
Lethem
Mains of Nairn
Gallowhill
ton Mill
Barkhead
Hillburn
Park corner
Fireside House
Church nians
Pitlochry
Drishmier
Cottertown
Middlebank
Upper
Benhall
Cambusmichael
Aikenhead
Loanfold
Ordie
Mill
Crosspites
Druim
ST° MAR
Gallybrache
Water
Marlhaugh
Over
Blind-wells
Wee
Gallybank
Cauldside
Mid Benhall
Collin
Maisbank
Northleys
Neth Benhall
Causeway
Pitlandy
Boghall
Bankhead
Dunalt
Rome
Neu mill
Parkhead
Lowstown
Cramphlate
Neth. Collin
ntendyne
Monedy
Regilny
Hillside
Luncarty
Gilkhead
Mill
Innerbuist
Lormont Mills
Cockston hill
Ardgillan
Scone's Lethends
Lawhead
Bullions Boat
Waukmill
Bushie
Dixons
New Mill
Blackhill
Turnagain
Willock Hutton
Gellshead
Blairhall
Langu
Cairnhall
Cudrochy
Batchfield
Denmark
Drumsheugles
Lochtown
Putmardily
Black
Grayswells
Sherifftown
Racend
Redgorton
PH
hall
Silver Castle
Ballou
REDGORTON
Brosie
Camp
Hole of
Scone
oatwells
Cotterhill
Neth Brosie
S
C
O
raigingall
Pitcairn
Green
Bertha
Rome
Scone
Manufactur
Cleanhill
Bridgend
Palace
Scone
Balforno
Park
Bamrich
Bridge
town
Balhouse
Pit
Easthaugh
Knowhead
Welltree
Haugh
Mill
Middlehaugh
Quarrie
Mill
Burngrove
Huntington
Moortown
Inver Ann
Picullo
Toft
Presthaugh
Bleachfield
Ballhouse
Kincarrothie
W. Mains
Newhouse
Tullach
Pp & AL
hills
Blackruthven
Barn
side
PH
Lethem
Hole of
Ruthven
Bleachfield
Goodie Burn
Den
KINNOU
Kingswells
MUIR
Codgerford
Bridgend
Tippermur
Hill of Ruthven
Kinnoul

1.

Houses and Offices in a Tasty Stile

Land Ownership and Agricultural Change

Stanley is situated seven miles north of Perth. It lies just south of the Highland Fault Line and east of the modern A9 (Perth/Inverness), in an area of relatively light and fertile soils. Three parishes meet in the Stanley area—Auchtergaven, Kinclaven and Redgorton. The area is famous for salmon fishing, as the fish lie in the pools at Stanley, below the Campsie Linn rapids, on their way up the Tay. The same rapids at Campsie Linn provided the fall for the waterpower at Stanley Mills, once a tunnel had been driven through the hillside. An export trade in salmon developed in the early eighteenth century, selling to the London market and even to the Mediterranean. (Defoe, 1724–6, 645 and OSA, XI, 521) Salmon fishing and the supply of fresh salmon was a continuing perk for the owners of Stanley Mills, as for the owners of other manufactories along the River Tay, such as Luncarty bleachworks.

In the seventeenth century, the land around Stanley belonged to the Nairne family, who were prominent supporters of the Stuarts. Robert Nairne fought on the Royalist side in the Civil War and was imprisoned for ten years in the Tower of London during the Cromwellian period. On the Restoration he was knighted, appointed a Lord of Session and raised to the peerage as Lord Nairne in 1681. His only daughter, Margaret Nairne, married Lord William Murray, fourth son of John, Marquis of Atholl and brother of the First Duke. (Rogers, 1886, 151)

Lord William and his wife lived in Stanley House, situated on the peninsula by the River Tay. It was 'an ancient house dating from the first half of the fifteenth century' with old yew trees and a beech avenue leading up to it. (*Ordnance Gazetteer of Scotland*, 1885, VI, 378). The yew trees and the beech avenue remain but the house is a ruin. The origin of the English-sounding place-name, Stanley, is after Lord William's mother, Lady Amelia Stanley, daughter of John Stanley, Earl of Derby. (*NSA*, X, 434)

The Nairne family were Jacobites and fought in both the 1715 and the 1745 Uprisings. A stone on the riverbank in front of Stanley House has the letters LJN and the date June 10, 1745. Lord Nairne took refuge in Stanley House after Culloden and

Opposite: *James Stobie's Map of Perthshire, 1805* (Perth and Kinross Libraries)

escaped from the dining room in the nick of time to avoid capture. He had to flee the country and his estates were forfeited and put up for sale. At the auction, the Duke of Atholl, who was a cousin of the Nairnes, made a bid for the Nairne estates. No one bid against him, believing that he was bidding on behalf of his exiled relative but the lands were added to the Atholl estates and the Nairne mansion house at Loak demolished. A member of the Nairne family commented 'a man's foes shall be those of his own household'. (Rogers, 1886, 151)

The area began to develop agriculturally in the latter part of the eighteenth century, responding to a growing population with more money to spend. Thomas Pennant, the English naturalist and antiquary, travelling through the Luncarty area in 1769 on his way to Dunkeld, wrote: 'The country is good, full of barley, oats and flax in abundance, but after a few miles travelling, is succeeded by a black heath'. (Pennant, 1769, 80) The *Statistical Account* for Auchtergaven parish, written in 1795, described a pre-improvement landscape of bleak, wet, moor ground, impassable roads and 'smoaky damp houses, built of turf and stone and thatched with straw or heath'. (OSA, XII, 35) This sounds an exaggeration, in view of Pennant's earlier description, and may reflect the way in which improvers emphasised the negative features of pre-improvement agriculture in Scotland. By 1795, farmers were using lime or marl on the land, the use of lime as a manure having been introduced some 30 years earlier and crop rotation was

Stanley House, c.1880 (Perth Museum)

practised with encouragement from the Duke of Atholl. *(OSA, XII, 35)*

In the same period, the Nairne estate in Redgorton parish had changed dramatically from 'two thirds heath land' to 'fertile fields of corn, wheat and grass'. (*OSA*, XI, 529) Industrialisation and the demand it created for agricultural goods, clearly had a major impact on the agriculture of the surrounding area. William Chalmers, the minister of Auchtergaven parish, reported that when Stanley mills were built:

> only a few families dwelt near Stanley; and except the land within the inclosures around Stanley House, most part of it, thereabout, was almost in a state of nature. His Grace the Duke of Atholl took under his own management 250 acres of this land, inclosed it, built upon it an elegant farm stead; and within the course of a few years, improved it so highly, that not long ago, this farm was let at the rate of £1 5s. per acre.
>
> (*OSA*, XII, 34)

The whole parish had been affected by 'the improvements in agriculture, in the manufactures, roads and buildings', which had been 'so rapid within these ten years past, that the country has assumed quite a different aspect from what it had before that time'. The turnpike road from Perth to Dunkeld, completed by 1795, encouraged agricultural development and many of the new farmhouses and steadings were built near it. (*OSA*, XII, 34) In the mid 1780s, 'there were not above three or four farms upon a regular plan' but ten years later, there were 'from 20 to 30 regular farms, from 80 to 200 acres each; and upon all of them, neat, elegant houses and offices covered with slate'. The farmers, following 'the method recommended by the proprietors' were using summer fallowing and mixing alternately, green and white crops. They were also growing wheat on a large scale encouraged by the 4th Duke of Atholl, who had built a flour mill on his estate in the parish. (*OSA*, XII, 33)

James Stobie, a land surveyor who factored the Nairne estate for the Duke, carried out improvements on his farm at Marlehall outside Stanley, where he 'erected houses and offices in a tasty stile'. (*OSA*, XI, 529) Land surveyors were at the forefront of agricultural change in eighteenth century Scotland, as they were required to draw up 'before and after' maps for enclosure plans—'the professional land surveyor emerged in the 1750s to reach his eighteenth century zenith in the year 1770'. (Adams, 1978, 84–5). James Stobie was particularly active—he drew up the original plan for Stanley village and for nearby Pitcairngreen, designed the tunnel through the peninsula that powered the water wheels for the first cotton mill and produced a detailed map of Perthshire in 1783. His death 'hastened by intemperance' took place on 30 July 1804. (*Chronicles of Atholl*, 1908, Vol. IV, 209)

Stanley was also affected by agricultural changes happening further north in the Perthshire Highlands. Some local historians have been rather coy about the Perthshire clearances and even Leah Leneman's excellent book about the Atholl Estates only has one reference to sheep in the index. This is a Gaelic poem, entitled *Salute to Atholl*, dated 1781, in which the poet, after extolling the virtues of Atholl, continued:

Your people live in tranquillity and sufficiency;
They put by in times of such peace and plenty;
They have good things instead of junk,
And a sufficiency of sound education.
Your new generation are promising to give pleasure
Both to their good king and to their land.
May he not have heirs who value them less
Than the sheep who come from the Lowlands.

(Leneman, 1986, 66–7)

A less idyllic picture of life in Highland Perthshire is given in another Gaelic poem, *Song on the Enemies of the Tenantry* by Alexander Robertson of Bohespick on the Atholl Estates, just north of Tummel Bridge. The poem, which is undated but may be from around 1715, was inspired by the imposition of a tax on the tenantry by the local wadsetter or mortgage holder. The poem is an astonishing attack on the landlord class and nails the myth of Highland passivity and quiescence in the face of population clearances for sheep:

Oh People (the nobles), face the truth
In the entirety of your minds
And be sure not to earn vengeance
Upon the generation that comes after you
There is no one who is accustomed
To have some arable for himself
Who does not find it sufficient for his craft and conversation
To have a grassum in his mouth.

When you (the nobles) gather together
Strong and firm would be your accord
To increase the rent of the land
For the poor people upon it
You would not listen to mercy
You would consider such talk worthless
Unless you give them an hour's respite
The Clearances will come upon them all.

Lord, help the children of the tenantry
There are many spectres chasing after them
There are lords and landlords
Forever seizing their possessions
Smiths and millers
Are eager for their share
There are tinkers and bards and beggars

And the caulker down the road

(Leneman, 1986, 83–4)

Clearances of population for sheep took place at different times on the Atholl and Breadalbane estates. (Mackenzie, 1883, 242–7, Gillies, 1936, 211–2 & Richards, 2000, 75) The ministers compiling the *Statistical Accounts* for the parishes of Highland Perthshire described the changes in the 1790s in somewhat coded language, so as not to offend powerful patrons like the Dukes of Atholl and the Earls of Breadalbane. In Killin on the Breadalbane estates, the Rev. Patrick Stewart wrote in 1794 that:

> It might be apprehended that this parish has been greatly depopulated within these past 60 years, by the union of farms, and the number of sheep introduced into it; and it must be admitted, that owing to these causes, the number of the people has decreased considerably in the higher parts of the parish in that period.
>
> (OSA, XII, 483–4)

However, the population of Killin village had actually increased in the same period. In Dull, Perthshire, in 1791, the Rev. Archibald Menzies reported that the population had fallen from 50 years earlier because of the practice of farm amalgamation 'perhaps three or four families lived where only one now lives. In the higher parts of the country, sheep farms have also been united'. (OSA, XII, 301) A different tale came from Weem, where the Rev. James M'Diarmid claimed, in 1791, 'Few or none have emigrated from this parish, but whole troops of boys and girls go annually to the low country for service, and of late to the cotton works, many of whom settle there'. (OSA, XII, 813)

As early as 1768, when Lord Kames drained Kincardine Moss, near Stirling, he employed '170 families, primarily from the Perthshire Highlands'. (Richards, 1985, Vol. 2, 205) Deanston Mills were quite close to Kincardine Moss and like Stanley, lay on the edge of the Perthshire Highlands. Here, it was reported in the 1780s:

> from the great wages which the people earned, the better part of the surrounding population were ultimately attracted to the works. The first supply was chiefly from the Highlands, where, from the introduction of sheep, the farmers and small cotters were forced away to seek employment in such establishments. Many of the offspring of the old stock still remain. It has been uniformly found that the people of the immediately surrounding neighbourhood have proved the best population, and these works have been an asylum for many a reduced farmer, with his family, and for the widows and orphans of the agricultural and village population.
>
> (Fitton, 1989, 205)

In the sprawling parish of Fortingall, which included Glen Lyon in the north west corner of Perthshire, the Rev. Duncan M'Ara complained in 1790:

crofters, cottagers, and day labourers, who can earn no bread at home set out for the great towns to get employment. Our extensive sheep walks are certainly, in that respect, a loss to the public. It is now exceedingly difficult to raise recruits amongst us. Attachment to lairds and chieftains is dying away.

(OSA, XII, 435)

David Stewart of Garth, near Fortingall, a sympathetic observer of the Highland scene, wrote in 1822 of the impact of the changes taking place:

it has converted whole glens and districts, once the abode of a brave, vigorous and independent race of men, into scenes of desolation; it has torn up families, which seemed rooted, like Alpine plants, in the soil of their native region . . . and forced them thence, penniless and unskilful, to seek a refuge in manufacturing towns, or, in a state of helpless despair, to betake themselves to the wilds of a far distant land.

(Stewart, 1822, Vol. 1, 123)

Perthshire was also affected by population changes happening further north. In 1802, Alexander Irvine described how in the Highlands:

To equipoise population, they spread themselves begging. For instance, the higher parts of Inverness-shire in summer pour in upon the Counties of Perth and Angus so that I have seen, in seasons of scarcity, twenty or thirty served at a door, in one day, consisting mostly of women and children. The prevalence of beggary in the Highlands, requires attention, if it be caused by a defect of economy or arises from excessive population.

(Richards, 1985, Vol. 2, 202)

Macinnes has written perceptively about the demise of clanship and the rise of a more commercial ethos in the Highlands. (Macinnes, 1998, 178) The Rev. Alexander McLagan, the minister of Blair Atholl and a noted collector of Gaelic poetry, wrote in 1799 that after the Jurisdiction Act, landowners no longer saw their tenants as fighting men but as rent paying tenants:

Then the rents began to be raised, the farms to be enlarged, much land to be taken into the landowners' domain, and the shepherd and his dog to be the inhabitants of farms, that formerly maintained many families; though this last particular is not, as yet, so much the case here, as it is in many other places. In consequence of these changes some of the tenants are

Opposite: *John Murray, 4ᵗʰ Duke of Atholl (1755–1830)*
(Sir Thomas Lawrence, Perth Museum)

become cottagers; some have removed to towns, to gain a livelihood by
labour; and a few have emigrated to America, though that spirit is not
become very common here as yet.

(OSA, XII, 101)

Stanley was promoted by the 4th Duke of Atholl as a way of dealing with these cottagers,
who were moving or being moved off the land. It was part of a wider effort to improve
an area on the southern boundary of the Atholl estates, to increase rentals and to
provide work and housing for Highland and lowland tenants. In this, Atholl was following
the example of the 3rd Duke, who was involved in negotiations over water rights at
Luncarty bleachfield and a paper mill at Huntingtowerfield. The 4th Duke himself was
involved in negotiations for a bleachfield at Huntingtowerfield, on the Atholl estates.
(Leneman. 1986, 210–11)

In the lowland parts of the Atholl estates, agricultural change led to the clearance of
smaller tenants, who could not measure up to the 'new farming' and were being steered
towards the textile industries. On 2 November 1786, the 4th Duke wrote a memorandum
in his own hand, which showed paternalism but also a streak of ruthlessness and the
new commercial ethos:

Tennents Warned from Nairne Estate
Cottartown
Letham
Wetlands
Kilburnie

Encouragement held out to any of the tennents in the above farms who
follow trades are industrious and have families of three children and
upwards the Duke will give them as much ground near Stanley as will be
sufficient to erect a house upon with a little garden behind for potatoes the
Duke will furnish the necessary wood and give them that and the ground
gratis for their prospective lives the neighbouring works (Stanley cotton
mill) will give constant employment to their children who instead of being a
burthen to their parents will help materially to support them. Any old
tenant having no family who can bring proof of his being on the ground 30
years upwards the Duke will assist in building a house and give a small
piece of ground to at an easy rate provided he bear a good character Those
of the above tenants who are wise enough to see their own interests in
accepting the above conditions will give notice to Commissary Bisset (the
factor) that the Duke may give orders about the laying out of the ground.
Those that do not accept of them will do well to look out for possessions
elsewhere as the Duke is determined not to let his lands again in such small
farms.

(Leneman, 1986, 34–5)

These close links between agricultural change, population movement and industrialisation are illustrated by accounts from neighbouring parishes, such as Little Dunkeld. Here, the Rev. John Robertson reported that the fall in population between 1776 and 1792:

> can in no way be accounted for but by the uniting of farms, and by the migration of some of the inhabitants to Perth and its neighbourhood, for employment at the bleachfields and extensive manufactories lately erected there, and to the village of Stanley in the parish of Auchtergaven, where there is a considerable cotton work carrying on.
>
> (OSA, XII, 411)

The growing manufacturing population in and around Perth created an increased demand for food, which was partly met by bringing under cultivation pasture or waste, using 'new' fertilisers, 'new' crops and 'new' methods of crop rotation. (Whyte, 1998, Vol. 1, 95) A description, in 1799, of a method of reclaiming moorland, 'recommended by a gentleman on the Nairne estate between Dunkeld and Perth', began with paring and burning the moor, then spreading the ashes with lime and sowing turnips to be fed off with sheep the first year. Turnips were sown again the following year and fed off in the same manner, followed by barley and grain seed the next year. Crop rotation on the banks of the Tay followed a six year cycle—first year fallow with lime and clay, second year wheat, third year peas and beans, fourth year barley with hay seeds, fifth year hay and sixth year oats. (Robertson, 1799, 138, & 266) A modern rotation might be— first year oats and barley, second year potatoes, turnips, kale and cabbage, third year barley undersown, fourth year hay and fifth year grazing.

Wages for agricultural labourers were rising in the 1790s because of competition with manufacturing industries, such as flax and cotton spinning, weaving, bleaching, dyeing and printing, in Perth and places like Stanley, Luncarty, Cromwellpark, Pitcairnfield and Huntingtowerfield. In 1795, a day labourer in Redgorton parish was asking a shilling a day and 'can scarce be hired at any rate'. Yearly wages for men had risen to £7 to £10, from £4 to £5 twenty years earlier and for women to £3 to £4 a year, compared to 30 to 40 shillings. (£1.50 to £2.00) (OSA, XI, 536) Labourers worked from 6.00 am to 6.00 pm in summer with an hour for breakfast and an hour for dinner. In winter, they worked all daylight hours. Often, agricultural workers lived with the farmer but there was increasing social segregation, with farm workers being given a house, a garden, a cow's grass rent free, fuel and 6.5 bolls of meal. Maidservants usually lived with the family. (Robertson, 1799, 341–2)

James Craig, who managed Stanley Mills from 1801 to 1814, took a great deal of interest in agricultural improvement and had acquired three farms in the Stanley area by 1823 (Stanley New Farm, Burnside Farm and Farm of Drumbeath), with a total acreage of 141 acres. (Atholl Mss., D3, 81/18) His acquisitive nature aroused mistrust amongst the Duke of Atholl's factors and amongst the Dale trustees, who bankrolled the mills during Craig's management. In 1808, Robert Owen, who was supervising the mills on behalf of the trustees, complained to Craig 'all your land speculation promises to do better than the spinning'. (Atholl Mss, 25, XI, 92–4) In 1829, Craig applied to the Highland Society for a Gold Medal for improving waste ground at Stanley. (Atholl Mss, 69, 5, 226)

By 1838, further changes had taken place. There were 140 ploughs in Auchtergaven parish and livestock had been greatly improved in quality with large draught horses, cross-bred Shorthorn and Ayrshire cattle and Leicester sheep. The main grain crops were oats and barley with some wheat. A fifth of each farm was always under turnips and potatoes, the latter being shipped from Perth for the London market. Leases were generally granted for 19 years and most farmers lived in well built and furnished two storey houses. The best land rented for £2 10s. (£2.50) an acre, the average rent being £1 5s. (£1.25), which was the rent the 4th Duke of Atholl had received for his best land forty years earlier. Wages for a labourer were 2 shillings (10p) a day in summer, 1/6d (7.5p) in winter and a weekly wage came to 9 to 10 shillings (45–50p) compared to the 13 to 16 shillings (65–80p) that a male cotton spinner earned in a week. A good ploughman earned £12 to £14 a year plus allowances of oatmeal and milk, whereas women farm servants earned only £5 to £7 a year, plus bed and board. (NSA, X, 437–9)

Stanley provided a market for local farmers and pendiclers, particularly for the sale of milk. (NSA, X, 1135) The system of smallholdings known as pendicles was a remarkably resilient one. In 1795, the pendicles in Redgorton parish were described as 'many small possessions, having attached to them one to ten acres'. (OSA, XI, 531) The minister at Kinclaven testified in 1843 that Stanley had been of great benefit to farmers and 'pendiclers' in the immediate neighbourhood, by giving them a market for liquid milk. (NSA, X, 1135) Fifty years later, there were still crofts on the outskirts of Stanley, known as the Tofts. Many of the crofters were employed on the large farms and looked after the crofts in their spare time. They usually had a cow each, one or two sheep, pigs and hens. (Ferguson, 1893, 114)

The land continued in the hands of the Atholl family until the depression of the 1930s. The Atholl estates insisted on good farming practice from their tenants. In 1915, tenants were bound by the terms of their lease not to take two white or corn crops in succession from the same field without an intervening green crop, grass or fallow (flax on no account to be considered a green crop). A five shift crop rotation had to be strictly followed: one fifth oats after lea; one fifth drilled green crop or fallow, sufficiently cleaned and manured; one fifth wheat, barley or oats; one fifth sown grass to be cut or pastured in the tenant's option; the remaining fifth pasture. Tenants had to keep their farm roads in good repair and the situation and arrangement of the farm steadings and all other houses and fences was subject to the approval of the proprietor. (Cooke, 1977, 9) The Strathord Estate at Stanley was sold in October 1936 to the Abbey National Building Society, who sold it to the Marquis of Bute in 1944. In 1952, it was acquired by its present owners, the Eagle Star Insurance Company. (Cooke, 1977, 9–10)

2.

An Erect and Outlooking Spirit Abroad

Factory Villages and the Scottish Cotton Industry

The cotton industry played a major role in early industrialisation in Scotland, which was noted by contemporaries. The *Old Statistical Accounts* recorded the general level of excitement, with reports from Renfrewshire that there was 'great speculation in the cotton business at the moment,' or from Glasgow, where 'cotton mills, bleachfields, and printfields have been erected on almost all the streams in the neighbourhood'. (Hamilton, 1966, 124) In *Annals of the Parish*, the Rev. Mr. Balwidder reported from his fictional parish of Dalmailing that when Mr. Cayenne, the Virginia planter, built a cotton mill on the Brawl Burn in 1788:

> The minds of men were excited to new enterprises; a new genius, as it were, had descended upon the earth, and there was an erect and outlooking spirit abroad that was not to be satisfied with the taciturn regularity of ancient affairs.
>
> (Galt, 1919 edition, 178)

However, this 'erect and outlooking spirit' was not confined to the central belt of Scotland. In the far North, George Dempster, writing of the ill-fated cotton mills at Spinningdale in Sutherland, in 1794, described how: 'The weavers at the cotton work begin to remove to their parents' houses with their looms and a little beginning is made towards converting Sutherland into a Lancashire'. (Cooke, 1995, 91) In Kirkcudbright, in the South West of Scotland, the local minister reported 'a spirit of cotton manufacture got amongst us'. (Hamilton, 1966, 129) Mrs. Hannah Cowley, a London poetess, writing in 1786, compared the hamlet of Pitcairngreen in Perthshire to Manchester:

> Go Manchester and weep thy slighted loom
> Its arts are cherished now on Pitcairngreen . . .
> Thus blest, this village shall some unborn aye

> Behold a city, grac'd with many a dome;
> Of note in commerce and of arts the stage
>   (Cooke, 1984, 52)

George Penny, remembering the 1780s in Perth, reported: 'Various fabrics were by times introduced in the cotton line. As the trade was at first very prosperous, a manufacturing mania seemed to pervade society. Every gentleman who had a second son of the requisite age, put him apprentice to the loom.'However, mania usually ends in tears and this was no exception. A crash in 1810 virtually wiped out the cotton industry in Perth leaving Stanley Mills and bleachfields like Luncarty as almost the sole survivors. Penny described the boom before the crash: 'For some time previously, the cotton manufacturers had flourished beyond example, giving employment to an immense number of hands, at very high wages . . . . Such was the demand, that not a herd boy could be found in the country; all flew to the loom.' (Penny, 1836, 251–256)

Historians have disagreed about the impact of the cotton industry on the Scottish economy as a whole but most have acknowledged its importance. Mantoux's 1928 classic *The Industrial Revolution in the Eighteenth Century*, highlighted the importance of new technology and invention. 'The use of machinery, even if not in itself a sufficient definition or explanation of the industrial revolution, remains at any rate the leading fact, in relation to which every other fact in that great historical process must be studied.' (Mantoux, 1964 edition, 189) Wadsworth and Mann's *The Cotton Trade and Industrial Lancashire, 1600–1780* emphasised industrial continuity. 'It is not without interest to note that the features common to the two centres, Manchester and Glasgow, where the cotton industry flourished and expanded, was the prior and continuous existence of a linen industry side by side with cotton.' (Wadsworth and Mann, 1931, 171)

Hamilton's *The Industrial Revolution in Scotland*, published in 1932, followed the Wadsworth and Mann thesis of industrial continuity. Whilst Hamilton recognised the revolutionary impact of the cotton industry on the Scottish economy, he acknowledged the base laid down by the linen industry, which had developed skills amongst the workforce and entrepreneurial flair amongst merchants. He also noted the effects of the American War of Independence, which had a devastating impact on the Glasgow tobacco trade and on Scottish linen exports. (Hamilton, 2nd edition 1966, 120)

At the beginning of the 1960s, the American economist W. W. Rostow developed a theory outlining five stages of economic growth—the traditional society; the preconditions for 'take off'; the 'take off'; the drive to maturity and the age of high mass consumption. Rostow believed that the cotton industry was the leading sector in the 'take off' of the British economy and that 'take off' could be dated between 1785 and 1803. As evidence, he cited the spectacular increase of raw cotton imports into Britain, which went up by 319 per cent from 1781–1791 and by 67 per cent from 1791–1801. (Rostow, 1960, 4–12, 53–4) In Scotland, raw cotton imports into the Clyde rose from 137,160 lbs. in 1775 to almost 2 million lbs. in 1790 and over 11 million lbs. in 1812. (Hamilton, 1966, 7)

Campbell, in 1964, returned to the Wadsworth and Mann/Hamilton industrial continuity thesis, stressing the importance of the Scottish linen industry as a nursery for the skills required by the new cotton industry:

> To explain the rise of the (cotton) industry solely on the basis of the new technology misses the point. The industry depended on the technical inventions, but that it was so successful in Scotland, especially in the west of Scotland, at that time depended on the favourable environment already formed by the linen industry and on two aspects in particular: first, the special skills and abilities, particularly in finer fabrics, of the linen weavers of the west of Scotland, and, second, the commercial acumen of the merchants who organised the expansion of the linen industry.
>
> (Campbell, 1971 edition, 97–8)

Smout's *History of the Scottish People*, in 1969, followed Hamilton in arguing that cotton played a key role in industrialisation in Scotland. Smout laid more emphasis than Campbell on the role of technology and the importance of English models. After discussing how the Scots copied agricultural methods from the English and improved them, Smout continued: 'The same story of an English technology, enthusiastically borrowed in the first instance and then still more enthusiastically adapted and advanced by native ingenuity, can be found in the cotton industry'. He emphasised the entrepreneurial skills of Scots merchants, citing the way in which Lancashire manufacturers sought an outlet for their surplus yarn amongst the West of Scotland weavers and then found the Scots outselling them in the market place. (Smout, 1969, 254) Samuel Salte, Samuel Oldknow's London agent, complained, in 1786, 'The Scotch Impudence and perseverance is beyond all'. (Unwin, 1924, 66)

Harte, in the early 1970s, emphasised industrial continuity and the links between Lanarkshire and Lancashire:

> The cotton industry was enabled to grow dramatically once its inherent technical potentialities were realised because of its long roots in the linen industry. In Lancashire (as in Lanarkshire) there were established skills to be drawn on and there was a nationwide commercial superstructure of provincial drapers and London warehouse men.
>
> (Harte, 1973, quoted in Berg, 1994, 213)

Lythe and Butt linked the transition from linen to cotton in terms of changes in raw material prices, as flax prices increased, alongside a halving of the price of raw cotton coming into the Clyde between 1776 and 1780. They added 'the process would have met with more difficulty had not Scotland already accumulated resources of capital, entrepreneurship, technical skill and labour'. (Lythe and Butt, 1975, 184) The Checklands took a different position, emphasising the way in which cotton had impacted on the whole industrialisation process.

It was the manufacturing activity centred upon cotton that had given the necessary primary impulse to West of Scotland engineering, ironfounding and blacksmithing. For the factories required machines, engines, shafting, and cast and wrought iron components.

(O. and S. Checkland, 1989, 20)

Rostow's theory has been challenged by more recent historians, who have characterised British industrialisation as a peculiarly 'fractured' process, rather than a series of distinct stages. (Stedman Jones, quoted in Berg, 1994, 21) Others have argued that the cotton industry was atypical and questioned whether it really played such a central role in the transformation of the British economy. Chapman, for example, calculated that cotton only accounted for some 5 per cent of British national income, similar to the contribution of the iron industry in the same period. (Chapman, 2nd edition 1987, 54)

In what has become 'the new orthodoxy', historians have challenged the whole concept of an Industrial Revolution, arguing that economic growth was slower, and smaller firms and traditional industries more important in the British economy, than previously recognised. Crafts wrote 'not only was the triumph of ingenuity slow to come to fruition but it does not seem appropriate to regard innovativeness as pervasive'. (Crafts, 1985, 87) In a phrase of striking inelegance, he described the inventions in cotton textiles as 'random exogenous shocks'. (Crafts, 1994, 58) An earlier article stressed the slow rate of change, pointing out that much of British industry in the first half of the nineteenth century was traditional and small scale and catered to local domestic markets. This sector, responsible for perhaps 60 per cent of industrial employment, experienced low levels of labour productivity and slow productivity growth, 'it is possible that there was virtually no advance during 1780–1860'. (Crafts, 1989, 425) Rodger noted 'the coexistence of small firms with their larger brethren', questioned how typical the large factory workplace was in mid-Victorian Scotland and highlighted the ways in which different sectors of the economy displayed widely varying degrees of modernity and traditionalism. (Rodger, 1988, 85)

Undoubtedly, the revisionist approach helped correct the overly cotton-centric view of early industrialisation by emphasising continuity in industrial development. However, its highly quantitative approach did have major drawbacks, an obvious one being the lack of adequate figures for significant sectors of the British economy such as 'food processing, metal wares, distilling, furniture, shipbuilding, chemicals, engineering, pottery, glass and clothing'. Berg pointed out that Crafts used new social and occupational tables by Lindert and Williamson, with an error margin as high as 60 per cent, for his calculations. These tables were based on occupational data for adult males whereas 'women and children were a vital and growing pillar of the manufacturing workforce'. The 'special place' that female and child labour occupied in 'the modernised progressive sectors' of the British economy finds parallels today in the textile mills and sweatshops of the Third World but was not fully recognised by the revisionist historians. (Berg, 1994, 24)

Certainly, contemporaries believed they were living through a period of major change.

This was particularly true in Scotland, where the sense of excitement, (or unease) at the changes taking place extended from agriculture to manufacturing industry, from urban to rural and from the English speaking South West to the Gaelic speaking West Highlands. This feeling showed up in the (uniquely Scottish) *Statistical Accounts*, compiled in the 1790s, under the direction of Sir John Sinclair, by ministers and teachers, who generally knew their own parishes intimately. They described rapid population increase, agricultural change, growing urbanisation, the growth of manufacturing industry and accompanying changes in social attitudes and behaviour.

Examples could be drawn from all over Scotland. The Rev. John Dunbar, minister of Nairn, described how, in 1790:

> The present possessors, finding that there are not so many rooms as formerly for farmers, breed their children to handicrafts; and these, not finding employment at home, push their way to Edinburgh, Glasgow, Paisley, or London, from whence they seldom find their way back to settle here. This cause affects most of the northern districts, where manufacturers do not meet with the attention and encouragement they deserve.

On the opposite side of the country, in the West Highland parish of Lochalsh, the minister in the 1790s welcomed 'The emancipation of the lower classes . . . from the remains of feudal oppression,' whilst in Kirkcudbright in the South West, the Rev. Alex Maclean, minister of Kirkmabreck, explained that the population increase in the parish from 680 in 1764 to 1088 in 1794 was due to inoculation for smallpox, the improvement of waste ground and 'recently established manufactures'—i.e. a cotton mill in Creetown. (Cooke et al., 1998, Vol. 5, 75–79)

Whatley has argued that Scotland followed a significantly different course to England in this period—'Scotland did experience an Industrial Revolution, . . . this started later and was more compressed than its English counterpart' and concluded 'whatever doubts there may be about the applicability of the term 'Industrial Revolution' to England, arguably, there are fewer in Scotland's case'. (Whatley, 1997, 6) This is in line with recent research, which viewed industrialisation in Britain as a phenomenon that varied between different regions and localities and therefore one that cannot be understood on a purely national level. (Hudson, 1989, Richards, 1993)

A recent book on the Scottish cotton industry emphasised its central role in the industrialisation process, moving towards mass production and mechanisation:

> it was cotton which more than any other Scottish industry stimulated moves towards industrialisation, particularly in the west of Scotland. Nine out of ten manufacturing workers in Scotland in 1826 were in textiles, with a ratio of six workers in cotton to three in linen, to one in woollens. But it was cotton with its novel method of organising work, its rapidly changing technologies and its dynamic growth, which acted as the lead sector. Between 1790 and 1820 Scotland's cotton industry was more dynamic

than England's, as it took the lead in the use of the power-driven mule and, later, the self-acting mule.

(Knox, 1995, 1)

Cooke and Donnachie agreed. 'The changes in the textile industries at the end of the eighteenth century can be described as revolutionary since they introduced mechanisation and large scale mass production for the first time.' (Cooke and Donnachie, 1998, 142) Devine described the Scottish cotton industry in 1830 as 'the jewel in the nation's economic crown' and emphasised its contribution to urbanisation in Scotland. 'The main engine of urbanisation was industrialisation and down to c. 1830 the main motors of growth were the textile industries of cotton, linen and wool.' (Devine, 1999, 149 & 108) This followed earlier work, in which he explored the ways in which the Glasgow tobacco trade provided capital for investment in the cotton industry and trading and commercial links with the important North American markets and raw material supplies. (Devine, 1976, 1–13)

Whatley returned to the Wadsworth & Mann/Hamilton industrial continuity thesis and emphasised the role played by traditional textile industries in laying the groundwork for the cotton industry:

contrary to the long held view that the Scottish cotton industry emerged as a result of capital being transferred from the tobacco trade following the blows to its prosperity caused by the American War, its entrepreneurial roots lay primarily in the flax, linen and silk trades.

(Whatley, 2000, 224)

Linen was the dominant manufacturing industry in Scotland prior to 'take off'. It accounted for two thirds of Scottish exports in 1700 and by one estimate employed 180,000 women (four fifths of the adult female population) from time to time in spinning linen. (Durie, 1979, 159, Whatley, 1997, 27) Although linen manufacturing was found all over Scotland, there was a strong concentration in Lanarkshire and Renfrewshire in the West and Angus, Fife and Perthshire in the East of Scotland. Within this distribution pattern, there was a marked degree of specialisation. The West of Scotland specialised in fine linens, the East of Scotland in coarser and cheaper fabrics. Although Forfarshire (Angus) produced almost half the linen cloth stamped for sale in Scotland in 1782, its value was less than a quarter of all cloth sold. Perthshire produced 1,699,682 yards of linen cloth in 1782 worth £81,195, out of a Scottish total of 15,348,744 yards worth £775,100. (Hamilton, 1966, 91)

Linen production was also important in England, where a petition to the House of Commons in 1713 claimed there were 60,000 people engaged in linen manufacture in Lancashire. (Daniels, 1920, 29) Here, there was an obvious connection with the development of cotton manufacturing, as South Lancashire specialised in the manufacture of fustians, which were a mixture of linen and cotton yarns. (Chapman, 1987, 11) The Scottish connection with Lancashire went back well before the Act of Union. A petition from Lancashire fustian manufacturers and London cloth merchants, dated 1621, referred to:

> the trade of making of other Fustians, made of a kind of Bombast or Downe, being a fruit of the earth growing upon little shrubs or bushes, brought into this Kingdome by the Turkie Merchants, from Smyrna, Cyprus, Acra and Sydon, but commonly called Cotton Wooll; and also of Lynnen yarne most part brought out of Scotland, and othersome made in England, and no part of the same Fustians of any Wooll at all, for which said Bombast and yarne imported, his Majesty hath a great yearly sum of money for the custom and subsidy thereof.
>   (Daniel, 1920, 9, & Wadsworth and Mann, 1931, 15)

In 1682, Thomas Marsden of Bolton in Lancashire was dealing in fustians, linen and woollen cloth and in yarn, including deliveries to his factor or agent, Hugh Pickering of Nether Darwin, Lancashire, of 'Scotch or English yarn'. In Glasgow, a cotton-linen industry producing checks and cloths for printing had developed out of the existing linen trade. Checks, which could be made out of linen or cotton, were made in Glasgow as early as 1702 and by 1727, the Scots were manufacturing 'short pieces made entirely of cotton,' according to regulations laid down for the industry. (Wadsworth & Mann, 1931, 83, 113, 116 & 128)

As the English cotton industry expanded, Scotland came to seem more of a threat. A contemporary account of the life of Samuel Crompton, the inventor of the spinning mule, described how: 'The Scotch in Lanarkshire, Renfrewshire, being long in the habit of weaving fine cambric from flax yarn and silk friezes, had also turned their hand to the manufacture of fine cotton fabrics, principally from the fine yarns produced by Hargreaves' and other subsequent machines'. (Daniels, 1920, 131) The weavers of Anderston, in Glasgow, claimed to have been the first in Britain to produce a web of muslin in 1769. (Campbell, 1995, 185)

In England, Samuel Oldknow pioneered muslin production, first at Anderton in Lancashire, in 1782, and later at Mellor, near Stockport. (Unwin, 1924, 3) Samuel Salte, Oldknow's London agent, wrote to him, on 10 May 1786, 'Arkwright must lower his Twist and he must Spin finer, tell him the reputation of our Country against Scotland is at Stake'. On 23 May 1786, Salte wrote again to Oldknow:

> You have Enemies and we have Enemies in abundance—Some to dispericate & others to rival us, in better goods they try at a lower price. Our Ears are stressed every day with the Excellence of Scotch and Lancashire Muslins, if cheapness proves any excellence they have it indeed. . . . The Scotch Impudence and perseverance is beyond all, but there is a Manufacturer in Lancashire makes Excellent goods in Muslins and sells them by Comission in London, we cannot get at his name.
>   (Unwin, 1924, 65–6)

Salte returned to the theme of Scottish competition on 5 June 1786, when he wrote to Samuel Oldknow:

> The Scotch have done much better this two months in the same. Do not make any Shawls, they are totally unsaleable, we mentioned that some time since . . . . We hinted at first our doubt about any demand—low 6/4 Striped will not do any longer, the Scotch have routed them out. Fancy broad Stripes are the fashion & good quality from 42s. to 60s. (£2.10p to £3.00) . . . indeed the Scotch perseverance and ingenuity are doing wonders, the Lancashire People are all exerting themselves, & no less than three or four houses opened to sell Lancashire Muslins by commission, & the accounts of buyers are much in their praise for Execution and Cheapness. The Scotch have sent up many Spotted Muslins, indeed too good and too cheap.
>
> (Unwin, 1924, 67)

Samuel Oldknow evidently shared Salte's fears of Scottish competition. He wrote to his brother Thomas from London on 19 October 1787:

> Nobody will buy till the India Sale is over . . . . The Jamdannies we must very much improve in fineness & in taste in patterns—I am told how the Scotch out do us in all respects in these articles.
>
> (Unwin, 1924, 97)

In the early days of cotton manufacture, cotton yarn could not be spun strong enough for the warp and linen yarn continued to be used as warp, with cotton as the weft. The invention of the water frame, patented by Arkwright in 1769 and 1775, meant that it was now possible to give the threads a firm enough twist to make them suitable for warps, so that pure cotton goods could be made for the first time. (Hamilton, 1966, 105)

   A shift in fashion began to take place from traditional linens, woollens and silks to British manufactured cotton, aided by rapidly falling prices for cotton yarn and fabrics. Just as there were strong links between linen and cotton and between Scotland and Lancashire, there was an important link between calico printing and cotton manufacture. Much of the new demand for cotton textiles was due to the increasing popularity of printed fabrics. By 1792, nearly a million pieces of white cotton cloth were produced in Britain of which 60 per cent was sent to the printers. (Berg, 1994 edition, 213) An East India Company Report in 1793 described how 'every shop offers British muslins for sale equal in appearance and of more elegant patterns than those of India, for one-fourth, or perhaps, one-third less in price'. (Bremner, 1869, 281) In 1785:

> A handsome cotton gown was not attainable by women in humble circumstances, and thence the cottons were mixed with linen yarns to make

reduce their price. But now cotton yarn is cheaper than linen yarn, and cotton goods are very much used in place of cambrics, lawns and other expensive fabrics of flax; and they have almost totally superseded the silks. Women of all ranks, from the highest to the lowest, are clothed in British manufactures of cotton, from the muslin cap on the crown of the head to cotton stockings under the sole of the foot. The ingenuity of the calico printers has kept pace with the ingenuity of the weavers and others concerned in the preceding stages of the manufacture, and produced patterns of printed goods which, for elegance of drawing, far exceed anything that was imported; and for durability of colour, generally stand the washing so well as to appear fresh and new every time they are washed, and give an air of neatness and cleanliness to the wearer beyond the elegance of silk in the first freshness of its transitory lustre. But even the most elegant prints are excelled by the superior beauty and virgin quality of the muslins, the growth and manufacture of the British dominions. With the gentlemen cotton stuffs for waistcoats have almost superseded woollen cloths and silk stuffs, I believe, entirely; and they have the advantage, like the ladies' gowns, of having a new and fresh appearance every time they are washed.

(Bremner, 1869, 282)

In spite of the social disruption caused by the change from linen to cotton, from the proto-industrial, domestic system to the factory system and from hand to water and steam-powered production, there are few recorded instances, from the textile areas of the East of Scotland, of machine breaking. Whatley has challenged the 'orthodoxy of passivity' amongst the Scottish working class in the period 1707 to 1830 and argued 'there was a higher incidence of riot and other symptoms of social conflict than was thought previously'. (Whatley, 2000, 143) Although this is true, there are few Scottish examples of the kind of widespread machine breaking that took place all over England. As early as 1737, the women of Macclesfield, Cheshire 'rose in a mob and burnt some looms, and when their leaders were arrested, released them from prison'. (Berg, 1994, 150) In 1779, when manufacturers in Blackburn, Lancashire began to introduce large spinning jennies into a factory setting:

A mob rose, and scoured the country for several miles round Blackburn, demolishing the jennies, and with them all the carding engines, water frames, and every machine turned by water or horses. It is said, that the rioters spared the jennies which had only twenty spindles, as these were by this time admitted to be useful; but those with a greater number, being considered mischievous, were destroyed, or cut down to the prescribed dimensions. It may seem strange, that not merely the working classes, but even the middle and upper classes, entertained a great dread of machinery

(Baines, 1835, 159)

Arkwright's mill at Birkacre, near Chorley, was attacked on 4 October 1779 by a mob 'to the number of 4 or 5,000 with considerable Quantity of Fire Arms and other Offensive Weapons and meeting with little or no resistance . . . broke into the Mill and destroyed all the Machinery then Attacked the Building with Pickaxes Hatchets &c to demolish it but at last as a shorter method . . . set fire to it & burnt it to the Ground'. (Fittton, 1989, 51) Elsewhere, 'spinning machinery was widely resisted in the West Country' and the flying shuttle was 'resisted in East Anglia, Lancashire and the West Country'. (Berg, 1994, 253)

In 1812, a year of widespread machine breaking in England, there was an attempt to destroy power looms at Deanston in Perthshire and there was fear of trouble at other Scottish mills. Five years later, stocking makers at Jedburgh, who had undercut agreed rates, had their stocking frames broken during a brief wave of machine breaking. (Fraser, 1988b, 94, & Donnachie, 1995, 16) In 1819–20, the introduction of female spinners at Broomward Mill in Glasgow led the men to burn the mill down and a woman was shot. (Knox, 1999, 53)

Scottish workers, including weavers, colliers, and shoemakers, campaigned actively for political change in the 1790s and during the 'Radical War' period of 1820. Fraser commented: 'The government, in the shape of the Lord Advocate, Alexander Colquhoun, and the Home Secretary, Sidmouth, seem to have feared Luddism less than a recurrence of political unrest, since there were increasing reports of political activities'. (Fraser, 1988b, 94) Workers attacked blacklegs and those who worked for lower wages than the norm, as in the Glasgow Cotton Spinners' Strike of 1837, a particularly bitter dispute, which centred on resistance to wage cuts, the introduction of larger spinning mules and the threat of the introduction of self-acting mules. The targets for violence, here, however, were mill managers and owners and other workers, who were brought in by the employers to work the new machines, rather than the machines themselves. (Fraser, 1988b, 152–5 & Knox, 1999, 48, 53–5)

Berg argued that labour resistance to new technology in the English textile industries 'was part of the story of industrial decline', adding 'the textile industries experienced widespread differences in their patterns of technological diffusion and labour resistance'. (Berg, 1994, 253) However, Blackburn in Lancashire, which saw large jennies destroyed as early as 1779, was no economic backwater but at the forefront of textile technology, being the birthplace of James Hargreaves, inventor of the spinning jenny. Similarly, Arkwright's spinning mill at Birkacre, Chorley, which was attacked and burnt to the ground in the same year, was state of the art in terms of its technical development.

Perth's radical history, which is largely unwritten, would certainly repay investigation. In *Traditions of Perth*, published in 1836, George Penny described the Perth meal mobs of the 1770s, demonstrations by the Friends of the People and the United Scotsmen in the 1790s and protests by Perth weavers in 1819. However, what he did not describe were any attempts to smash machinery or to stop new technology being introduced into the industry he knew so well, as a weaver and the son of a weaver.

The first cotton mills in Scotland were built in 1778 at Penicuik in Midlothian and

Rothesay on the Isle of Bute. Both had strong English and indeed Arkwright connections. Penicuik was built 'under the inspection and direction' of James Hackett, a former workman of Arkwright and an acquaintance of James Hargreaves. It was financed by Bertram, Gardner and Co., Edinburgh bankers, on land feued from Sir James Clerk of Penicuik. Rothesay was built by three Sheffield manufacturers on land leased 'on very liberal terms' from the Earl of Bute. In 1778, David Loch noted that three weeks before his visit an English engineer had planned 'the buildings, water courses, dams and machinery for a large spinning manufactory to be erected above the town, where the mills for beating lint formerly stood'. In December 1778, two of the partners withdrew from the mills, whereupon the remaining partner, James Kenyon, had 'the address to buy off from about Arkwright's works some men who were known to understand the construction and making of machinery'. (Fitton, 1989, 70–1)

This set the pattern for the development of the industry in Scotland. Richard Arkwright was involved personally with New Lanark, Stanley and Woodside near Aberdeen, where he trained workers at Cromford and licensed Gordon, Barron and Co. to use his patents. Arkwright also introduced his millwright, Thomas Lowe of Nottingham, to David Dale and Claud Alexander, who hired him to build the first four water wheels at Catrine in Ayrshire. The Buchanans of Glasgow had strong links with Arkwright. They were his first agents in Scotland and Archibald Buchanan was trained at Cromford by Arkwright. (Cooke, 1979, 197) This formed part of a more general 'English invasion' of the Scottish cotton industry. 'Apart from Brotherston, Kenyon and Burns, at least ten other individuals between 1779 and 1795 were associated directly or indirectly with English mill practice.' (Lythe and Butt, 1975, 186)

Arkwright's influence on the Scottish cotton industry continued even after his death. In 1839, the *Inverness Courier* gave an account of Deanston cotton mills in Perthshire, which showed his influence on the mill's management. This is hardly surprising, since Deanston was managed by Archibald Buchanan on his return from training at Cromford, in 1787, at the age of eighteen:

The general order of management of the Deanston Works is very much on the principle of Arkwright—a proof of the talents of that eminent person. There is a head or superintendent to each department—everyone has his own allotted part—and in most cases they are paid by the piece—not in weekly wages. They receive the amount of their earnings every Thursday morning (that being the market day), and the youngest individual about the works is paid his or her wages into their own hand, which seems to give them an idea of personal consequence. They have all the privilege of leaving any moment they choose, without previous warning; and we were informed that this is found to insure a more steady, agreeable, and lengthened service than could be obtained by the firmest indenture. There is no fine or punishment, excepting for damage to the works through evident carelessness. The order of the establishment is preserved by the dismissal of offending individuals or their banishment for a limited period. By 'stopping

the supplies' every member of the family is interested in the good conduct of the whole, and a banished child, man or friend, finds no rest at home. The morals of the people are in general very correct—no drunkard is permitted about the establishment.

(Fitton, 1989, 205–6)

Similar principles operated at Catrine cotton mills, which Kirkman Finlay, a cousin of the Buchanans, bought in 1801. He installed Archibald Buchanan as manager, who re-organised along Arkwright lines:

a system of management was adopted, and is still acted upon, which has had a very salutary effect, both as regards the conduct of the establishment with regularity and satisfaction to all parties, and also as regards the comfort and respectability of those employed in it. In the works there are 21 different rooms or departments; in each of these the master or overlooker is at liberty to chose his own hands; and in like manner, the workers have it in their power to change at the end of every week, and to go to any room within the establishment, where the master of that room can employ them, upon giving six days' previous notice to the master they leave. In this way, each master soon gathers around him a set of workers to his mind; and in reality there is very little changing from one room to another. The master, as well as all the workers, with the exception of learners and extra hands, are paid by piece work; of course it is in his interest to have the best workers he can get, and, should a worker not be able to obtain employment from any master, it is pretty evident that the fault lies with the individual, who must choose some other employment. No corporal punishment has ever been permitted; and the above regulation is a check on the severity on the part of the master, as his workers can leave him at any time, upon giving the proper notice.

(Fitton, 1989, 206)

No detailed descriptions have survived of the management methods at Stanley Mills, although it seems likely that they would be similar, as the first manager was Andrew Keay, who was trained at Cromford.

In 1796, there were 39 water mills in Scotland with 124,800 spindles on water frames, as well as 187,200 mule and jenny spindles. Once Samuel Crompton's spinning mule became established, it swept all before it, as it could spin the finest counts of cotton. William Kelly, at New Lanark, was the first person to successfully apply water power to the mule for spinning cotton in 1790. Two years later, Kelly took out a patent for a self-acting mule but this idea only became viable thirty years later, when the Manchester engineer, Richard Roberts, invented a fully automatic mule. (Donnachie & Hewitt, 1993, 53–4) Coincidentally, Roberts designed a pendulum clock for the Great Exhibition

Opposite: **Richard Arkwright (1732–1793)** (Joseph Wright of Derby)

of 1851, which was acquired by Samuel Howard for the church tower at Stanley. In 1806, Deanston Mills were bought by James Finlay and Co. and were reorganised the following year to become the first integrated cotton mills in Britain, where all the processes—washing, preparing, spinning and weaving—were carried out on the same site. (Fitton, 1989, 80, & Smout, 1969, 254) Both Deanston and Catrine cotton works were experimenting with power looms as early as 1807. (Fraser, 1988b, 114)

In 1812, there were 310,516 spindles on water frames, 158,880 on jennies and 4,209,570 on mules in the British cotton industry. In Scotland, there were 120 cotton mills with a total of 900,000 spindles, 800,000 being mule twist, 100,000 water twist, the jenny having disappeared. 20,000 people were employed in Scottish cotton mills, of whom 18,000 were women and children and the total capital invested was £1,400,000. (Lee, 1972, 4 & 7)

Whereas the spinning process was mechanised and factory based, weavers usually worked from home and formed the majority of the estimated 150,000 cotton workers in Scotland in 1812. (Whatley, 2000, 225) Power looms were slow to be introduced into Scotland, although by 1813 there were about 1,300 in operation. (Fraser, 1988b, 114) Change came slowly, partly because not all types of cotton cloth were suitable for weaving on power looms. The Glasgow cotton magnate, Kirkman Findlay, gave evidence in 1833 that:

> A grand mistake exists in supposing that the power loom supplants the hand loom universally: the power loom used in Scotland manufactures a kind of goods in general, which the hand loom weaver of Scotland was not in the practice of working at all. . . . I would also say that the hand loom weaver can work a great many things which it would not be in the interest of any power loom manufacturer to make, especially all the finest goods, fancy goods of all kinds.
>
> (Berg, 2nd edition, 1994, 252)

In 1825, out of a total workforce of 154,000 in the Scottish cotton industry, 66 per cent were women and young people. Sir John Sinclair regarded manufactures as generally beneficial. 'They are a nursery for the army; they enlarge the ideas, enlighten the minds, and promote a spirit of liberty, (which is sometimes apt, however, to degenerate into licentiousness), and they materially tend to augment the population, and to furnish it with useful employment.' He worried, however, about the cotton industry's impact on morals and family life, as well as its adverse effect on the native woollen and linen industries 'numbers of all ranks now being clothed in cotton, who formerly wore linen and woollen goods'. (Sinclair, 1825, 207, 320, 324 & 335)

By 1833, the number of mills in Scotland had increased to 134 but the number of spindles had almost doubled. There was increasing concentration in the West of Scotland, with 74 mills in Lanarkshire and 41 in Renfrewshire. There were only 17 mills outside Lanarkshire and Renfrewshire—Stanley being one of a handful of large mills outside the 'magic circle'—others being Deanston in Perthshire, Catrine in Ayrshire,

Ballindalloch in Stirlingshire and Woodside Mills outside Aberdeen. (Hamilton, 1966, 135) Leonard Horner, one of the Factory Commissioners, commented in 1834 on the dominance of Glasgow ownership in the industry:

> in Scotland there are 134 cotton mills. With the exception of some large establishments near Aberdeen, and one at Stanley, near Perth, the cotton manufacture is almost entirely confined to Glasgow and the country immediately adjoining, to a distance of about 25 miles radius; and all these cotton mills, even including the great house at Stanley, are connected with Glasgow houses, or with the Glasgow trade.
>
> (McLean, 1901, 146)

Scotland was losing out to England in cotton manufacturing. By 1835, 90 per cent of British cotton manufacturing was concentrated in the North of England, as compared to 70 per cent at the end of the eighteenth century. (Chapman, 1987, 19) Because of its superior resources of water-power, Scotland was slower than the North of England to make the changeover to steam power. In 1800, there were only 8 steam engines in Scottish cotton mills with a total power of 128 h.p., whereas the Birmingham firm of Boulton and Watt alone had built 84 steam engines in English cotton mills by the same date. (Lee, 1972, 28) In 1835, the North of England had 934 cotton mills with steam power producing 26,513 horsepower and water power only 6,094 h.p. By contrast, Scotland had 125 cotton mills with steam power producing 3,200 h.p. and water power 2,480 h.p., a much more even distribution between the two forms of power. (Chapman, 1987, 19) Scotland's relative decline can be measured by the fact that in 1833 there were no longer any cotton mills in Scotland which employed over 1,000 people, whereas in the Manchester area alone there were seven mills with over 1,000 workers. The largest mills in Scotland in 1833 were still the early water powered mills of the 1780s—Ballindalloch, Blantyre, Catrine, Deanston, New Lanark and Stanley. Largest of all were Walker and Co. at New Lanark with 930 workers and the Buchanans at Stanley with 920. (Pollard, 1965, 93)

In 1838, there were 85,000 hand-loom weavers in Scotland weaving cotton and linen. The bulk of cotton weavers were in the Glasgow/Paisley area and only 3,500 cotton looms were in the East of Scotland, the principal weaving centre here being Perth, with 1,335 looms. (Murray, 1978, 24) Earnings for cotton weavers went into steep decline from the 'glory days' between 1780 and 1800, when a good weaver could earn from 30 shillings to 40 shillings (£1.50 to £2) a week. Linen weaving was less well paid, even in the 'glory days'. For example, William Crichton's earnings in Perth from linen weaving in 1787, were only 15s. 4d. (77p) per fortnight. By 1840, earnings for a skilled muslin weaver in Glasgow had dropped to 7s. 6d. (37p) a week and average earnings for weavers were only 4 shillings to 8 shillings (20p to 40p) gross in Glasgow and 4s. 9d. to 7s. 9d. (24p to 37p) in Perth. (Hamilton, 1966, 139). As late as 1871, there were still 348 cotton weavers in Perth, a figure which fell to 79 ten years later. (Murray, 1978, 41, & 71)

From the 1830s, a shift from water to steam power took place in the Scottish cotton industry. The number of cotton mills in Scotland fell from 134 in 1834 to 98 in 1871 but total horse power increased from 10,152 h.p. to 20,122 h.p. with water power falling to an insignificant proportion of the total. (Knox, 1995, 29) The centre of the industry was Lanarkshire, which accounted for 1,138,602 spindles (over half the Scottish total) in 1861 and employed 27,065 people, which was more than half the total workforce in Scotland. (Bremner, 1869, 287)

This picture of steady expansion received a shock with the outbreak of the American Civil War in 1861. British imports of raw cotton, of which 80 per cent came from the southern states of the USA, fell from a total of 1,261 million lbs. in 1861 to 533 million lbs. in the following year and did not recover to 1861 levels until 1865. Average prices of Middling Orleans (Upland) at Liverpool increased from 6.25d. (2.5p) per lb. in 1860 to 27.5d. (13p) in 1864, then declined to 19.0d. (9p) in 1865 and 10.5d. (5p) in 1868. The value of English cotton exports fell from £40 million in 1860 to £28.5 million in 1862 but recovered steadily to reach £58 million in 1866. The Cotton Famine caused huge human distress. By November 1861, 49 mills in Lancashire had stopped and 119 were on short time. Out of 500,000 cotton workers in Lancashire, over 250,000 were receiving poor relief in November 1862 from Boards of Guardians and by 7 December 1862, outdoor relief was costing £13,743 a week. (Henderson, 1964 edition, 35,13 & 53)

Manchester bankruptcies totalled 1193 in 1861–64 and between 1861 and 1868 338 cotton mills closed and the number of power looms fell by 20,663. The number of spindles actually increased by 1,612,541 in this period, whereas the number of workers fell by 50,505. The crisis led to a 'speculation mania' in cotton futures and a general banking crisis in the Spring of 1866, when the London bank, Overend, Gurney and Co. Ltd., stopped payment with liabilities of nearly £19 million. (Henderson, 1964, 23–26)

The Cotton Famine hit Scotland equally hard. In 1861, there were 161 factories in Scotland with nearly 2 million spindles and 30,000 power looms, employing over 40,000 people. Raw cotton imports into Scotland fell from 172,055 cwt. in 1861 to 7,216 cwt. in 1864 and exports fell from 150 million yards of cloth in 1861 to 94 million yards in 1864. Unemployed Scottish cotton workers were in a worse state than in Lancashire, where able-bodied but unemployed workers received outdoor relief or workhouse relief. In Scotland, the Royal Commission on the Relief of the Poor ruled 'relief to able-bodied persons from funds raised by assessment is neither necessary nor expedient' and 'nothing herein contained shall be held to confer a right to demand relief by able-bodied persons out of employment'. (Henderson, 1964, 120–3)

Hamilton (1932) and Henderson (1934) believed that the Famine dealt a death blow to the Scottish cotton industry and 'marked a stage in the permanent decline of the industry which had already begun with the financial crisis of 1857'. (Henderson, 1964, 131) Knox has challenged this view, pointing out that cotton yarn exports from Scotland, which amounted to 6.5 million lbs. in 1861 declined to 5.5 million lbs. in 1862 but recovered to 9.5 million lbs. by 1867. The value of these exports increased from £468,000 in 1861 to £842,000 in 1867. However, the industry ceased to be a major employer of labour, even in its Lanarkshire heartland. In 1861, the cotton industry employed 23.6 per cent of the total female workforce in Lanarkshire but by 1901 this had declined to a mere 4.7 per cent (Knox, 1995, 23 & 37)

The reasons for the decline of the cotton industry in Scotland are complex and hard to unravel. Some contemporary observers followed the old British tradition of blaming the workers. Wages in the Scottish cotton industry were lower than in England. In 1886, the highest paid cotton workers in Britain were in Burnley with 35.4 per cent of its workforce consisting of men and an average wage of £42 per year. In Scotland, only 10.6 per cent of the workforce were men and average wages were £28. However, productivity was higher in England. A factory inspector claimed in 1883 'Even though lower wages may be paid in Scotland, it is doubtful if the cost of production is not even greater'. The English cotton industry produced an average 87.5 lbs. of yarn per worker per week in 1867, compared to only 56 lbs. in Scotland, giving a competitive advantage to England. By 1907, the lead had grown with England producing 132.4 lbs. of yarn per week per worker, whilst Scotland averaged only 64 lbs. English yarn output grew from a weekly total of 17.5 to 29 million lbs. between 1867 and 1907, whilst the workforce only increased from 200,000 to 219,000. In Scotland, production fell from 0.95 million lbs. in 1867 to 0.19 million in 1907 and the number of spinners fell from 17,000 to 3,000. (Knox, 1995, 89–91)

Between 1867 and 1907, the number of cotton weavers in England doubled from 153,000 to 304,000, whilst in Scotland, the weaving workforce fell from 22,000 to 11,000. Output of cotton piece goods doubled in England from 68.25 million yards in 1867 to 134 million in 1907, whilst in Scotland they halved from 5.19 million to 2 million yards. (Knox, 1995, 91–92) In 1886, out of 2,660 power loom weavers in Scotland, 2,100 (79 per cent) minded two looms and only 560 (21 per cent) looked after three looms, whereas in Lancashire, three or four looms per weaver was the norm. The Chief Factory Inspector, Henderson, claimed in 1890:

> There are no operatives of whom I have ever had an experience who work with so much energy as the Lancashire people, and the contrast between a Scotch and a Lancashire weaving factory in this respect is very remarkable. The Lancashire weaver works with a will, she earns a high wage (on average double that of her Scotch sister on the same class of work) and is anxious to maintain it. She will take charge of four power looms without hesitation; and indeed, her energetic industry is not unfrequently an embarrassment to the inspector, for it makes her indifferent to the provisions of the Act of Parliament, which has been passed for her protection. She has practically to be driven from her work . . . . In Scotland, . . . it is common to find weavers of long experience with only two power looms, and it is with difficulty that they can be persuaded to take a third. Such is the recognised contrast between the two classes of cotton operatives
>
> (Knox, 1995, 69)

Some contemporaries blamed the demise of the Scottish cotton industry on the failings of the employers, rather than the inefficiency and restrictive practices of the workers. The *Textile Trade Review,* in 1883, contrasted the hard working, practical, first generation Glasgow cotton masters with their spoilt successors with gentlemanly aspirations 'Born with silver spoons in their mouths . . . with little love for the practical work of their fathers'. Margaret Irwin, writing in 1893, accused the Scottish cotton manufacturers 'of lacking in commercial enterprise'. (Knox, 1995, 115–116) Campbell believed that the Scottish industry's decline was due to its 'relative backwardness in the introduction of the mechanical devices' and its dependence on textile machinery developed and manufactured in Lancashire. Henry Houldsworth, a prominent Glasgow cotton manufacturer, acknowledged this in the 1830s, having 'no doubt that Manchester is the leading place for machinery' and that 'good improvements' there in the previous two or three years were only adopted slowly in Glasgow because of competition from Lancashire. (Campbell, 1995, 197)

Another theory, developed by Bolin-Hort, argued that the decline of the industry in Scotland was due to greater worker efficiency in Lancashire, based on regional piece rates after 1850. These agreements, which were upheld by unions and management in Lancashire, meant that greater worker efficiency, such as minding more looms, led to increased earnings. After the Glasgow Cotton Spinners' strike of 1837, piece rate lists were abolished and every employer fixed their own rates. After 1837, there appeared to be organised trench warfare between workers and management in the West of Scotland and all attempts at increasing efficiency were resisted by workers, because there was no guarantee it would increase earnings. (Bolin-Hort, 1994, 63–83) Another factor, not mentioned by Bolin-Hort, may be the presence of large numbers of Irish workers in the West of Scotland cotton industry leading to sectarian and racist responses from employers which were less prevalent (although not unknown) in Lancashire.

The Scottish cotton industry only survived in a much reduced form by entering specialised 'niche markets' such as cotton thread in Paisley or cotton belting for steam engines, as in the case of Stanley Mills. Knox divided the industry into 'losers, hangers on and winners'. (Knox, 1995, 173) If the Perth cotton industry as a whole was an early loser, Stanley was a survivor for an amazing two centuries before it succumbed to global competition.

3.

Several Gentlemen in the Mercantile Line in Perth

The Foundation of Stanley Mills
and the Arkwright Connection, 1784–1800

Stanley lay on the southern fringe of the Atholl Estates and its development was overseen by factors like James Stobie of Marlehall on behalf of the 4th Duke of Atholl. The bend of the River Tay at Stanley is situated just downstream from the rapids at Campsie Linn, giving access to unrivalled resources of water power. Lord Nairne was the first to exploit this resource, when he drove a tunnel through the peninsula and built a corn mill in 1729. This mill was used by Dempster and Company for cotton spinning before the Old Mill was built in 1786.

Stanley did not develop in isolation but was part of a well-established textile industry in the Perth region, centring on linen and cotton manufacture plus associated bleachfields, dyeworks and printworks. The region around Perth had water-power in abundance, being at the confluence of the Rivers Almond, Earn and Tay and was linked to the London market through Perth harbour. Flax was grown extensively in Perthshire and the town was known for its skilled workforce and the enterprise and ingenuity of its merchants.

Linen manufacture was certainly important for the Perthshire economy as a whole. As early as 1689, Thomas Morer, a Londoner who had served as 'chaplain to a Scotch regiment' reported 'The trade of the town depends chiefly on linen, which the Highlanders bring thither, and which they export to the value of 40,000 l sterling per annum'. (Hume Brown, (ed.), 1891, 286) In 1724, Daniel Defoe, who had spent some time in Scotland earlier as a government spy, described Perth's linen manufacture in glowing terms:

> The chief business of this town is the linen manufacture: and it is so
> considerable here, that all the neighbouring country being employed in it,
> that there is a wealth to the whole place. The Tay is navigable up to the
> town for ships of a good burthen; and they ship off here so great a quantity

of linen (all for England) that all the rest of Scotland is said not to ship off so much more . . . . The linen trade, too, which is their main business, has mightily increased since the late Act of Parliament in England, for the suppressing the use and wearing of printed calicoes; so that the manufacture is greatly increased here, especially of that kind of cloth which they buy here and send to England to be printed, and which is so much used in England in the room of the calicoes, that the worsted and silk weavers in London seem to have very little benefit by the bill, but that the linen of Scotland and Ireland are, as it were, constituted in the room of the calicoes.

(Defoe, 1981 edition, 645–6)

In spite of Defoe's enthusiasm, there were limits to the affluence and sophistication of Perth. Until 1725, women in the town 'whose riches or circumstances intitled them to Cloathes tolerably decent or genteel' sent to Edinburgh to have them made, while others made or mended their own. Perth may have appeared 'douce' to an English traveller, even a well-informed one like Defoe, but it was a town with a lawless edge to it, like many others in contemporary Scotland. In 1722, the local customs officers, learning of the withdrawal of troops from the town during a parliamentary election, declared that unless half the garrison remained 'we shall certainly be mobbed and our warehouse be broke open'. (Whatley, 2000, 76, & 172)

Half a century later, during a meal riot in 1773, the 'Enraged and Desperate Multitude' released some of those who had been imprisoned earlier. Perth women were heavily involved in the rioting and 'to show that Sex gives no privilege to commit Mischief' it was decided that they should be arrested and brought to trial. (Whatley, 2000, 199) George Penny reported:

Between the years 1770 and 1777, there occurred a succession of bad seasons and wet harvests; and as a natural consequence, provisions were both dear and scarce, and of very inferior quality . . . . During Provost William Stewart's authority, Meal Mobs were frequent and outrageous. There were three worthies then alive who were particularly active in fomenting and heading these riots . . . . The first, James Wilson, by trade a barber, was a tall, gaunt looking personage, with a spare cadaverous visage; knock-knee'd, and splay-footed; he dressed in tawdry clothes, with tie, wig and cocked hat; his shoes often disencumbered of soles, and his stockings ornamented with needlework up to the knees. Wilson possessed that essential to every popular leader,—an unbounded stock of impudence; he had also a good deal of satirical wit, and had made some appearance as a poet . . . . The second, Blair Flight, by trade a watchmaker, was an odd looking figure. His countenance was of that description which indicates a mind capable of any mean action . . . . The third, Ned Keillor, like Tom Thumb, a little hero with a great soul. A weaver to trade, he stood, when his legs were out of the treddle hole, nearly five feet high. He wore a short round jacket, wide Dutch-fashioned breeches, a large broad blue bonnet, and a leather apron. When excited, whether by liquor or otherwise, Ned had one of the most loquacious, unscraped tongues that ever existed . . . . If at any time the price of meal advanced, these distinguished fountains of wisdom were sure to get up a mob. Notice was sent through the weaver's shops; the men turned out in a body; and came down the streets hallooing and smashing the windows of the offenders; and sometimes gutting the houses of everything valuable.

(Penny, 1836, 46–8)

The reaction of the Perth magistrates to this was predictable. In 1778, after a meal riot, they applied to the Board of Ordinance for '200 Stand of Fire Arms for the use of the Inhabitants to be Lodged at the Artillery Barracks & to be used at the Order and at the direction of the Magistrates'. (Whatley, 2000, 207–8)

By the early 1780s, cotton manufacturing was being introduced into Perth. An aristocratic French traveller and part-time industrial spy, Faujas de St. Fond, visited Perth in 1784 and described how:

Machines for carding and spinning cotton had just begun to be introduced into Perth when I arrived there. We saw the first of them at the manufactory of an individual who had them made in Manchester. He found it impossible, however, to convey them out of that town, except by night; so jealous are the manufacturers of Manchester of this happy invention of Arkwright, which has given wide celebrity and immense advantage to the commerce of that town.

I saw a loom for weaving very large bed-sheets, in one piece, by means of shuttles fixed on small rollers . . . (and bought) at a manufactory of table-linen a dozen small napkins and a tea-cloth . . . . I was glad to carry them to France by way of models.

(Faujas de St. Fond, 1784, 1907 edition, 183–3)

Two years later, another French aristocrat, Alexandre de Rochefoucauld, who was making the 'Industrial Grand Tour' of Britain, accompanied by his Polish mentor Lazowski, visited Perth and enthused:

This town is greatly increased by the manufacture of cloth in Scotland. Here, the manufacture is carried to great perfection and on a large scale. One of the manufacturers alone has working for him 200 looms every day, from which you will see that as the looms are multiplied, the town is more and more occupied by cloth-workers and cloth-workers.

Here, they make cloth of all kinds; in cotton, linen thread, hemp and damask. This manufacture is the more precious for Scotland as it all profits the country, except the raw cotton. They spin the cotton in the new mills, one of them is established three miles from Perth and two more are being built. This invention has greatly increased the output of these linen cloths, of which shirts are made for export to the coast of Africa, and in these islands. The people in the north are themselves beginning to make use of them. They are now making cloths 122 inches wide, using the English shuttle. The damask is superb, and perhaps you already know that it is better—better made and marketed—in Scotland than in any part of England. I've seen magnificent examples and they will carry out the designs one orders.

When an individual wants to have a damask made to order he goes to see the workman and pays him so much a yard, and provides the thread. The craftsman provides the loom and equips it: he is paid three shillings a yard for the most beautiful damask, and earns about 1 shilling and 6 pence a day. But as he has to spend so much time servicing his loom, he can't count on making more than a little over a shilling. The cost of the material plus workmanship works out at between 4 shillings and 4 shillings and 6 pence per yard for this fine damask. The fine thread generally costs 4 shillings a pound weight.

If the damask workers earn only a little over a shilling, the others earn less: on average 11 pence seems to be the sum.

The women and girls are all employed in spinning, not only in the town, but in all the country around. They spin as I remember I told you I saw it done last year in Leicester, spinning with each hand, but with the utmost speed, on wheels of the kind I described in Leicester. Passing through the villages, I have seen spinning by spindle, but seldom, and by old women, earning at most 4 pence a day. They can never lack work; those who can't afford to buy the flax or hemp to spin and sell on their own account are employed either by the manufacturers or by merchants trading in the business. Finally, there are establishments where all those who come asking for work receive it: these are storehouses of hemp, flax and yarn where both the merchants who organise the trade and the manufacturers who are prepared to sell the finished cloths come to stock up with the raw materials. It is this spinning-business that is replacing the wool-spinning in England: there is this difference, that here the poor can only gain assistance by working: they work harder and live less well, for here there is no Poor Rate.

(Scarfe, 2001, 134)

Rochefoucauld's description of the wonders of textile manufacture in Perth is only matched in its enthusiasm by Defoe's account of the weaving country around Halifax in the 1720s.

A modern historian has described Perth as:

perhaps one of the most interesting provincial towns at the end of the
eighteenth century, for it borrowed almost equally from the characteristics of
Edinburgh and Glasgow; it was renowned on the one hand for its academy,
its assemblies, its genteel society and its literate interests, and on the other
for its linen industry, its cotton work at Stanley, its boot and shoe
manufactories, its paper mills, its printing works, and its exports of fresh
salmon refrigerated on blocks of ice for the London market.

(Smout, 1969, 365–6)

A great deal of flax was grown in Perthshire. A survey of 252 Scottish lint mills (used
to prepare flax) in 1772 revealed that the largest number (73) in any one county was in
Perthshire. (Warden, 1864 & McLain, 1970, 300) In Little Dunkeld parish, the
minister reported in 1792 'Lint (flax) is another article of great importance to the
inhabitants of this country. Potatoes and lint may be called the two feet that support
them'. (O.S.A., XII, 409)

In Highland Perthshire, the income from the sale of linen yarn and cloth was 'the
staple for cash rents in much of the Highland area of Atholl'. (Leneman, 1986, 210)
A petition from the tenants of Atholl, Strowan and Glengarry in 1763 described how
'the tenants and their little ones are all winter employed in spinning, which draws
considerable money into them yearly, and former indolence and sloth banished the
country'. (Hamilton, 1966, 90) The 4th Duke of Atholl was appointed a member of
the Board of Trustees for Manufactures and Fisheries in 1781 and followed the example
of his predecessors in promoting the linen industry by distributing flax seed amongst his
Atholl tenants. The Rev. James McLagan, minister of Blair Atholl parish, underlined
the importance of the linen industry locally and the threat it faced from cotton manufacture
in 1790:

Our exports are a few black cattle, sheep and linen yarn. It was the last
article which principally brought ready money into the country to pay the
rents. The materials were raised at home; and almost everyone had a share
in that business. It has already felt the baleful effects of the cotton
manufactures, the materials of which are brought from afar, and by which
few gain in proportion.

(OSA, XII, 103)

However, as late as 1807, it was reported from Perthshire that: 'By the industry of the
people here in raising flax and in spinning yarn for sale, all the rents, as well as the
tradesmen's accounts due by the tenants are paid from the produce of the linen yarn'.
(Richards, 1985, Vol. 2, 430), which suggests that the linen industry in Highland
Perthshire had a fairly long shelf life. In Scotland as a whole: 'Linen output continued
to rise, tripling in volume between 1773–77 and 1813–17 to an annual average of
26.6 million yards, some of this woven from yarn spun in mills which from the mid
1790s had retreated from cotton back into flax'. (Whatley, 2000, 229)

The 4th Duke of Atholl took a keen interest in the development of Stanley Mills and village, particularly in the early stages. This was typical of many Scottish landowners, who had a strong involvement in industrial development on their estates. Early cotton manufacture required the co-operation of the local landowner, because of the need for access to water power and land. This was true of Lord Braxfield at New Lanark, of Sir Claud Alexander, (a former Paymaster of the East India Company) at Catrine in Ayrshire, or Sir William Douglas at Newton Stewart in Dumfrieshire. (Smout, 1970, 96, Donnachie & Hewitt, 1993, 13–15, Cooke & Donnachie, 1998, 139)

Some Scottish landowners were hostile to industrial development, 'from an unfounded apprehension that the privacy of their demesnes would be invaded and that fresh burdens would be entailed upon them for the support of the poor'. However, finding that the value of land was enhanced by greater consumption of its products and 'that the mills were yielding large returns to the proprietor, many landlords soon evinced a desire to have similar establishments on their own estates'. (Marwick, 1924, 203)

John Murray, 4th Duke of Atholl (1774–1830), succeeded to the Dukedom at the age of 19. He was committed to agricultural improvement and the development of forestry on his estates, introducing exotic North American species and creating the Hermitage at Dunkeld. The Duke claimed;

> In 8 years, that is from 1791–1799 inclusive I continued still further to decrease the Planting of Scotch Fir and to increase Planting of Larch and Spruce Fir. In these 8 years I planted . . . in all about 800 acres, about 600 of which were either entirely Larch, or to such an extent as to be able to thin out leaving the Larch.
>
> (Dingwall, 1987, 23)

Atholl was a patron of the great Scots fiddler, Neil Gow, who lived on the Atholl estates at Inver near Dunkeld. Robert Burns dedicated a poem to the Duke after a visit to Blair Atholl, where he 'had the honour of spending nearly two days with his Grace and Family'. (Dingwall, 1987, 21) During the famine of 1782–3, Atholl bought 500 bolls of meal and sold it at a reduced price to the poor of Dunkeld and neighbourhood. However, in January 1783, the Atholl Highlanders, who had signed up for three years' service during the American War of Independence, mutinied on being told they were embarking for India, in spite of the American peace treaty being signed. None of the Highlanders was punished for the mutiny but it bred great hostility towards the Atholl family, particularly Major-General James Murray. (Leneman, 1989, 116, 142–3)

The 4th Duke had a serious interest in industrial development on his estates, which he shared with his predecessors. In 1711, coal was discovered at Blairingone in Clackmannanshire. Successive Dukes developed the mines at Blairingone and the 4th Duke extended his landholdings in the area in 1783. The historian of the Atholl estates commented:

> while Blairingone may not have actually made a loss, its profitability had

little to do with the Duke's fascination for it. Like improving the home farm or beautifying the castle, operating a coal mine simply happened to be the sort of thing an eighteenth century landowner *did*—though it seems likely that many made a better job of it than the Dukes of Atholl.

(Leneman, 1989, 205–206)

The 4th Duke encouraged flax growing on the Atholl estates and took great exception in 1784 to a proposed duty on printed and stained linens and calicoes, which he thought would hit tenants' income and encourage emigration from the Highlands. (Leneman, 1989, 210) Atholl took the initiative at Stanley, by sending Robert Graham of Fintry to Cromford to view Arkwright's mills, by advertising in the Manchester papers for cotton manufacturers, by meeting Arkwright in Perth and by advancing £2,000 to the Company to build the village. Atholl's factor, James Stobie, designed the tunnel through the hillside at Stanley, which brought water to drive the millwheels, and he laid out the village on a regular plan.

Whatley has argued 'at its core, the Scottish Enlightenment was intensely practical'. (Whatley, 2000, 120) Many landowners felt it showed their belief in science and rational improvement to become involved in economic development, particularly if it boosted agricultural rents, or led to mining royalties, or increased feu duties from textile factories or planned villages. At Stanley, there was active involvement by the Duke of Atholl, an aristocratic grandee, and by two middling landowners, George Dempster of Dunnichen and Robert Graham of Fintry, who were both partners in the Company.

Cotton manufacture was introduced into Perth in 1782 by George Penny, who began to weave fine muslins. Penny's son later recounted how Stanley Mills developed:

> Mr William Sandeman, the proprietor of Luncarty Field, a gentleman of great enterprise, had seen and admired the muslins referred to. The Duke of Atholl and Mr Arkwright, having met at Perth, at the King's Arms Inn, Mr Sandeman introduced Mr Penny, and recommended his fabrics to the notice of these distinguished individuals, who expressed themselves delighted with his success. They inquired if he could weave them himself and teach others? On his answering in the affirmative, Arkwright said, that was all they could desire; that the erection of the mills could be immediately proceeded with;—there could be no fear of success.
>
> (Penny, 1836, 251)

On 19 February 1784, the *Nottingham Journal* reported 'very large cotton works are going to be erected at Glasgow, Perth and Lanark under the patronage of Messrs. Dempster, Arkwright and some capital Merchants and Manufacturers of that Kingdom'. Three days later, the *Manchester Mercury* warned its readers of 'the very great preparations making in Scotland by Mr. Arkwright, joined by several of the most Conspicuous in the Landed and Commercial Interests of that kingdom'. (Fitton 1989, 75)

An undated memorandum, *Considerations on the Cotton Manufacture*, stressed the novelty of the industry. 'It is in all our Memories that there was not a single piece of entire cotton cloth woven in Great Britain.' It set out Arkwright's achievements—his interest in 'eleven different engines', sales of 'not less than from £12,000 to £15,000 a month' and annual profits of up to £40,000. Some had bought the privilege of using Arkwright's patent at £7 per spindle, others contended it and 'foiled him at law'. The patent did not extend to Scotland and several 'engines' had been erected there. A new engine had been invented called a mule, which worked by hand and spun yarn of great strength, which could be used for warp but was finer than yarn produced by water frames. High wages were paid in cotton; children earned 2s (10p) a week at eight years old, no weaver had less than that sum a day and many earned 30s to 35s (£1.50 to £1.75) a week. Female spinners could earn 2s (10p) a day. The writer believed the linen industry would find it impossible to compete with cotton:

> I know but two reasons by which the Linen Manufacturers can escape
> being ruined by the rapid progress of the cotton Manufacture, one is the
> Invention of a means of spinning Linen yarn by Machines. Mr Arkwright
> is said to have discovered the art of doing so, But he is too old and too rich
> to prosecute an uncertain and labourious discovery. The other is for the
> linen manufacturers to betake themselves to the Manufacturing of
> Cotton . . . . The more quietly this is undertaken the better chance it has to
> succeed. Little should be said till we are fully possessed of every Machine
> whether for weaving or spinning that is known and used anywhere else
> (Atholl Mss. 25, IX, 1).

On 16 July 1784, the Duke of Atholl wrote to Major-General James Murray:

> I was at Perth two days ago and held a good deal of conversation with the
> most Intelligent People belonging to the Linnen Branch what effect the
> proposed new Duty would have on that Manufacture. It was their
> unanimous opinion that it required all the skill and Industry the
> manufacturers of Linen in this country possessed to be able to vie with the
> People of Ireland who had the superior advantage of paying no Duty . . . if
> a Tax is laid on the Manufacture which that Manufacture cannot bear, that
> Tax must be unproductive and the manufacture be so checked as never to
> recover. Its positive Consequence; the Numbers of People leaving the North
> Highlands this Season for America is very great the Highlands of
> Perthshire have alone been flourishing these two last years partly by the
> attention of the gentlemen in procureing proper seed corn, and partly from
> the money the linnen Trade has brought and yet government are going to
> take off the only means which will enable these People either to pay their
> rent or live in this Country.
> (Atholl Mss. 65, 5, 22)

On 28 August 1784, the Duke drew up a letter of agreement with the Company to feu 70 acres of ground at Stanley to commence at Whitsuntide 1785 for 31 years. The Company consisted of Richard Arkwright, George Dempster, of Dunnichen, M.P. for the Perth burghs, William Sandeman of Luncarty bleachfield and four Perth merchants—Patrick Stewart, William Marshall, William Keay and Andrew Keay, who became the first manager after training at Cromford. (Atholl Mss, 25, IX, 1)

In October 1784, Arkwright visited Scotland and was presented with the freedom of the burgh of Glasgow. The *Glasgow Mercury* gave an account of the visit:

> George Dempster, Esq. of Dunnichen, member of Parliament for the Boroughs of Dundee, Perth, &c. arrived here on his tour through Scotland, to procure information relative to the state of the Manufactures, Fisheries &c. Richard Arkwright, Esq; of Cromford in Derbyshire, the ingenious manufacturer of cotton- yarn, was in town, on a tour to visit the manufactures of Scotland, previous to Mr Dempster's arrival. On Friday, they were entertained by the Lord Provost and magistrates in the Town-hall, and Mr Arkwright presented with the freedom of the city, Mr Dempster having received that honour on a former visit. They were invited to dine with the Lord Provost at Kelvin Grove on Saturday. The manufacturers of Anderston, through which they had to pass, in order to testify their gratitude to Mr Dempster, the patron of manufactures in Scotland, and their esteem for Mr Arkwright, assembled their workmen to receive them. On their arrival, the workmen wanted to unyoke the horses from Mr Dempster's carriage, in order to draw him to Kelvin Grove. This honour he declined, as it has been his uniform wish and practice to lead his countrymen to freedom, rather than put them under the yoke. Mr Arkwright however was forced to comply with their offer, and the cavalcade proceeded, in a triumphant manner, to the Lord Provost's country seat.
>
> The inhabitants of Anderston, to testify their joy still further, lighted up bonfires, and prepared flambeaux to accompany them with in the evening upon their return to this city—The procession entered about half past eight, which consisted of five carriages; in the first the Lord Provost, who was followed by Mr Dempster in the second; his carriage was preceeded by a large transparent gauze-lanthorn, raised upon the top of a pole, inscribed with these words, on the front and back, *The Patriot of his Country.* On the sides, *The Guardian of our Manufactures.* The other carriages were taken up by the Lord Advocate, member of Parliament for this city &c. Mr Arkwright, Colonel Campbell of the 9th regiment, &c. In this manner they proceeded to the Saracen's head, where they alighted, amidst the acclamation of many hundreds of the inhabitants.
>
> (*Glasgow Mercury*, 7 October 1784)

This was part of a triumphant Scottish tour for Arkwright. At Paisley, on 29 September

1784, 'for his good deeds done and to be done for the well and utility of the Burgh . . . (he) was by the magistrates and Town Council . . . Made and Created a free Burgess'. On 4 October 1784, he was presented with a Lanark burgess ticket in recognition of his involvement at New Lanark. Finally, on 27 October 1784, Arkwright arrived in Perth where 'a deputation the Magistrates and Senate . . . presented him with the freedom of that city' for his part in the planning of Stanley Mills. (Fitton, 1989, 72–4)

The next month, William Sandeman of Luncarty travelled south to meet Arkwright. He wrote from Nottingham on 15 November 1784 to the Glasgow merchant Gilbert Hamilton, James Watt's brother in law:

> One great object I had in this Journey was to look into the Cotton manufactures in Lancashire being somewhat inspired with the idea of a great riseing trade from the Spirited beginning I had the pleasure to see in your thriving city of Glasgow. And from the short acquaintance I had got of the great Mr Arkwright when lately with you I had some desire to visit him and see his great Cotton Mills I have now had that Satisfaction and much pleas'd I am with my visit . . . . I am sorry that Mr. Arkwright does not stand so high in esteem with many in his own Country as his Merit deserves I have had access to See both Sides. And if through his means a part of the great Cotton Manufacture now carrying on to the employment of many thousands not only in Lancashire but in Derby and in this County Shall be brought to Scotland We will have reason to hold him in that high point of view wherein Mr Dempster introduced him to us and your great & thriving city of Glasgow will not repent the honours paid him there. It is possible that the honours he met with there which spread thro' Britain may have occasion'd some little envy from his owne Country for fear of consequences
>
> (Fitton, 1989, 76)

The Duke of Atholl took a cautious line and, on 20 February 1785, wrote to Major-General James Murray:

> I have an Idea of establishing the Cotton Manufacture in this part of the World, and I have received proposals for Erecting Mills &cr in which the famous Mr Arkwright is to be materially concerned; I thought it such an object that Fintry took the trouble of going the length of Derbyshire to be satisfied of the Utility and to induce Arkwright to be concerned in this Country; Arkwright in consequence means to be here sometime in March till then I shall enter into no agreement tho' some of the Men of most Capital and Spirit in Perth want to begin instantly a great supply of water is necessary and no where in the Kingdom is there such a Command as at Stanley & by perforating the Hill I can bring in any quantity of the Tay I please.
>
> (Atholl Mss, 65/5/43)

In April and May 1785, Atholl took adverts in the *Manchester Mercury* aimed at English cotton manufacturers, setting out the advantages of Stanley:

TO MANUFACTURERS

The Proprietor of a Situation where Mills may be erected, and a Power of Machinery worked, hitherto unattempted at any one Place in Great Britain, calls the Attention of those Manufacturers, whose Business may require a great Command and Weight of Water, especially those concerned in the **COTTON BRANCH.** The populous and thriving Port of Perth, in Scotland, from whence there is a constant and easy Access to the London Market, lies within seven measured Miles. Coal is reasonable, Labour cheap and the adjacent Country populous. Workmen being already engaged, and all Materials for Building collected, extensive Works may be prosecuted immediately.

The Proprietors sole view being the Establishment of a considerable Manufacture, Individuals or a Company, of Capital and Spirit, will meet with the most liberal Terms, and every further Particular may be known, by Letters addressed to the Duke of Athol at Dunkeld. Proposals unaccepted of shall be kept Secret, if desired.

(*Manchester Mercury*, 5, 26 April, 10, 17 May 1785)

The Duke entered into a formal agreement with Dempster and Company on 17 May 1785. They were to pay £69 10s. (£69.50) annual rent for the corn mill and the exclusive privilege of water power. The Duke agreed to 'the sole Expence of Building a house fit for the necessary Machinery,' plus workers' housing and enlarging the lade. It was agreed the Duke would grant a 21 year lease for 30 acres of ground to build a village and advance £2,000 for putting up buildings, to be supervised by Dempster and Co. and maintained by them. The Company agreed to pay 7.5 per cent interest on the Duke's advance. Richard Arkwright was appointed 'sole arbitor' on such matters as the length of the lease, the annual rent and the Duke's expenses. No rent was fixed for the 30 acres and 70 acres of ground leased but James Stobie, land surveyor at Roseland, and John Donaldson, farmer at Dron, were appointed to inspect the land and fix a rent. (NAS SC., 49, 59, 99, fos. 307–322)

On 2 June 1785, a draft lease was drawn up for the Duke of Atholl and the Stanley Company for 30 acres of land, although the Duke gave the land for streets and squares. The rights of timber and fishing remained with the Duke, who also agreed to advance £2,000 to the Company at 7.5 per cent to be advanced at various times as necessary. The land had to be used for cotton manufacture and the Company accepted damages for inconvenience and disruption to the river bank. The Company had exclusive rights of water from the Tay. Houses in the village had to be of equal height and no dung or rubbish was to be left in the streets. The High Road was to be 10 feet in breadth, between the present road to Stanley and the terrace on top of the bank on the left.

(Atholl Mss. 25, IX, 1, underlining in original)

The Company had the rights to work quarries, take stone from the 30 acres and employ the soil to make bricks. Atholl advanced £1,000 to the Company on 14 March 1786 and it repaid him £500 on 22 November 1787 plus £84 13s. 2d. interest. The remainder of the capital was paid on 15 May 1788 plus £11 19s. 9d. interest. (Atholl Mss., 25, X, No. 4) A Minute of Agreement dated 24 July 1786 fixed the feu duty at £2 per acre, half of which the Duke would pay back to the chief Magistrate of the free barony to be laid out in the town. 30 shillings (£1.50) an acre was to be paid for the ground containing the mill and £1 an acre for making use of the clay pits. Two days later, the Duke wrote to George Farquhar, his Edinburgh lawyer, that he wished to apply for a Charter of Barony for Stanley and asked Farquhar to send him a copy of Lord Gardenstone's charter for Laurencekirk. (Atholl Mss., 25, IX, 1)

James Keay, the Company's lawyer, wrote to Farquhar in Edinburgh on 23 August 1786 that they were hoping to have the scroll of the feu right—'some of the Coy are impatient to have it settled before Mr Dempster leaves this County'. (Atholl Mss., 25, IX, 1) Six days later, Farquhar forwarded the scroll for the Stanley Company to the Duke of Atholl. The feu included the mill and 4.5 acres of adjoining ground with a tack of 70 acres with houses, if any, thereon. Farquhar also enclosed papers regarding Gardenstone's village, as he was still applying for a burgh of barony. (Atholl Mss. 65, 5, 132) In late December 1786, Andrew Keay, the manager, told Robert Graham of Fintry that he had written to Perth informing the partners of what was proposed regarding the £2,000. He couldn't yet determine thirlage for the corn mill as 'we have not yet had the Corn Mill going above ten months'. (Atholl Mss., 25, IX, 1)

Village planning was fashionable amongst Scottish landowners in this period, often associated with manufacturing industry or fishing villages. Between 1770 and 1799, 164 planned villages were laid out in Scotland with a further 119 in the next two decades, including fishing and coastal villages in the North East of Scotland and in the Highlands and Islands. (Lockhart, 1983, 133–6) James Stobie drew up plans for Stanley for the Duke of Atholl and for nearby Pitcairngreen for Thomas Graham in 1788. (Cooke, 1984, 49) In the same year, George Dempster of Dunnichen, one of the Stanley partners, laid out Letham village on a greenfield site on his estate. The *Statistical Account* reported in 1791:

> In the year 1788, a farm of 66 acres, called Letham, has been laid out by the proprietor of Dunnichen for a village. Streets have been marked out on a regular plan, and lots of any extent are let upon perpetual leases, at the rate of £2 an acre. It contains already about 20 families, and new houses are rising in it daily . . . here a fair or market has lately begun to be held, once a fortnight, on Thursdays, for the sale of cloth, yarn and flax; and £400 or £500 are sometimes returned in one market day.
>
> (OSA, XIII, 201)

Lord Gardenstone planned Laurencekirk in Kincardineshire with 'bleachfields, a printfield, linen workers, stocking-knitters, cabinet makers, smiths and other sorts of country tradesmen'. John Ramsay of Ochtertyre commented in 1800 that he had 'surely succeeded in converting a paltry kirk town into a neat and flourishing village. It is a Herculean task to think of establishing manufactures in a country ill provided with fuel and at some distance from the sea'. (Smout, 1970, 94) Laurencekirk was founded as a burgh of barony, which gave various trading privileges and a degree of self government to the villagers. However, James Keay, the Stanley Company's lawyer, was reported on 14 August 1786 as advising against this 'as giving the Government of it to those elected by a parcel of low manufacturers might be a source of discord instead of utility'. (Atholl Mss 65/5/128) This reflected unease amongst many Scottish landowners about local democracy. 'A watchful eye ought to be kept over villages no less than other collections of men, and that the reins of government ought to be held by a steady hand'. (Robertson, 1799, 67–8)

Although the Duke of Atholl's involvement was crucial in terms of access to land and water rights, there were other requirements for Stanley to succeed, some of which were mentioned in the adverts. Access to the London markets via the port of Perth was considered an important factor, as was local expertise in textile production and the low cost of local labour. Other key factors were entrepreneurial experience and capital from local merchants and industrialists, including William Sandeman of Luncarty bleachfield, and a number of Perth merchants. However, the technology of cotton spinning had to be imported from England and here Arkwright's involvement, which was crucial, was secured by the intervention of George Dempster.

In a letter to Sir John Sinclair, dated 21 January 1800, Dempster described how he became involved in the development of cotton spinning in Scotland:

> I cannot trace that business to its very source, for cotton was spun by mills at Pennycuik in Mid Lothian, and in the Isle of Bute, before ever I had heard of such an invention. But as I had some concern in engaging Sir Richard to instruct some of our countrymen in the art, and also to take a share in the great cotton-mills of Lanark and Stanley, it may not prove unentertaining to one of your turn for statistical inquires, to mention a few particulars to you; more especially as mere accident occasioned my having any concern in that matter.
>
> Ever since the tax on post-horses, it had been my custom, to perform my journeys to and from Parliament, with my own carriage and horses, making time, as other mechanicians do, supply my want of pecuniary power. To amuse my wife and myself, and to rest my horses, I generally halted a few days at the different watering places by the way; and in the year, I think, 1796, (actually 1783) being particularly captivated with the romantic scenery of Matlock, we staid a week or ten days there. In the course of a forenoon's ride, I discovered in a romantic valley a palace of a most enormous size having, at least, a score of windows of a row, and five or six stories in height. This was Sir Richard Arkwright's (then Mr. Arkwright)

George Dempster of Dunnichen, MP (1732–1818) (George Willison)

cotton-mills. One of our mess-mates being known to the owner, obtained his
permission to see this stupendous work. After admiring everything I saw, I
rode up to Mr Arkwright's house—knocked at the door. He answered it
himself, and told me who he was. I said my curiosity could not be fully
gratified, without seeing the head from whence the mill had sprung. Some
business brought him soon after to London. He conceived I had been
useful to him; and offered to assist me in establishing a cotton-mill in
Scotland, by holding a share of one, and instructing the people. Private
business carried him the following summer to Scotland, where he visited
Perth, Glasgow and Lanark, and, I believe, Stanley, for I was not then in
Scotland. Mr. Dale and I became partners in mills to be erected in Lanark.
A company of five or six Perth gentlemen, he and I, entered into
partnership in mills to be built at Stanley in Perthshire. Some

misunderstanding happening between him, and Mr. Dale, which they submitted to me, I met them both at Sir Richard's house at Cromford in December 1786. Each gentlemen offering to take concern and to take my share also, I awarded the whole to Mr. Dale, as being most convenient to him to manage. Mr Dale thinking, I had made him a valuable gift of my share, offered me £1,000 Sterling, by way of equivalent for it, but I was too glad to be rid of so extensive a concern to accept of any compensation for it. Sir Richard instructed Mr Dale's artists and young children gratis, as he did those sent from Stanley. From this last concern I was never able to extricate myself, although it was my intention to do so, as soon as it should become profitable to the adventurers. Mr Arkwright resigned. The war surprised us just when we were beginning to reap the profit of our labours. The price of cotton rose, the value of cotton-yarn fell, and considerable loss was incurred. In the year 1799 the company was dissolved, and those admirable mills are now on sale.

(NAS, RH, 449, 2, Vol. 3, 266–8)

Why did Arkwright become involved in the development of the Scottish cotton industry in general and of Stanley in particular? Towards the end of 1785, he was involved in a scheme to secure a statutory monopoly of wool spinning, helped by Sir Joseph Banks, the great botanist, then President of the Royal Society. Banks undertook to bring Arkwright's proposals to the attention of his 'parliamentary friends'. (Fitton and Wadsworth, 1958, 87–90) Dempster was one of those friends and wrote to the Earl of Buchan about the application of Arkwright's machinery to the spinning of wool. (Laing Mss, II, 588/1)

Although this project fell through, Banks and Dempster feature prominently in a (rather supercilious) account of Arkwright's knighthood, by the aristocratic Mrs George Murray in a letter to her husband, Captain George Murray, dated 25 December 1786. The occasion was the presentation of a loyal address by Arkwright to George III on the failure of an assassination attempt by Margaret Nicholson on the King. Mrs Murray described how they had driven to Soho Square, where she:

was much entertained at the scene they had had the Morning before, in the arrival of the <u>Great</u> Mr Arkwright who came to Sir Joseph's in a black wig, brown frock, worsted stockings and Boots to ask him to go with him to the levee when he was to present an address on Margaret Nicholsons affair. Sir Jos too good-natured to refuse agreed but asked him about his dress. Mr Arkwright proposed going as he was, for he was not afraid they were but Men—and so was He—however it was agreed he should take off his boots & return with good shoes at the proper hour our friends had a hint he would be worth seeing so took care to be in the way, but were not a little surprised to see little fatty appear a beau with a smart powdered <u>bag</u> wig so tight that coming over his ears it made him deaf: a handsome striped sattin

Waistcoat & proper coat with a sword which he held in his hand, all
provided it is suposed by Mr Dempster, to crown the scene Mr More
introduced him telling Sir Joseph he did not know if he was prepared for
the ceremony but Mr Arkwright intended to accept the Honor his Majesty
offer'd—this surprised all the company but . . . Sir Joseph carried off his
Beau and Brought him back Sir Richard Arkwright. What a pity you
happened not to be there then as the scene was excellent, the little great
Man had no idea of kneeling but crimpt himself up in a very odd posture
which I suppose His Majesty took for an easy one so never took the trouble
to bid him rise.

(Atholl Mss. 65, 5, 171, underlinings in the original)

Both New Lanark and Stanley may have been a reward for Dempster's contribution
towards easing Arkwright, however uneasily, into the Court and smart London society.
(Cooke, 1979, 200–1) However, another explanation is the way in which English
merchants and manufacturers saw the Scottish cotton industry as a threat, so that Stanley,
New Lanark and Woodside, Aberdeen can be seen as Arkwright's revenge on his
English competitors, who had successfully overturned his patent rights in the courts.
Baines claimed:

The Lancashire spinners, were indeed Arkwright's great enemies. Owing
partly, perhaps, to his humble origin, and partly to the doubt whether he
was the author of the inventions, 'he had no honour in his own country'.
Being of an irritable temperament, he resented this treatment, and exerted
himself to raise up a successful rivalry to Lancashire. He therefore favoured
the Scotch spinners as much as possible and formed a partnership with
David Dale Esq of Lanark mills; in allusion to which, and probably by way
of retorting the unworthy taunts of his opponents, relative to his former
occupation, he said, that 'he would find a razor in Scotland to shave
Manchester'.

(Baines, 1835, 193)

Andrew Keay, the first manager at Stanley, was sent to Cromford to be trained. He
wrote from Cromford, on 17 June 1785, to William Sandeman, one of the partners.
Keay had received Sandeman's letter of the 8th from Luncarty, and presumed he had
not yet recovered from 'the hurt' he got. The boys who had left Perth 'Monday sennight'
had not yet arrived. Arkwright was still in London, so Keay had not had the opportunity
of telling him what Sandeman said about the canal:

We must on no account be Short of Water for the Cotton mill but do not
you think that it would be proper to begin the work according to Mr. A.s
directions when on the spot by repairing the old one—he says you will have
plenty of water for the whole mill which I hope we shall but if not a new

Cutt can be made and surely it ought to be as wide as you mention in that case I believe we can get some of the lime you speak of from near Chesterfield by the canal to Hull which will be much less expense than buying it from Wales. The water which according to the plan I sent is intended to use about 70 tons of water . . . so that some judgement may be formed of whether more water will be necessary than there is in the old Canal—40 tons however will drive all the machinery we shall have for sometime.

(NAS GD. 151, 12, 21)

James Stobie of Marlehall, the Duke's factor in the Stanley area, was the man charged with putting these plans into practice. His plan for the new mill lade, dated 1785, showed a tunnel 776 feet long with a fall of 1 foot 4 inches, at a depth of 127 feet below the hill. (Atholl Mss D1/2) In Stobie's plan of Stanley the mill lade emerged from a tunnel in the hillside to run parallel to the river, before taking a right angled turn to the mill and splitting into two channels to discharge into the Tay. (Atholl Mss A/6) An undated plan showed the same configuration for the lade but with three channels exiting into the river, labelled 'Spinning Mill shoot'. (Atholl Mss B/14)

James Stobie's Plan of Stanley Mill Lade, 1785 (Atholl Mss.)

(1)

Contract of Co-partnery

Betwixt

Richard Arkwright Esqr. and others

At Perth the first day of January Seven:
:teen hundred and Eighty Seven Registered
In presence of David Smyth Esqr. advocate
:sheriff Depute of Perthshire Patrick Duncan
and James Chalmers Procurators

It is Contracted and Agreed upon
Betwixt Richard Arkwright Esquire at
Cromford Derbyshire South Britain George
Dempster Esquire of Dunichen Robert Graham
Esquire of Fintry William Sandeman
Merchant in Perth Patrick Stewart Mer:
:chant there and Andrew Heay Mercht.
Whereas the Said parties Having intend:
:ed to enter into Co-Partnership for the pur:
:pose of carrying on the business of prepar:
:ing and Spinning cotton-wool in this
Country in the way and manner in
which it is carried on by the Said Richard
Arkwright at Cromford aforesaid and
other branches of Trade connected there:
:with Did in prosecution of their Said
intention enter into a Submission with
his Grace John Duke of Atholl for a Lease
of the Cornmiln at Stanly aqueduct thereat
and exclusive priviledge of the water
and

The Contract of Partnership for the Company was drawn up in December 1785 and registered in January 1787, under the name Dempster and Co. The partners were: Richard Arkwright, George Dempster of Dunnichen, Robert Graham of Fintry, William Sandeman of Luncarty, Willliam Marshall, Patrick Stewart and Andrew Keay, all of Perth and the partnership was for 'preparing and spinning cotton wool in the way and manner in which it is carried on by Richard Arkwright at Cromford'. Each partner held one share of £1,000 in the Company, making a total capital of £7,000, and the Duke of Atholl advanced £2,000, towards the cost of building houses, on which the partners would pay 7.5 per cent. They entered into indentures with different people to be sent to Cromford, to learn to make cotton spinning and preparing machinery. Profits and losses were to be shared according to the partners' interest in the business and they could not sell shares, except to other partners, without majority consent. An exception was made for Richard Arkwright that, when operations became profitable, he could sell his shares to George Dempster or, if Dempster declined, to anyone he saw fit. Andrew Keay was appointed as manager to sign all bills, orders, letters etc., although at present, he was absent in Cromford. It was agreed to take out a cash account with the Perth United Company or any other company up to the value of £3,000. (NAS, SC49, 48, 104, fos. 1–5) The Stanley Company's capital of £7,000 in 1787 compared with a Scottish average, in 1795, of £5,000 for cotton mills for insurance. (Cooke, 1995, 91)

The partners brought a range of expertise to the Company. Richard Arkwright (1732–1793) had established the world's first modern cotton mills at Cromford, Derbyshire in 1771. He had worked as a barber in Preston, Lancashire but had moved into cotton spinning—first in Preston, then in Nottingham. At the time that Stanley was planned, he was fighting a bitter battle in the English courts about patent rights for the water frame, a revolutionary water-powered machine for spinning cotton. In February 1785, Arkwright won his case in the Court of Common Pleas but was challenged by Thomas Highs of Leigh in Lancashire. Highs had built a machine identical to Arkwright's in 1767 with the help of John Kay of Warrington, who was employed a year later by Arkwright to build the water-frame. The cotton industry mobilised against Arkwright, the case was reopened and in July 1785, 'after a great display of hostile witnesses,' Arkwright lost his case. (Mantoux, 1964 edition, 228–9, Fitton, 1989, 127–8 & Fitton & Wadsworth, 1958, 86)

Whatever Arkwright's dubious claims as an inventor, he did have unrivalled skills as a manager, entrepreneur and organiser of a workforce. Baines attributed his success to:

> his wonderful ardour, energy and perseverance. He commonly laboured in
> his multifarious concerns from five o'clock in the morning till nine at
> night . . . Arkwright was a severe economist of time; and that he might not
> waste a moment, he generally travelled with four horses, and at a very rapid

Opposite: **Contract of Co-Partnery, Stanley Mills, 1 January 1787**
(National Archives of Scotland SC49/48/104)

speed. His concerns in Derbyshire, Lancashire and Scotland were so
extensive and numerous, as to shew at once his astonishing power of
transacting business and his all-grasping spirit. In many of these, he had
partners, but he generally managed in such a way, that whoever lost, he
himself was a gainer.

(Baines, 1836, 195–6)

Arkwright trained the Stanley manager and workforce at Cromford and clearly had a
hand in the design of the Old Mill at Stanley, which is built on Derbyshire lines. He
also advised on water-power installation at Stanley.

George Dempster of Dunnichen, (1732–1818), was MP for the Perth burghs,
which included Cupar, Dundee, Perth and St. Andrews, from 1761 to 1790.
Dempster's father (like his father before him) was a corn merchant in Dundee and
became the target for a Dundee meal mob, in February 1720. They damaged his
townhouse and furnishings and he described Dundee thereafter as a 'wicked place'.
(Whatley, 2000, 192, & 204) Dempster Senior died in a fall from a horse in 1754.
His son went to grammar school in Dundee and to the Universities of St. Andrews
and Edinburgh. He entered the Faculty of Advocates on 1 March 1755 and Parliament
in 1761. In 1763, he founded the Dundee Banking Company and in the same year
became a member of the Scottish Order of the Thistle. (Boase, 1867, 69–73, Foster,
1882, & Lowson, 1893)

Dempster's career received a setback when, at the age of 35, he was accused of
bribery and summoned to be tried before the High Court of Justiciary, on 7 December
1767. The case involved £60 in Dundee bank notes that had been given to one of the
deacons of a trade in Cupar, Fife. Dempster appealed on the grounds of Parliamentary
privilege and the Court of Session ruled that he could not be tried while Parliament was
sitting. He was arraigned in Edinburgh in August 1768 for bribery and corruption but
the case was dismissed. (Boase, 1867, 69–73)

Dempster recovered from this setback and he became a director of the East India
Company, Provost of St. Andrews from 1774–1780 and, with the 4th Duke of Atholl,
a Commissioner of the British Fisheries Society. He knew most of the key figures of the
Scottish Enlightenment and people further afield—he corresponded with the philosopher,
David Hume and the Icelandic antiquary, George Thorkelin, knew James Boswell,
was praised for his honesty by Robert Burns and was a friend of the great English
botanist, Sir Joseph Banks. (Fergusson, 1934)

In 1786, Dempster bought the estate of Skibo, in Sutherland and carried out
improvement schemes, building Scotland's most northerly cotton mill at Spinningdale,
on the Dornoch Firth, with assistance from David Dale and a group of Glasgow
merchants. (Richards, 1985, Vol. 2, 19–25, & Cooke, 1995, 89–94) This was an
attempt to counteract population clearances for sheep, which distressed Dempster. 'People
need not be driven out of the country because the sheep are introduced into it. Villages
may be built for them where they might be employed in manufactures'. He enlarged on
his ideas for planned manufacturing villages in the Highlands:

It is one thing to build a village, to which people may resort if they choose it, and another to drive them from the country into villages, where they must starve, unless they change at once their manners, their habits, and their occupations. How much better it would be gradually to introduce spinning wheels and looms into their houses, than to drive them from their houses, their gardens and their little fields.

(Cooke, 1995, 90)

Richards saw Dempster as an influential figure in the debate on the 'Highland problem'. 'Three men in particular—Adam Smith, George Dempster, and Sir John Sinclair— were influential in moulding the intellectual and psychological content for the further transformation of the Highlands.' (Richards, 1985, Vol. 2, 14) Dempster supported the Scottish cotton manufacturers in their campaign against the tax preference given to muslin and calicoes imported by the East India Company and presented a petition to Parliament in 1784 signed by 12,000 operative weavers. (Fraser, 1988b, 61) He was the key person in persuading Arkwright to become involved at Stanley (and New Lanark), having met him in Derbyshire on his way back from Parliament and toured his mills. (NAS, RH 449, 2, Vol. 3, 266–8) As a founding partner of the Perth United Bank, in 1766, Dempster was the Stanley Company's main channel of access to local credit.

Robert Graham, twelfth of Fintry, (1749–1815) came from a landed family with estates at Linlathen, just outside Dundee. In 1785, Graham had to put his estates in the hands of trustees for the benefit of his creditors. He was taken under the wing of the Atholl family and carried out various services for them. (Mudie & Walker, 1964, 17) Graham successfully lobbied on behalf of Dundee linen manufacturers in 1792, when a regulation was brought in for 'the inspection of public stampmasters'. (OSA, XIII, 164)

William Sandeman of Luncarty (1722–1790) was the owner of Luncarty bleachfield on the Tay three miles downstream from Stanley. He was a member of the Glasite Church founded by John Glas of Tealing near Dundee, who broke away from the Church of Scotland in 1730 after challenging the authority of the Presbytery in favour of congregational authority. The Glasites enforced strict discipline over their membership and formed an influential business network. Their membership included the Baxters, linen merchants and manufacturers in Tealing, Glamis and Dundee and the Turnbulls, who were partners with Sandeman at Luncarty. (Cooke, 1980, 16, & 1984, 3)

Sandeman was appointed a lapper and stampmaster of linen by the Board of Trustees for Manufactures on 13 June 1746 and became the main channel of communication for their activities in Perthshire. He was the man the Board turned to in the early 1750s, when they wanted someone to distribute flax seed and spinning and reeling machinery in Highland Perthshire. In 1752, Sandeman began to lay out a bleachfield at Luncarty and over the next two years spent £1,300 'levelling and laying out twelve acres of bleaching ground'. Later, he acquired another bleachfield at Tulloch, near Perth. He took an active interest in Stanley and travelled to Nottingham

William Sandeman of Luncarty (1722–1790) (artist unknown)
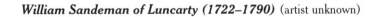

to see Arkwright's mills. (Durie, 1979, 85 & 1996, 77, Cooke, 1984, 1–3 & Fitton, 1989, 76)

The remaining partners– Patrick Stewart, William Marshall and Andrew Keay— were Perth merchants and would be familiar with sales of yarn and cloth, if not production. Keay became manager, after training at Cromford, and wrote to Sandeman about water-power for Stanley. (NAS, GD.151, 12, 21) It seems likely he was related to James Keay, the Edinburgh–based lawyer for the Company. Andrew Keay was succeeded as manager by David McVicar, another Perth merchant, who presumably was the same David McVicar, who was town treasurer of Perth in 1787. (Cant, 1806, 223–230)

Marshall is a common name in the Perth area and a Thomas Marshall was provost of Perth in 1784 and 1785 but William Marshall may also have been related to John Marshall, who became principal partner at Luncarty bleachfield in 1837, having begun his working life there as manager and junior partner. Patrick Stewart was probably the person of the same name, who served as merchant bailie in Perth in 1784–85. (Cant, 1806, 223–230 & Cooke, 1984, 5)

The Company opened an account with the Perth United Banking Company, on 4 July 1785, in the name of 'William Marshall for the Stanley Cotton Company' with an upper limit of £1,000. Munn described how 'the proprietors of the Stanley Mill used their cash account to provide themselves not only with a source of circulating capital but also with a long term loan'. Between July 1785 and May 1787, when the Perth United Bank closed, the Stanley balance only fell below £700 in November 1786 and in most months it was much larger (Munn, 1984, 118 & 212) Whatley commented on the importance of bank lending to the Scottish cotton industry for capital needs and for shorter term credit through bill discounting. By 1793, the number of provincial banks in Scotland had risen to 21 and a further 12 formed between 1802 and 1810. In 1802, Scottish bank assets were £12 million, a higher per capita level than England (Whatley, 2000, 224), which challenges notions of Scotland's economic backwardness in this period.

Most provincial banks did the majority of their business with merchants rather than manufacturers. In 1787, 38 per cent of cash credits with the Perth Bank were with merchants, 18 per cent being with landowners and 14 per cent with manufacturers. Between 1802 and 1805, 42 per cent of cash credits of the New Dundee Banking Company were with merchants, 14 per cent with landowners and 14 per cent with manufacturers. (Munn, 1984, 196) However, the number of Perth merchants amongst the original partners of Dempster and Company suggests that the categories of 'merchant' and 'manufacturer' were blurred in this period.

The Company had easy access to the Perth United Bank, as George Dempster was one of the Bank's founding partners in 1766. Dempster was a champion of small provincial banks, being a founder member of both the Dundee Bank and the Perth United Bank. In 1790, he wrote to Henry Dundas, Viscount Melville, who, as well as being Lord Advocate, was also Governor of the Bank of Scotland, to protest about a bill to tax bills of exchange. Dempster argued 'many small banks are infinitely preferable to one or a few great ones the advantages of which are very much confined to the places where they are established'. (Munn, 1984, 20 & 45)

When the mills started, the area was a green field site, except for Stanley House and the corn mill. The Duke of Atholl demanded control over the development of the village and plans were drawn up by his factor, James Stobie, on a rectangular gridiron plan, which survives in its essentials down to the present day. The first street to be laid out was King Street with its continuation Duchess Street running roughly parallel to the River Tay. A rough sketch, formerly at Stanley Mill, named the square as Arkwright Square, later changed to Duke Square.

The Stanley feu contract, dated 13 February 1787, referred to the partners having begun operations at Whitsuntide 1785. William Stewart was named as a new partner, in place of Arkwright, who had withdrawn from the Company, as he had done at New Lanark. The reasons for this are not entirely clear. Arkwright was at the height of his powers, having been knighted in 1786, although his health was poor and he was never the easiest man to fit into a partnership. (Cooke, 1979a, 200) The Company were given the right to make bricks, in common with the inhabitants of Stanley, from the spot allocated by the Duke. The feu contract also gave the right to quarry and take off stone from Hilltown Quarry and Whinstone Rock, near Thistle Bridge, a rock formation on the Tay to the West of Stanley. (NAS SC49, 59, 104, fos. 120–129) A plan of

Duchess Street, Stanley, c.1900 (National Monuments Record of Scotland)

Stanley, which predated the cotton mill, showed a circular 'kill' (kiln), either a grain drying kiln or a brick kiln, to the west of the corn mill. (Atholl Mss B/14)

An agreement between Atholl and the Company, on 13 February 1787, insisted that the village must follow the plan laid out by Stobie. It was hoped to get a Charter from the Crown, failing which, the village would be subject to the regulations of the Barony of Nairne. Feuars must conform to the plan regarding the breadth and lines of the streets and the feu duty was to be £2 sterling per scotch acre. The village was eventually intended to cover 30 acres. Villagers had to build alongside existing buildings 'so that the buildings fronting the streets or square may be in one continuous line without any Empty spaces intervening, Excepting Entries of four feet or thereby where necessary to the Gardens behind'. (NAS, SC49, 59, 104, fos. 129–132) This was common practice amongst improving landowners in this period, going back at least as far as John Cockburn at Ormiston, who wrote in 1742 'I can give my consent to no houses being built in the Main Street of the town but what are two storys high'. (Smout, 1970, 86)

The first cotton mill at Stanley, known as the Old Mill, the Brick Mill, or the Bell Mill, was begun in the Spring of 1786 and was finished by 13 February 1787, when the feu contract referred to 'the Stanley Corn miln and a Cotton miln and other Buildings thereto belonging . . . erected situated along the side of the River Tay'. (NAS, SC49, 59, 104, fol.129) The name 'Bell Mill' is a later title—in the 1830s it was referred to as the 'Old Mill' or the 'Brick Mill'. The Old Mill is a handsome six storey building—the two lower floors built of stone, the rest of brick with segmentally arched sash windows. The internal dimensions are 90 feet by 28 feet, the size of brick is 8.5 inches by 4 inches by 2.5 inches, laid in Flemish bond. The use of brick was very early in this part of Scotland and showed the influence of Arkwright and the early Derbyshire mills. There are wooden beams and floors supported by a single row of cast iron columns placed off centre. This is the oldest known use of cast iron columns throughout a textile mill, making the building a landmark in the development of iron framed buildings, the ancestors of the modern skyscrapers. An oral tradition attributed the manufacture of these cast iron columns to the Carron Iron Works but there is no documentary evidence for this.

Early cotton mills followed a standard (and functional) layout, described in Ree's *Cyclopaedia* of 1812:

> A large cotton mill is generally a building of five or six stories high: the two
> lowest are generally for the spinning frames, if they are for water twist,
> because of the great weight and vibration caused by these machines. The
> third and fourth floors contain the carding, drawing and roving machines.
> The fifth floor is appropriated to the reeling, doubling, twisting and other
> operations performed on the finished thread. The sixth, which is usually in
> the roof, is for the batting machine or opening machine and for the cotton
> pickers, who for a large mill are very numerous. This last is not always so
> occupied, many manufacturers thinking it better to have outbuildings for
> these parts of the process and only to have such parts in the mill as require

the aid of the large water wheel or steam engine, which turns the whole mill. If the mill is used for spinning instead of the water frame, then the cards are usually put below, because they are then the heaviest and most powerful machinery.

(Fitton, 1989, 148)

Brick making continued in Stanley and the manager, David McVicar, commented, on 16 March 1791, 'the privilege of making bricks is of much consequence to the inhabitants and ought not to be given up—The Company have that privilege mentioned in their feu but are excluded from selling any'. He was also concerned about the privilege of quarrying stone at the Mitton quarry or the whinstone quarry at the Thistle Bridge. (Atholl Mss, 25, IX) In 1795, it was reported in Redgorton parish 'there are many clay pits from which they make excellent bricks'. (OSA, XV, 540) Brick was also used in the construction of the tenement on Store Street, which was built under the Buchanan regime in the 1820s. However, the East Mill and the Mid Mill, most of the housing and most of the other buildings such as the churches and school were built of stone. Slate was the main roofing material, probably from the slate quarries on the Atholl estates around Dunkeld. A Valentine's photograph of the late nineteenth century showed a kiln situated to the west of the modern school, which was marked as an 'old brick kiln' on the 1901 OS map. (NMRS, PT, 5126)

Stanley was a large mill by contemporary standards. A Board of Trade Report, in 1788, said Stanley Mills contained 3,200 spindles and was valued at £13,000. In 1795, the mill contained 2,000 spindles, whereas most of the early English mills averaged 1,000 spindles. (OSA, XV, 529, & Chapman and Butt, 1988, 106) However, New Lanark was much larger—in 1795 it contained 12,000 spindles and employed 1,300 people, according to an American visitor, John Aspinall. (Donnachie & Hewitt, 1993, 55)

In January 1792, George Dempster told David McVicar, the manager, that they should be covered for insurance in 'this cold weather and these long nights'. He added 'I'd sooner underwrite a Fireship or a Powdermill and as far as fire goes sooner be concerned in either'. (NAS, GD. 151, 12, 20) The Company took out a policy with the Sun Fire Office and a Sun Fire Office plaque survived on the gable of the Brick Mill until mill closure in 1989. In 1796, the insurance valuation was £10,500, including a cotton mill valued at £2,500, a 'New Cotton and Flax Mill near unfinished' at £2,000 and millwrights' work with 'all the going gears therein' at £2,500 for the cotton mill and £750 for the unfinished mill. 'Clockmakers Work Carding and Breaking Engines all moveable utensils therein,' came to £2,000 for the cotton mill and £250 for the unfinished mill and stock, including flax, was valued at £500. The annual premium for the policy was £50 13s. 0d. (£50.65) (Guildhall Library, Sun Fire Office Policy 640186)

In 1794, it was reported that:

At Stanley, there is a considerable cotton-mill for spinning twist by water, the first that was established in the neighbourhood; in which Sir Richard Arkwright interested himself much in the outset, George Dempster, Esq. and Company. The proprietors here have lately built another mill, which will probably be employed soon in spinning linen yarn by water.

(OSA, XI, 494)

The building of a flax mill, on the site of the East Mill, suggested that the Company planned to produce either fustians, which were a mixture of cotton and linen or a fabric known in Perth as 'blunks', a combination of linen warp and cotton weft, which was preferred by the local printers. (Penny, 1836, 250)

The Literary and Antiquarian Society of Perth produced a Report on the Perth textile industry, dated 10 June 1794. Linen was still the dominant textile, in spite of the advent of cotton. The total value of textiles in the Perth area was estimated at £220,000, of which £160,000 (72 per cent) was linen. The Report placed an annual value of £120,000 on 'brown and white fine threaded linens, denominated *Silesias*, chiefly printed for handkerchiefs; with *Britannias*, *Kentings*, &c. for export trade', for which Perth was famous. 'Stout Holland sheetings' were valued at £12,000 per annum and an annual value of £20,000 was placed on 'Four-fourths wide brown and white country linen, chiefly used for hat linings, buckrams, &c. Brown Hollands, Hessians, pack-sheetings, and other coarse fabrics, manufactured in the neighbourhood; including soldiers shirtings, with a few coarse sheetings, and Osnaburgs purchased'. An annual value of £8,000 was given to 'Five-fourths wide umbrella linens, and linens for window blinds, &c'. (OSA, XI, 492–495) The dominance of linen in Perth was confirmed by a claim, in 1795, that there were 1,500 looms in the burgh and that linen was still the 'staple manufacture' of the town. (Murray, 1978, 3)

The main goods produced from cotton yarn in Perth were 'Shawlcloths, calicoes and muslins with a very few pulicate handkerchiefs,' which were shipped from Perth, chiefly for the London market, at an annual value of £60,000 sterling. The Report added: 'The cotton manufacture was rapidly extending; but met with a severe check last summer, by a reduction of the goods manufactured, and has not yet recovered its former vigour. The shock did not affect the linen manufactures in a similar degree.' The water-powered works of Stanley, Cromwellpark, and Stormontfield produced some £30,000 worth of cotton twist yarn annually between them and there were three printfields in the area—Ruthvenfield, Cromwellpark and Tulloch and four bleachfields—Luncarty, Tulloch, Huntingtower, and Stormont. (OSA, XI, 492–494)

Textile printing was one key to Perth's success:

The produce of these works, is shipped at Perth, chiefly for the London market. The printers here have a full command of the article of Silesia linen for handkerchief printing, being the staple manufacture of the town and neighbourhood; they likewise supply part of the country demand, in England and Scotland.

(OSA, XI, 494)

The Duke of Atholl had an ambivalent attitude towards Stanley. He had gone to great effort to establish it in the first place and advanced £2,000 of his own money towards buildings but he feared social disorder if the mills closed down, to say nothing of the effects on the poor rates (and his pocket), of large scale unemployment. These fears surfaced in June 1790, when James Keay, the Company lawyer, was sent a draft feu contract 'for regulating the buildings and for preventing the Poor collected there by that Coy from becoming a burden upon your Grace as heritor of the parish'. (Atholl Mss. 25, IX, 1)

The Atholl estates dragged their feet over the granting of a charter. James Keay, the Company's Edinburgh lawyer, wrote to George Farquhar, the Duke's lawyer, on 16 December 1790, enclosing minutes of agreement. Keay asked Farquhar to make out a charter by the Duke and added 'it has been a great loss to the Coy that they had it not sooner as it prevents their going on with the village with forwardness they would otherwise have done'. On 9 March 1791, Keay told Farquhar that he had received a letter from the Stanley manager 'complaining of the delay in the granting of a Charter of the Village to the Coy and that many people had been prevented from taking feus from the Coy on that account'. He hoped that a Charter could be made out soon 'otherwise the Coy will be under the disagreeable necessity of establishing their feudal rights in some other manner'. He would expect the scroll in a day or two. (Atholl Mss. 25, IX, 1)

A new feu contract between the Duke and George Dempster and Company was registered on 26 April 1792. The new partners were George Dempster, Robert Graham of Fintry, Patrick and William Stewart, James Keay, writer in Edinburgh, Alexander Keay, accountant in Edinburgh, Thomas Marshall, merchant in Perth and David McVicar 'formerly merchant in Perth, now at Stanley'. William Sandeman, William Marshall, and Andrew Keay, the former manager, had all died since the agreements in January 1787. The Company agreed to feu an extra acre of ground, making a total of 7 acres in all. If it was not built on in 15 years, it would revert to the Duke. The feu duty was fixed at £2 an acre, £14 a year in total. (NAS, SC49, 59, 116, fos. 235–244)

The Duke's worst fears were realised in the early 1790s, when a combination of trade depression and radical ideas spreading from France led to the spectre of social breakdown. The Friends of the People Societies, which had branches all over Britain, were inspired by Tom Paine's *The Rights of Man*, published in 1791, advocating universal suffrage, redistribution of property, and political reform through 'a general convention elected for the purpose'. (Smout, 1969, 442). The Societies were supportive of the French Revolution, at least in its early phases, and of the ideals of Liberty, Equality and Fraternity. By 23 September 1792, Perth was reputed to have four Societies, with a total membership of a hundred. (Meikle, 1921, 91–2)

A report in 1792, estimated that the Perth Society of the Friends of the People had 1,200 members, contrasting with another estimate of 100 members. The leadership was largely middle class, including merchants, a surgeon, a minister, a solicitor and other 'persons of some little respectability in the Town' but the bulk of the membership consisted 'chiefly of operative weavers, of which there are a vast number' and 'operative people in the various trades of Perth'. It was reported 'the lower Class of People talk of nothing but Liberty and Equality—No Dundas—No Bishops—and No King. Nothing but a republic for us'. (Fraser, 1988b, 65, 67) In Aberdeen, Perth and Dundee 'and almost every village in the North of Scotland,' the mob burnt an effigy of the Home Secretary, Henry Dundas, Viscount Melville. (Meikle, 1912, 81)

Perth was a hotspot for radical activity at this time. It lay on the southern edge of the Perthshire Highlands in a key strategic position, on a major river crossing. It was a first port of call for Highlanders moving south to seek work and as such had the air of a frontier town, with Gaelic being in daily use. The burgh had an important textile industry and weavers had a long-standing reputation for radicalism. Perth was a substantial town by Scottish standards. In 1755, its population was 9,019, compared with the 47,815 of Edinburgh, the 30,000 of Glasgow, Dundee's 12,477 and Paisley's 6,799. In 1790, the population of Perth had grown to 19,871. Five years later, Edinburgh's population was 71,645, Glasgow's 56,028, Paisley's 24,592 and Dundee's 23,500. (Meikle, 1912, 63)

Perth's reputation also owed something to its longstanding role as a garrison town, including its role in the Jacobite period. After the 1745 Rebellion 'an encampment of 5,000 German troops formed upon the North Inch; the more effectually to overawe, and secure the submission of the country'. (Penny, 1836, 43) Soldiers often brought their own problems of discipline and, if they were German, English or Irish, there was always the danger of a nationalist or sectarian backlash from the local population.

However, the reaction of the Perth population was not always predictable. A Company of Irish troops, known as the White Boys, was stationed in Perth. They were badly treated by their officers and following a particularly brutal flogging on the North Inch, a group of soldiers was rescued by the outraged Perth washerwomen 'who, with their laps full of stones, and backed by the willing multitude, broke through the line, drove the officers from the circle, and liberated the prisoners'. The women seized the adjutant and gave him 'a handsome flogging on the bare posteriors, in the presence of thousands'. (Penny, 1836, 63) Clearly, Perth women were not averse to taking direct action when required.

The King's Birthday was celebrated on 4 June as a holiday, the streets decked with flowers 'the bells were set a ringing; the great guns fired a royal salute; the military fired a feu de joie; and the whole town turned out to see the sights'. 'Reform and Retrenchment' brought about dramatic changes. 'Democrats began to make their appearance; dead cats and basses were hurled about, and dirt thrown; and the birthday fell into great disrepute.' (Penny, 1836, 38–9) There were similar incidents in Glasgow, where the night of George III's birthday in June 1792 saw 'a loose disorderly rabble throwing brickbats, dead dogs and cats, by which several of the military were severely cut'. (Whatley, 1995, 383)

Lord Adam Gordon described Perth as 'a very dangerous place' and the sheriff reported that it was not uncommon for even boys in the west end to shout 'liberty, equality and no king!' On 6 November 1792, 'several hundreds of the lower class' burnt Henry Dundas in effigy and little more than a fortnight later the entry of Dumouriez into Brussels was celebrated by the erection of a Liberty Tree at the Perth Cross. The bells were rung from eight in the morning till six at night and people were forced to illuminate their windows. (Meikle, 1912, 81, 96) George Penny described how:

> The Perth Hunt, then newly instituted, having assembled at the races, the Friends of the People took the opportunity of displaying their sentiments in a way which could not be mistaken. The assemblies were then held in the Glover's Hall and the ordinaries in the George Inn. At the time appointed for the meeting of the assembly, a numerous body of Friends ranged themselves in two compact lines, forming a lane betwixt the inn and the hall, along which the gentry had to pass. . . . Every individual who was supposed to be a friend to the rotten constitution had a severe ordeal to undergo; even the best of them had to walk, hat in hand, and make obesience to the *Majesty of the People*. When the Duke of Athole appeared a terrible clamour was produced. The cry arose 'There comes citizen Murray, Black Jock who sold the Highlanders. To the guillotine with him, that he may receive his deserts'. Mr Dundas also received special notice. Many of the nobility came in chairs, but this did not save them; the occupant was examined: and even ladies were compelled to endure the insults of the rabble.
>
> (Penny, 1836, 70–71)

In December 1792, the Nine Societies in Perth sent nine delegates to the First General Convention of the Friends of the People in Edinburgh. This compared with only one delegate from Dundee (Thomas Muir) but a staggering two delegates from the tiny Kincardineshire village of St. Cyrus. In September 1793, the Reverend Thomas Palmer, an English Unitarian minister and graduate of Queen's College, Cambridge, who had been a minister in Dundee, was tried in Perth and sentenced to seven years transportation to Botany Bay. Palmer was 'a disciple of Priestley's' responsible 'for the promotion of levelling doctrines' and for a riot in Dundee in 1792. He was a delegate (from Forfar) to the First General Convention of the Friends of the People held in Edinburgh on 11–13 December 1792. (Meikle, 1912, 98, & 240)

Palmer had been a marked man for some time. On 29 July 1793, the Lord Advocate wrote: 'You may rest assured, from the accounts I have received from Glasgow and from Perth and Angus, that those rascals have laid a plan for exciting the country again to discontent and disorder on account of the war, and that this is the topic on which they are to dwell'. He enclosed an address on the subject, printed in Dundee and circulated in Edinburgh—'Palmer, the Methodist (sic) clergyman who lately went over to Dundee, is strongly suspected. If he is the man, I shall not doubt his being got hold of; which he was artful enough to keep clear of last winter'. In August, the Lord Advocate described Palmer as 'the most determined *rebel* in Scotland'. (Meikle, 1912, 129)

Palmer's crime was publishing a handbill written by a Dundee weaver, George Mealmaker, which 'described the King and Parliament as in League to enslave the country and exhorted the people to combine to take decisive measures in their own defence'. (Fraser, 1988b, 68) In February 1794, the Relief church minister in Perth was reported to have been preaching sedition by denouncing the wars with France. In April, firearms from England were allegedly delivered to 'Evil disposed persons' in Perth and the bridge over the Tay was daubed with slogans such as 'Damn all Kings' and 'Who would want a King to eat the Bread of twenty five thousand men?' (Whatley, 2000, 303)

In April 1794, Robert Watt, a former government spy employed by the Lord Advocate, was put on trial for sedition along with an associate, David Downie. They were accused of running a Committee of Union in Edinburgh, which was corresponding with radicals in Perth, Paisley, Strathaven and Dundee. Robert Watt had ordered the manufacture of pikes and halberds. He was found guilty and hanged at the Tolbooth of Edinburgh, his body was cut down, the head cut off and displayed to the crowd with the age-old words—'This is the head of a traitor'. (Meikle, 1912, 152–3) In September 1794, there were mass arrests in Paisley, Perth, Stirling, Dundee, Edinburgh and Glasgow. (Fraser, 1988b, 69) In 1795, a poor harvest sent grain prices spiralling. An additional six troops of dragoons were stationed in Perth but this only exacerbated the situation, as the new regiment was Irish. Horse patrols went through the town with drawn sabres, which the magistrates believed put 'an end to Civil Authority' and on 31 October 1795, they requested the 'immediate Removal' of the 31st Regiment. (Whatley, 2000, 303)

George Mealmaker, Thomas Palmer's associate in 1793, a Dundee weaver and a member of the United Scotsmen, somehow escaped prosecution then but was eventually arrested and tried in January 1798. He was charged with sedition, with publishing inflammatory pamphlets and administering unlawful oaths. Robert Dundas, 2nd Viscount Melville, wrote: 'It is of essential importance, that Christie, Campbell and Mealmaker should be sent to Botany Bay as soon as possible. The discoveries we are daily making of what is going forward amongst the United Scotsmen warrant me in what I am now stating'. Mealmaker was duly dispatched to Botany Bay for fourteen years. (Meikle, 1912, 188 & Smout, 1969, 445)

The United Scotsmen were particularly strong in Tayside. Burns identified twenty six Societies in Scotland, half of which were in Tayside, drawing support from parishes with large numbers of weavers and large Seceder congregations. (Fraser, 1988b, 71) George Penny reported that both the Friends of the People and the United Scotsmen attracted mass support in Perth, especially from weavers and shoemakers. Penny claimed to be scandalised by the egalitarian and irreligious behaviour of the United Scotsmen in Perth:

> This society (United Scotsmen) was started in Perth by a stranger from
> Glasgow, who was introduced to Robert Sands, the Secretary to the
> Friends of the People. Their ostensible object was Universal Suffrage, and
> Annual Parliaments; but their ulterior aim was purely Republican . . . .
> Vast numbers were sworn in, among whom was James Thomson, one of the
> town officers . . . Liberty and equality became such cant words, that

ignorant and deluded people were encouraged in the belief that equality of property was their grand aim, and that a speedy division was to take place;—that the banks were to be plundered, and the spoil divided;—that the taxes were to be abolished, and the exciseman would cease from troubling;—that all invidious titles of distinction were to be annulled, and the only terms by which men were henceforth to be known, was that of citizen. Extravagant as were these political nostrums, they were innocent compared with the flood of immorality, profligacy, blasphemy, and infidelity, which rapidly spread to the most deplorable extent. Heads of families renounced the Christian religion, and adopted Paine's infidel notions as the standard of their creed. The Bible was declared to be a silly fable; and some of the deluded wretches actually burnt the sacred scriptures at their profane meetings . . . . Many of these misguided men persevered in these courses till they had reduced their families to misery and want. Their work was neglected, and much of their time occupied during the day with political pamphlets and discussions, and in the evenings their earnings were squandered at club meetings. The weavers and shoemakers, the trades which chiefly distinguished themselves in these matters, had good wages at the time, and were enabled to sport away for a time, particularly the weavers, who, in addition to high prices for their labour, had their time in a great measure at their command. But these habits soon involved them in debt, to an extent which constrained many to leave the town, and to abandon their families to the utmost distress; thus demonstrating, that no species of tyranny is so pernicious as the want of self government.

(Penny, 1836, 68–69)

In 1797, Henry Dundas, Viscount Melville, the Secretary of State for War, wrote to the Lord Advocate about raising a Scottish militia of 6,000 men to 'preserve the *internal Tranquillity*, and to repel *foreign Invasion*'. The Scottish Militia Act of 1797 obliged schoolmasters in every parish to make a list of all able bodied men, between the ages of 19 and 23, to raise a militia. There was great popular opposition to the Act, the most serious being at Tranent in East Lothian, on 29 August 1797, where a crowd of 200–300 toured the neighbouring villages, beating drums and shouting 'No Militia! To Tranent!' and threatening the lives of the schoolmasters, until they handed over the parish registers to the crowd. Government troops reacted by opening fire and killing eleven men and women. (Meikle, 1912, 179–180, 277, & Fraser, 1988b, 71)

On 27 August 1797, James Stobie reported to the Duke of Atholl that a threat had been made to the life of the schoolmaster at Auchtergaven, adding: 'I am happy to mention that no person about Stanley or anywhere in the neighbourhood is making the least disturbance'. (Atholl Mss. 59, 4, 345) Several country schoolmasters were attacked in Perthshire and session books were burned. 'Two troops of the Ayrshire cavalry were lying here at the time; and every day expresses arrived from different quarters for troops to keep down riots and quell disorders.' The main resistance to the Act in Perthshire came from Highland parishes, which 'had become extremely outrageous: they became organised into regular bands, under the guidance of one Cameron, and opposed the cavalry'. Rumours spread that Blair Castle had been burned down and, although Cameron was arrested and imprisoned in Perth, he escaped almost immediately. (Penny, 1836, 84)

On 26 March 1798, Stobie told the Duke that George Mellis had stopped working his cotton mills at Cromwellpark on the River Almond and 'hundreds of very worthless people are cast loose on the world'. (Atholl Mss. 59, 5, 88) Trading conditions during the French Wars grew increasingly difficult and in September 1799, the new flax mill at Stanley was burnt down and the mills put on the market. Stobie told the Duke, on 20 December 1799, that the Stanley Company 'have at last advertised their magnificent works, as they call them'. No date had been fixed for the sale but the Company had named people 'to be enquired at' including the former manager, David McVicar. (Atholl Mss., 59, 6, 152) George Dempster wrote to Sir John Sinclair in 1800 'the war surprised us just when we beginning to reap the profits of our labours. The price of cotton rose, the value of cotton yarn fell and considerable loss was incurred.'(NAS, RH, 4, 49, 2)

Very little of this political and economic turmoil was picked up by Robert Heron, the Galloway-born biographer of Burns, who passed through the area in 1799. He described Perth as 'a very flourishing town, A great linen and cotton manufacture is here established . . . . Bleaching and printing of linen and cotton is carried on in its vicinity to a great extent'. (Heron, 1799, 149) Heron also visited Stanley. 'At Stanley, on the west side of the Tay, there is a cotton work, and a handsome village, built on a regular plan, and containing about four hundred inhabitants.' Another traveller was more realistic, when he noted: 'Flax works were lately erected at Stanley, but were burnt almost to the ground in September 1799. The whole of the machinery is now on the market. Three channels over 12 feet wide and arched with stone, merge in a great canal 20 feet deep and 4 feet deep. The fall is from upwards of 20 feet onto the wheel.' (Campbell, 1811, Vol. I, 310)

The bleachfield at Luncarty was described by Heron in glowing terms—'(the fields) were now covered with linen-cloth or luxuriant crops of wheat or other grain'. (Heron, 1799, 144–5) In 1800, an English traveller, John Leyden, toured the area and was also impressed. 'We passed beneath Birnam to Stanley, a small town the situation of which is extremely sweet and romantic, and proceeded to Taymount to see the Linn of Campsie, a small fall of the Tay.' (Leyden, 1903 edition, 268)

4.

A Positive Greedy Fellow

James Craig, David Dale, Robert Owen, and the Dale Trustees, 1800–1823

Stanley mills had shut down by 10 January 1800 and the Duke of Atholl's factor, James Stobie, told the Duke that the workers 'are but a worthless sett but it is dismal to see the state they are now in'. Stobie was suspicious of the Company's intentions. 'The Stanley Company hold the Sparrow in their hands. They say to everybody make an offer and we will tell you if this is accepted or not this is in plain English after offers have been made they will roup the Subject which is using offerers very ill.' (Atholl Mss. 48, 1, 3) In the same month, he told the Duke 'the Starving Thieves at Stanley have been committing depredations for which if nothing else can be got, they must be put in prison'. (Atholl Mss. 48, 1, 7)

The Duke of Atholl put out feelers regarding alternative uses for Stanley. John Borland, of Stormontfield bleachfield on the Mansfield estates, on the other side of the Tay, wrote to the Duke on 6 March 1800 with a proposal for a bleachfield at Stanley. He had devised a plan for a canal from the mouth of the Anaty Burn to the back of the mills, where the canal would be navigable to Stanley. He proposed to convert the park at Stanley into a printfield and bleachfield, if coal could be carried by water instead of overland. He asked the Duke to discuss it with Lord Mansfield, the owner of the land over which the canal would pass. Five days later, Borland wrote to Atholl again to report that he had written to Lord Mansfield. He had previously said that the canal at the back of the mills was navigable to Stanley but the truth was it could be made navigable if £4,000 was subscribed by Atholl, Mansfield and others as a 'free gift', which would enable Borland to construct a canal capable of carrying barges of 10 to 20 tons. He believed the Board of Trustees had given £2,000 towards Luncarty, which was much less important, so the Board might contribute and the county might assist. (Atholl Mss., 48, 1, 27 & 34) A rough, undated, sketch of this canal survives at Blair Castle. (Atholl Mss., D1/4)

At the end of March, Stobie reported that the Company had not yet come to any conclusion concerning David McVicar's (the former manager's) decision to divide the falls and keep one himself, as the other partners were inclined to the whole going in one lot. Another partner, William Stewart of Perth, had assured Stobie that there would be a public sale. The sale was eventually advertised on 7 May 1800 at Perth. (Atholl Mss., 48, 1, 49 & 58) The partners of the outgoing Company carried on the business until 17 September 1799, when it was disponed in favour of Archibald Campbell of Clathick, advocate. Campbell was presumably acting for David Dale, whose wife was a Campbell. There were 6 acres of ground Scots—King Street and Duke Street were largely built on and another acre, where Arkwright Square and Charlotte Street were built. (NAS, RS 52/69, fos. 65–69) Under a disposition of 6 March 1800 in favour of Archibald Campbell, the Company confirmed that 5 acres had been let for the Stanley Corn and Cotton Mill, 6 acres Scots for the village and a further acre feued for the village in 9 March 1792. A tack of 70 Scots acres, known as Drumbeath Farm, had been sublet to James Stobie for 31 years from Martinmas 1785. A factor, a clerk and agent were to be appointed to look after the property and to report to an annual meeting of former partners and trustees. Any income was to go to paying first the management, secondly, feu duties, tacks and other public burdens, thirdly, insurance in the Sun Fire Office and finally, the Company's debts. (NAS, B22, 8, 221)

Trade depression continued into the following year and Stobie told the Duke, on 31 March 1801, that a new company had taken over at Stanley but were 'not to proceed in much opperation before business appears to take a turn it will at any rate take them a considerable time to get all ready'. Trade conditions were generally grim—the Ruthven Company had stopped work the previous week and unemployment was causing great distress to the weavers—'a few years ago these people were so haughty as to disturb the state I think chastisement has fast followed them'. On 26 June 1801, Stobie was making a new street in Stanley (Atholl Mss. 48, 2, 58), which from a sketch of March 1803 was Percy Street to the north of King Street. The sketch showed housing on both sides of King Street and Charlotte Street, as well as on three sides of the Square. (Atholl Mss. 48, 4, 54a)

James Craig, a Glasgow muslin manufacturer and his partner, James Mair, 'Plantation merchant in Glasgow', bought Stanley Mills with financial assistance from David Dale on 21 January 1801 for the knock down price of £4,600, the original asking price being £6,500. James Craig was the principal partner and James Mair was cautioner. The company was registered on 28 January 1801 and began business on 9 February 1801, as 'Mair Craig and Co'. They had a Glasgow establishment, where goods were sent for sale and raw cotton was purchased, often from Robert Owen. The whole money transactions of the company were carried on in Glasgow, Robert Wilson being their Glasgow agent. They agreed to pay £1,000 in part payment at Candlemas 1801 and the remaining £3,600 in three yearly instalments of £1,200 with interest, at Candlemas. The mills re-opened in January 1802 and James Mair sold his half share of the business to Craig on 3 April 1802. (Atholl Mss. 25, XI, 3, & NAS, GD, 64, 1, 247, 58)

James Craig (1757–1839) was presumably the same Glasgow merchant mentioned in Owen's autobiography, who bought Sea Island yarn from Owen's Bank Top Mill in Manchester. Owen had pioneered the spinning of Sea Island cotton on 'new machinery through rollers,' which, although it looked dingy compared to French West Indian or New Orleans cotton, produced a better thread than either. Craig returned to Manchester to look for more Sea Island cotton, telling Owen it was the best quality he had ever seen and its dingy colour was no problem, as it bleached much better than the white yarn. (Owen, 1857, 84,) David Dale's next-door neighbour in Charlotte Street, Glasgow was called James Craig and it may be this link that led Dale to support Craig financially, a decision he came to regret. A Memorandum for the Duke of Atholl, in 1817, claimed that Craig was 'a relation of the late David Dale' but there is no other evidence for this claim. (Atholl Mss., 25, XI, 3)

James Mair was the son of John Mair, a Paisley-born merchant and manufacturer, who had started life as a mason then come to Glasgow and become a prosperous merchant there and in London. John Mair bought Plantation in 1793 from John Robertson, a Glasgow colonial merchant. The Glasgow Directory of 1803 listed John and James Mair as merchants living at 27 Hutcheson Street. They were admitted as burgesses and guild brothers in Glasgow, on 28 February 1801. The same Directory also listed James Craig, manufacturer, at 44 St. Andrews Square, Glasgow, which was the address Owen used in some of their correspondence and was situated in the same Square as the Lanark Twist Company's Glasgow warehouse. (*Old Country Houses*, 1878, 203, & Donnachie, 2000, 86)

David Dale, (1739–1806), was born in Stewarton in Ayrshire, the son of a grocer and general dealer. His background was humble:

> Originally a herd boy at Stewarton, and afterwards a weaver at Paisley, Hamilton and Cambuslang. He came here as a young man and became a dealer in linen yarn, tramping the country and buying in pickles from farmers' wives. From this small beginning he developed a large trade in importing yarn from the Low Countries.
>
> (Smout, 1969, 385)

In 1777, Dale married Anne Caroline Campbell, a descendant of the 1st Earl of Breadalbane, who was a member of the powerful Clan Campbell. Caroline's father was a cashier with the Royal Bank of Scotland, an extremely useful link for an up and coming merchant like Dale and five years after his marriage, Dale became the Glasgow agent of the Royal Bank. (Donnachie and Hewitt, 1993, 17–34) Caroline Dale was also related to Archibald Campbell of Jura, a wealthy improving landowner, who made a fortune from the sale of black cattle and became entangled in the financial affairs of the Stanley Company. Campbell was a member of the Committee of Management of the Board of the Cotton Trade in Glasgow, along with Kirkman Finlay. (Donnachie, 2000, 90)

In 1783, David Dale was appointed joint agent, with Robert Scott Moncrieff, of the Glasgow branch of the Royal Bank of Scotland, which owed a great deal to his family connections with the Campbells and explained why Craig was so eager to seek his patronage. Archibald Campbell of Jura placed his money in Dale's hands at a special fixed rate of 5 per cent interest regardless of the current rate. After Dale's death, Campbell and his family became vocal critics of the Dale trustees' role in financing Stanley with Campbell money.

Dale's connections with the powerful Clan Campbell were one of the keys to his rise from humble beginnings as a weaver and itinerant pedlar to becoming the founder of New Lanark and a partner in numerous Scottish cotton mills. They illustrate the importance of family connections in the early stages of industrialisation. Mathias, in his study of the English brewing industry, observed: 'Kinship . . . must be regarded as one of the most fundamental considerations in the study of entrepreneurship in the eighteenth century. Cousinhood can give the key to much success.' (Mathias, 1959, 271)

Dale was 'Pastor to the Independent Congregation in Glasgow, for which he was particularly fitted, by a thorough knowledge of the Hebrew and Greek languages (and) a steady friend to civil and religious liberty'. He was a member of the merchant guild of Glasgow, a burgess of the city and a founder member of the Glasgow Chamber of Commerce, the first of its kind in Britain. He was the key figure, with Richard Arkwright and George Dempster, in the foundation of New Lanark in 1784 and was its owner until Robert Owen, his son-in-law, and his partners, took it over in 1800. He was a partner, or had interests in, at least six large cotton mills in Scotland, including Stanley and Britain's most northerly cotton mills, at Spinningdale in Sutherland. (Donnachie & Hewitt, 1993, 17–34, 56, & Cooke, 1995, 89).

A Letterbook that survives at Blair Castle, contains 106 copies of letters, mainly from Robert Owen to James Craig at Stanley. Letters also survive from Robert Humphreys, Owen's under manager at New Lanark, a Glaswegian who had worked with him at Bank Top Mill, Manchester and was known as a 'good mechanic', and from John Wright, the book keeper who ran Owen's Glasgow warehouse, having previously worked for David Dale. (Chaloner, 1954, 94, Cooke, 1979b, 107–11, & Donnachie, 2000, 79, 111, & 173) Owen kept an eye on affairs at Stanley from New Lanark or Glasgow on behalf of the Dale trustees, giving advice to James Craig and buying raw cotton for him on the Glasgow cotton exchange. Owen also visited Stanley occasionally, to advise Craig on the spot.

Robert Owen (1771–1858) had moved to Scotland from Manchester on taking over New Lanark as Managing Partner in 1800. He was born at Newtown in Monmouthshire, Wales, the son of a saddler and retail ironmonger. He served his apprenticeship as an assistant with the McGuffogs, a Scottish family, who ran a haberdashery and linen merchants' shop in Stamford, Lincolnshire. Owen moved to London to work with Flint and Palmer, another haberdashery shop, in Southwark. In 1788, Owen, aged 17, moved from London to Manchester to a job with Sattersfield and Co., a firm of silk merchants and drapers, in St. Ann's Square, Manchester. In 1791, he went into partnership in Manchester with John Jones, another Welshman, and set up a firm making cotton-spinning machinery. A year later, he was appointed manager of Peter Drinkwater's Piccadilly, or Bank Top, Mill, Manchester, at a salary of £300 a year. He set up the Chorlton Twist Company in Manchester in 1794 or 1795. In 1800, Owen and his partners bought the New Lanark mills for £60,000, a substantial sum, though on very favourable credit terms, after Owen's marriage to Dale's daughter, Caroline, on 30 September 1799. (Donnachie, 2000)

The Letterbook gives very little hint of the future author of *The New View of Society* or of the man who claimed on taking over New Lanark 'my intention was not to be a mere manager of cotton mills, as such mills were at the time generally managed; but to introduce principles in the conduct of the people which I had successfully commenced with the workpeople in Mr. Drinkwater's factory'. (Owen, 1857, 56–57) In fact, the correspondence is very much that of the practical, hard-headed businessman, even down to the use of language. In February 1802, Owen urged Craig to 'push' his stocks of yarn as hard as possible, whilst later that year he enclosed a bill for £100 for Craig as 'you must now be short of the needful' The letters contain no references at all to schooling or education and the few references to the work force are those of any moderately enlightened employer. For example, in August 1802 Owen advised Craig to supply candles for the cotton spinners at Stanley, adding 'there is not anything lost by a fair encouragement of work people'. (Atholl Mss., 25, XI, 3, fos. 6–7, 14, 16–17)

Owen's humanitarianism finally emerged, in November 1808, during the American Embargo, when he wrote that prices for raw cotton were so high, it would be better to pay the hands full wages to do nothing than spin such expensive cotton. (Atholl Mss., 25, XI, 3, fos. 109–111) At New Lanark, Owen stopped the mills and paid full wages for four months, amounting to £7,000, during the American Embargo. (Owen, 1857, 64) Towards the end of Craig's management, in February 1811, Owen wrote that he must stop water spinning, the sooner the better 'but you cannot discharge any of the work people without giving them sufficient notice'. Craig should not dismiss anyone until Owen had visited Stanley but he was sorry to say that several Glasgow mills planned to discharge hands as soon as their stocks ran down. (Atholl Mss., 25, XI, 3, fos. 162–165)

Owen was not a partner at Stanley but kept an eye on the business for his father-in-law, David Dale, who paid the third instalment of the purchase price in 1803 and kept the business supplied with working capital to the tune of £24,270 until his death in 1806. (Atholl Mss. 25, XI, 3, & NAS GD. 64, 1, 247, f.43) This began a fraught relationship between James Craig, David Dale and Robert Owen, representing the Dale trustees, which eventually ended in tears and the law courts.

Stobie reported to the Duke, on 23 January 1802, that Craig had set the spinners to work and seemed anxious to feu or lease even more ground, although little could be done until more was known about the purpose for which the ground was required. Craig had only come to Stanley for a day. He had been held up by the high cost of insurance for the mills but had got his policy at 26s (£1.30) per £100, instead of the 42s (£2.10) per £100 formerly demanded. (Atholl Mss., 48, 3, 15) On 8 February 1802, Robert Owen was happy to hear that Craig had arrived at Stanley. The next day, Owen was going to New Lanark and would immediately put some webs to be warped, which would be sent to Stanley for the weavers. He had given instructions to John Wright, his book-keeper, to forward some warp immediately and as soon as possible thereafter some weft, which would give the quality desired but must in future be warped

½ inch narrower than Craig was currently doing. Craig should write to him at the Lanark Twist Company, Manchester with details of the cost of the goods he was making, including 'the price of 4/4 shawls cloths' and of 'callicoes'. He was glad to hear that the spinning was coming on and that Craig liked the cotton he had sent. 'Mr Scott Moncrieff on Saturday corresponded with the Perth Bank respecting discounting our paper.' (Atholl Mss. 25, XI, 3, fos. 1, 11–12) Robert Scott Moncrieff was Dale's fellow Glasgow agent for the Royal Bank of Scotland and had argued Owen's case in his successful courtship of Caroline Dale, with her sceptical father. (Donnachie, 2000, 75)

Owen had left Lanark on 11 February 1802, on his journey south, when news came that Mrs Owen was very ill. He had hurried back but found she was recovering. He had sent two bags of Georgia cotton to Craig, the price being 2/9d (13.5p). Prices for raw cotton were rather lower since Owen sent the last bag, as more cotton had come into Glasgow. Mr Scott Moncrieff, of the Royal Bank of Scotland, had written to David Walker regarding the discount on bills of exchange drawn on Glasgow at three months and had received a favourable reply. Walker, who presumably worked for the Perth Bank 'finds in a regular way, that Bills must be accepted by him before they were presented for discount' and he would only discount bills, the money for which was to be spent in the Perth area. Owen gave a detailed account of the price of spinning fine counts of cotton on mules at New Lanark and was anxious to see some of the goods which Craig had made and to know how much they cost. He would send some more twist and weft and instructions for another fabric or two in a few days time. He hoped to resume his journey to Manchester as soon as his wife recovered. (Atholl Mss., 25, XI, 3, fos. 3–6)

On 26 February 1802, Owen acknowledged Craig's letter of the 23rd giving details of the price of weaving calicoes at Perth, which appeared favourable to their views. He urged Craig to 'push' the low counts as much as possible and as soon as he had a piece of the new cloth to send it to Mr. Wright, who would soon know if it answered their customers' expectations. Owen's next letter was from Manchester, on 20 March 1802, to enthuse about his visit to one of the best and cheapest spinning mills in the country. The spinning mules contained 126 spindles each and 'one boy and a girl work two of them without any pain'. He was very enthusiastic about what he had seen. 'This is the cheapest spinning I ever saw and this is done within 7 miles of Manchester where living is very expensive.' The children produced 3,000 hanks of cotton per week once experienced and could exceed that in the summer, with good light. Owen had bought two pieces of Stockport cambric for inspection and was going to visit Mr Horrocks in Preston. He asked Craig to send him the price of Perth cambrics and warned: 'We shall have much to contend with in this County, but perseverance and attention will still I think put the advantage in our favour'. (Atholl Mss. 25, XI, 3, fos. 6–10) Horrocks, Miller and Co employed a particularly high proportion of children and young people— in 1816, 73 per cent of their workforce were under 18 and 13 per cent were under 10. (Pollard, 1965, 185)

On 8 May 1802, Stobie told the Duke that he had not seen Craig for a long time— he had been 'in the West Country' but was coming to live at Stanley at Whitsuntide.

Craig had 'got an English gentleman of great property a Mr. Owans to be his partner—Owen and Co have a great many cotton mills in Lancashire and lately bought Mr. Dales in Lanarkshire'. (Atholl Mss. 48, 3, 74) Five days later, Dale agreed to act as a cautioner for Craig for an account with the Perth Bank. Owen told Craig 'the old gentleman is in tolerable good spirits about your concern at present and I hope all things will now go on well'. (Atholl Mss. 25, X1, 3, fol. 11)

The Stanley Letterbook revealed some of the reasons for Robert Owen's success as a cotton spinner. Owen boasted 'my previous habits had prepared me for great nicety and exactness of action, and for a degree of perfection in operations to which parties then employed in cotton spinning were little accustomed'. (Owen, 1857, 29) This boast is confirmed by the Letterbook, which revealed his methods for checking on the efficiency of Stanley and keeping tight control of raw material and stocks of the finished product. He wrote to James Craig, on 13 May 1802: 'If you can prevent your Stocks of yarn from accumulating, so much the better, mule yarn is likely to be heavy'. The Letterbook gives a rare glimpse of the day to day problems of running a cotton mill in this early period of industrialisation, with insights into problems of credit and cash flow, quality control, the difficulties of coping with new machinery and of recruiting skilled labour to operate it. Entrepreneurs had to be able to negotiate with landowners and their agents for land and water rights, as well as seek out new markets in a period of major European wars and great political uncertainty, when European and North American markets were subject to sudden embargos.

James Stobie reported to the Duke on his negotiations with Craig for land on 22 May 1802. Craig seemed anxious to have the land but Stobie wondered whether he would give a good price. Stobie had offered 150 acres of muir at 1 shilling (5p) per acre for seven years, 4 shillings (20p) for the next seven and 8 shillings (40p) for the last seven—a 21 year lease in all. Craig wanted a longer lease but the rent should rise proportionately. (Atholl Mss., 48, 3, 78) Owen wrote to Craig, on 27 May 1802, telling him that he had just returned from New Lanark, was planning to visit Loch Lomond and Dunkeld and would visit Stanley the next week. (Atholl Mss., 25, XI, 3, fos. 10–12) In June 1802, Owen wrote to Craig at 'St. Andrews Square, Glasgow,' asking him to bring a copy of his monthly balance of warp in the weavers' hands, as he wanted to adopt a similar system at New Lanark. He was putting up a new water wheel at New Lanark made principally of cast iron and had improved the shuttles at work. Stanley Mills were lit by candles and, in August 1802, Owen advised Craig to find candles for the spinners adding 'there is not anything lost by a fair encouragement of Work people'. (Atholl Mss. 25, XI, 3, fos. 10–14)

After the Duke had visited the Mills, Craig wrote to him, on 14 August 1802, to ask for a perpetual feu or lease of the Stanley lands presently occupied by the Misses Robertson with the fishery on the Tay opposite, as he needed the 'entire command' of the banks of the river. The Duke's encouragement of the Huntingtower companies led Craig to hope for similar help 'which will bring money into the area, give work and prevent Perth manufacturers having to remit money for cotton yarn to Glasgow and Manchester'. He had gone to great trouble and expense getting the spinning to the state that the Duke saw, so it was not possible to build the few houses his predecessors had not finished according to the bargain. He had plans drawn up and would have finished a house at the end of the church, had the Duke not objected. Craig proposed building the flax mill on additional land, which would alter the line of the footpath to Stanley House. (Atholl Mss. 48, 3, 115)

Money continued to be a problem for James Craig. Owen wrote to him, on 8 September 1802, allegedly enclosing £100 'as I suppose you must now be short of the needful'. He was pleased to hear that the spinning and weaving at Stanley were coming on well. A note on the letter from John Wright, Owen's book-keeper in Glasgow, told Craig that Owen had set off before the bill could be drawn out and he would send it on to Lanark. Four days later, Owen wrote that he had received Craig's letter of the 9th and hoped that he had got the money, as he had sent it from Lanark. He had been thinking about the plans for a New Mill, which Craig had left with him and hoped to build a better one, when funds became available. In the meantime, he approved the plan to build on the Old Mill 'which will not require as much Capital'. It was very desirable to conclude something with the Duke about land, although Craig should not appear to be in too great haste. On 19 September 1802, Robert Humphreys, the under manager at New Lanark, wrote to Craig about the types of cotton they used for different spinning counts. For counts 20 to 24, they used half Orinoco and half Georgia cotton and for counts 20 to 25, they used good Demarara, or a mixture of Orinoco or Trinidad. He had sent some 22 and 24 weft to Glasgow and expected Mr. Wright, the Glasgow book keeper, to forward it to Stanley immediately. (Atholl Mss. 25, XI, 3, fos. 15–17)

A variety of spinning was carried out at Stanley, using throstles, a modified water frame, which could only spin the coarser counts of cotton and could be worked by women, unlike the spinning mules, which demanded great physical strength to operate and were worked by men. Owen advised, on 23 December 1802, that Craig should spin yarns of no more than 18 to 22 hanks in the pound on his water frames and recommended replacing some of his water frames by throstles 'because you can put more spindles in the same space' and they would work with less power and cost less to make. Owen promised to send drawings of the throstles—Mr. Robertson could see them at Lanark and Craig could have castings of most parts of the machine, which concerned the mechanics. The next thing to get forward with was mules to spin 'No. 18 weft'—the sooner the new building for these could be raised on the Old Mill, the better. He hoped that the building could be completed and all machinery got to work by the end of the summer. Mrs. Owen, who with her young son was doing well, and Mr. Dale, were obliged for Craig's present of a Tay salmon 'quite fresh when it came and most excellent in flavour', a continuing perk for those associated with Stanley. (Atholl Mss. 25, X1, 3, fos. 19–21)

On 9 January 1803, Owen reported that he would be visiting Stanley soon and was glad to hear of Craig's progress with the Duke. A week later, he wrote to Craig from Glasgow, acknowledging the arrival of 16 bags of Georgia cotton but complaining that only about 6 were worth sending. Sales of yarn were currently very brisk and he advised

Craig to increase his output of calicoes. Later that month, Owen wrote a detailed letter, about the price of Stanley mule yarn. He had bought 100 bags of Pernambuco (Brazilian)cotton for Craig at Dale's request and was expecting an answer from the London office before Craig's insurance matters could be settled. There had been complaints about the length of the Stanley calicoes—'we measure every piece at Lanark'. (Atholl Mss., 25, XI, 3, fos. 32–36)

Craig wrote to David Dale on 24 January 1803, about his land deals with James Stobie. Stobie was driving a hard bargain by insisting that Craig's offer of £3 10s. 0d. (£3.50) per acre, including wood, must be increased to £3 10s. 0d., with grain, wood, house and fishing all separate. Craig could not pay £1,320 to Mr. Keay on 2 February 1803—he had hoped for £700 for bleaching but Wilson had not got it and London sales had turned out little. He asked Dale to pay the sum 'as I know 'tis but a small matter to you'. Three days later, Dale agreed to pay the £1,320—Mr. Keay should call at the Royal Bank on the day the money was due. Dale had already advanced £580 to Mr. Wilson since Craig went away 'and if you cannot do without, I must advance £1,320 to pay the third instalment to Mr. Keay'. (Atholl Mss., 25, XI, 3,) This was the third instalment of the payment price of £4,600 plus interest; Keay was the Company's lawyer.

James Stobie told the Duke on 9 March 1803 that Craig was quarrying stone in the river quarry at Stanley, having received permission from the Misses Robertson. Stobie warned the Duke to beware of Craig when he came to London. Craig was 'a positive greedy fellow I am of opinion he will be troublesome to deal with'. Later in March, Stobie informed the Duke that Craig had left for London via Glasgow and another letter gave details of Craig's negotiations for part of the farm; apparently he drove a hard bargain. Stobie thought it strange that Craig had threatened that he would allow no villager except under him. 'Numbers of respectable people will always settle there if the Village is thriving and populous.' (Atholl Mss 48, 4, 38, & 53)

Owen wrote, on 23 April 1803, that Robertson had written for cotton and he had sent 15 bags of very good Narenham. The prices of weaving at Stanley were lower than in Glasgow, although a reduction was expected soon in Glasgow prices. On 24 May 1804, he had seen Craig's letter of the 20th to Dale, who had asked him to reply. As he was just newly arrived from Wales and his partners were expected at Lanark early in June, Owen would not be able to visit Stanley before their departure. However, Craig could take an account of cotton, yarn, machinery and all other stock and they could fix a value on it, as well as on the premises. Mr. Dale thought that the manufactory balance sheets should be produced as soon as convenient. Owen had much to say to Craig regarding the Lancashire manufacturers. (Atholl Mss. 25, XI, 3, fos. 38–40)

In July 1803, Owen wrote that they should meet in Glasgow and defer fixing prices of cotton spinning till then. He advised Craig to bring Stobie to a settlement soon. Owen's letters were nothing if not versatile, as he wrote, on 28 August 1803 advising Craig to give up his suit with the young lady of his interest, who was not reciprocating and to turn his attention instead to Dale's daughter, Owen's sister-in-law and make her Mrs. Craig. (Atholl Mss., 25, XI, 3, fos. 29–32). David Dale had four daughters and Owen had married Caroline Dale in 1799. John Wright, who was Dale's and then Owen's clerk at their Glasgow counting house, also had his eye on one of the Dale sisters but nothing came of either his suit or that of James Craig. (Donnachie, 2000, 111)

Owen's letters began to take a tougher tone, He wrote, on 3 August 1803, that he had just received Craig's request for the renewal of a bill due to be settled on the 10th. As the New Lanark Twist Company knew that Dale was a partner at Stanley and they had to pay him nearly £6,000 on the 15th, they could not renew the bill. Owen was still supplying Craig with cotton and, on 24 October 1803, reported that the price of raw cotton had gone up at least 2d (1p) in the pound, so it was a good idea for Craig to work up all the 'water' he could into weft for cambric. As yarn had not yet gone up in proportion, the more printed cambrics and the less yarn manufactured the better. (Atholl Mss. 25, XI, 3, fos. 27–29) Owen was concerned at Craig selling to a Perth house, on 12 December 1803, at less than the prime cost. David Dale was ill and wanted to settle his affairs on a permanent basis, Stanley being foremost in his mind. He wanted to know 'what probability there is of him being relieved from the concern' or otherwise, a contract would be made and the business finally adjusted. (Atholl Mss. 25, XI, 3, fos. 22–24)

A week later, Owen wrote that Dale was still ill and regretted getting involved with Stanley. 'Unless you advance an equal capital with him he will not enter into contract of Partnership nor will he advance any more capital into the business.' Owen added: 'He blames himself and me for having anything to do with the Stanley Property as it has again involved him in business and stocked up a large amount of Capital which he says he has great Occasion for'. Trade was difficult. 'There is never any Brasils and no Demerara in the Market, the Island is the most plentiful and cheapest. Demeraras and Americas are expected in about two months, and the price of cotton is likely to rise till then. If War continues, we cannot expect lower prices. The spinning trade was never worse and many are losing money.' (Atholl Mss. 25, XI, 3, fos. 24–27)

Raw cotton was bought on the Glasgow market and brought overland to Stanley by cart, a round journey of some ten days. This placed the Company at a disadvantage compared to its West of Scotland competitors and this can be documented during Craig's management. Owen bought a wide range of raw cotton for Stanley, including Georgia, New Orleans, Brazils, Carriacou, (a West Indian island), Pernambuco, Orinoco, Demerara and Trinidad. The main distinction between different types of raw cotton was between long and short stapled cotton. The long stapled included Sea Islands, Brazilian, Demarara, West Indian and Egyptian. Short stapled included cotton grown in the US interior, such as Upland or Bowed Georgia, New Orleans, Alabama and East India cotton such as Surat, Bengal and Madras. (Baines, 1835, 311)

Craig had a constant struggle with money problems and Owen spent a good deal of energy vainly trying to instil some financial discipline into him and to exert financial control, without much success. In January 1804, he told Craig that he would underwrite bills for him, which should carry him through his present difficulties. In February, Owen had not had time to look through Craig's monthly account but would do so in a few days time. This was following management practice that Owen had introduced at New Lanark, where he had 'a daily return presented to me every morning of the preceeding days operations, and frequent balances in every department'. (Owen, 1857, 80)

Although yarn prices were likely to rise, Owen warned on 9 March 1804 that Craig should accept current market prices as his capital was 'too limited to keep larger stocks at present'. He had wanted to see whether Dale would discount Craig's bill, which he had done or was inclined to do. Owen told Craig: 'We rate both Mills and village as commercial property and give in our estimate of income accordingly. I am afraid you will not have any Income Tax to pay this year.' Keeping him up to date with Glasgow gossip, Owen added 'Mr. Wright stands no chance of ever marrying Miss Dale'. (Atholl Mss. 25, XI, 3, fos. 56–7)

Owen told Craig, on 17 May 1804, that 'a clever person to manage the spinning would be a great advantage to you' but this post proved difficult to fill and not until December did Owen find a suitable person. He thought that weekly returns from Stanley would be useful and, after some experience, Mr Wright would have them correct and then Craig would be able to see which parts of the works required most attention. At present Owen's 'water' was less and his produce per spindle greater but, he added charitably, Craig might have the edge on quality. The sale of yarn in Glasgow was very bad. He wished Craig's dispute with Miss Robinson was settled, it did not 'appear favourable to the world to dispute with a female'. As Georgia cotton was the cheapest on the market, he recommended that Craig used it for all numbers. He would write to Glasgow to get six good bags forwarded immediately. (Atholl Mss. 25, XI, 3, fos. 52–55)

Owen wrote on 21 September 1804 that he had seen Mr Keith for the job that Craig was hoping to fill but did not think he had enough experience. Owen was at New Lanark but when he went to Glasgow he would look over the other application. By 11 December 1804, Owen had received the monthly report of the mills since August. It was not as large as hoped, also Craig was using more raw cotton for a pound of yarn than elsewhere but perhaps he picked it better. (Atholl Mss., 25, XI, 3, fos., 42–6, 48–51)

Owen's 'attention to detail' in his management was exemplified by the New Lanark Produce Books which 'itemised the number of spindles in use, the species of cotton and the quantity used, the time taken to spin the yarn with a note of any delays which occurred, the precise weight and number of hanks produced as well as the wages of all the workers'. (Donnachie, 2000, 97) This period saw 'the development of accounting as a tool of industrial management,' which included 'the adoption of regular, periodic returns in place of the ac hoc, waste book or journal type of book-keeping, the forcing of the natural rhythm of work into a strait jacket of comparable sections of time'. (Pollard, 1965, 215)

In December 1804, Owen finally recruited a manager for Stanley—Robert Barr—who came with a good reputation as a spinner and received a salary of £100 a year. This was at the bottom end of managers' salaries. Robert Owen's salary, as manager of

Peter Drinkwater's factory in Manchester in 1791, was £300 a year and at New Lanark he earned £1,000 a year as Managing Partner in 1800. Robert Humphreys, the under-manager at New Lanark, was recruited from Peter Drinkwater's mill in Manchester in 1803 at a salary of £350 a year plus a 2.5 per cent share of the profits. (Donnachie, 2000, 43 & 79) Even in Perthshire, where salaries were lower, Luncarty bleachfield recruited William Turnbull as manager in 1812 at a salary of £400 a year with a house and a riding horse, the nineteenth century equivalent of a company car. Turnbull's son, William, was appointed clerk to the Luncarty Company and assistant to his father at a salary of £100 a year and a riding horse. (Cooke, 1984, 4) Barr's modest salary suggested that Craig was running a bargain basement operation at Stanley. By 1830, top managers in British companies could earn up to £1,000 a year and managing partners as much as £2,000. (Pollard, 1965, 143–4)

Owen sounded a warning note on 6 January 1805, when he told Craig that Mr More, (of the Royal Bank of Scotland in Glasgow) was not yet in post and could not pay Craig's bills without the consent of all his creditors. The news from the Continent was bad, the yarn trade worse and Craig should only buy for immediate consumption. (Atholl Mss., 25, XI, 3 fos. 48–51, 72–73) He advised Craig, on 6 April 1805, that the market was such that a fortnight's stock of cotton was as much as he should purchase. He had some good Demarara cotton and Craig could have 66 bags, at 20 bags a time, at current market prices. The market was expected to pick up in about six weeks time but as Craig could not keep large stocks, he would do well to sell at current market prices. Owen hoped that Robert Barr's standing with the workpeople had improved. He wrote, on 7 July 1805, that he was sorry to hear that Barr had behaved in the way Craig described, for it would destroy confidence in him. Cotton yarns were falling in price and Craig should endeavour to sell. (Atholl Mss., 25, XI, 3, fos. 48–51, 63–70)

Owen was losing patience with Craig. He wanted to know, on 15 November 1805, why Craig wanted an additional £1,000 as he understood that the £1,500 already supplied would have supplied his needs for some months. Owen told Craig that David Dale was glad that he was planning to acquire more land at Stanley. In January 1806, Owen reported that Dale thought a fair price for the ground was £3 per acre, whereas the Duke was asking £4. He advised Craig to tell the Duke that he hoped to let it in small lots at £4 an acre to encourage settlement. (Atholl Mss., 25, XI, 3, fos. 70–72, 76–79)

Craig continued to be a drain on Dale's finances up till and after his death in January 1806, when the debts were taken over by Dale's trustees. (Donnachie, 2000, 92) Owen wrote, on 24 February 1806, that Mr. Wright had sold little or none of Craig's stock—'We are told you sell No. 18 wefts at 2s' (10p); this price, although made from waste, was below anything in the market. Owen was selling at 2/5d, (12p) and Craig ought to sell at 2/3d and 2/4d. For many reasons, Owen could not permit Mr. Barr (Craig's manager) to come to New Lanark for 6 or 3 days but he would tell Craig all he wanted to know in Glasgow. Sales of water twist had been very high. (Atholl Mss., 25, XI, 3, fos. 81–84) On 19 December 1806, Craig wrote to the Duke, offering feu duties of £73 10s. 0d. (£73.50) per annum for the feu at Stanley marked on a plan by Peter McNaughton, land surveyor, reserving ground formerly feued to George Dempster and Company. Craig undertook to pay £520 plus interest for the houses on the ground and would stand in the right of Dempster and Co., regarding the obligation of £6 for the improvement of the village. Six days later, Craig wrote to Palliser, Stobie's successor as factor to Atholl, that he had received the Duke's acceptance of the offer. Craig wanted an acre for a burying ground, church etc. and would like the Duke's advice as to where to site it. (Atholl Mss., 48, 7, 177 & 179)

Owen wrote from Braxfield House at New Lanark, on 17 February 1807, that he was sending details of top rollers for water frames, which were leather covered with sheepskins from Cummings of Kilmarnock at 20 shillings (£1) per dozen. They were oiled and dried according to a plan formerly mentioned to Mr. Barr. (Atholl Mss., 25, XI, 3, fos. 83–84) Owen's son, Robert Dale Owen, described how there were two sets of rollers on an Arkwright spinning frame, the top ones covered in leather. Spinning was through three machines, then the thread was made into rovings on a throstle frame, being loosely twisted in long cylindrical revolving cans. The yarn made on throstle frames had a much harder twist and could be used for warp, whereas previously linen had to be used. (Owen, 1874, 11–12)

On 9 March 1807, Owen wrote that he could not visit Stanley that month, as one of his partners from Manchester was coming to New Lanark. The price of wool and yarn was rather advanced by 1d (0.5p) per lb. for wool and by 2d (1p) per lb. for yarn, which was in demand in Lancashire. He hoped Craig was successful in his journey to London. It was not easy to give advice regarding the subscription to the New Perth Bank. Nine days later, Owen advised Craig to settle his dispute with Messrs. Stewart and NcNaughton and to stick to the agreement, however hard it might seem, for the sake of his reputation. (Atholl Mss., 25, XI, 3, fos. 84–88)

Owen noted the temptation of 'low priced second-hand machinery,' on 3 October 1807. Bargains of this sort were common in Lancashire, where they had recently been selling top quality spinning mules 'no worse for wear,' at 1p per spindle. He advised that if the machinery, which was near, was properly made and repaired, could spin the numbers which Craig required and above all was the size to fill his 'empty flat' without loss of room 'I think they cannot do you harm'. If they were deficient in any of these respects, then it became a matter for serious consideration. (Atholl Mss., 25, XI, 3, fos. 88–90)

Craig's financial problems continued. Owen told him on 7 January 1808 that he couldn't say whether Mr. More (of the Royal Bank of Scotland) would discount his bills or not but Craig would hear what he said to Mr. Wilson. His spinning New Orleans cotton at counts from 20 to 24 at 23/6d (£1.16) was a 'very serious losing part of your concern'. Yarn was costing Craig 2/4d (12p) per lb. to produce, whereas Finlay (Kirkman Finlay, of Catrine and Deanston Mills) was spinning it at 1/3d (6p). The other counts at Stanley were doing better except for the 17 to 20 counts, which ought to be spun into a quality worth 2/4d (12p) for 20. Owen feared 'all your land speculation promises to do better than the spinning' and he would be glad to hear what the Duke had to say about the 'muir'. He wished to interfere in Stanley as little as possible, partly because he was so busy at New Lanark. 'For some weeks past, I have been continually occupied from early and late with several heavy repairs which while they were doing kept between 3 and 400 people idle that I had not ever time to attend to many pressing matters belonging to the Lanark concern.' (Atholl Mss., 25, XI, 3, fos. 92–95)

Owen was upset to learn of Craig's distressed state on 30 January 1808 as he had hoped Craig would have made sales in Perth and relieved his financial position. He couldn't visit Stanley soon but would send Robert Humphreys (the under-manager at New Lanark) in 8 or 10 days to look at the water spinning which, in his opinion, was far from doing well. The demand for yarn was by no means brisk but prices were so low, it was a losing business, without the best management. New loose cotton was extremely good and could be bought in Glasgow at about 17d (8p) per lb. Two days later, Humphreys was on his way to Stanley via Edinburgh. He planned to stay one or two days in Stanley and look at the water machinery. A few days later, Owen hoped that Humphreys had arrived. Raw cotton was rising very rapidly in price, particularly New Orleans and an unidentified cotton, which was selling in 300lb. bags in London at 18d (8p) per lb. The quality was good and prices were expected to go up. (Atholl Mss., 25, XI, 3, fos. 96–98)

Ten days later, Owen reported that it was uncertain how long the rise in cotton prices would continue and it was as well to purchase as sparingly as possible. Craig could buy New Orleans and Demarara cotton from the New Lanark Twist Company but should only lay in 2 or 3 weeks stock. Craig was setting up carding at Stanley; John Whiteley and Co. of Halifax made the type of card that Humphreys mentioned and 70 carding machines would do well for the amount and range of yarn spun. Owen thought that cast iron frames for cards were not worth attention, unless 80 or 100 carding machines were wanted. Half of the carding machines at New Lanark were of wood and this made little difference to quality. Demerara or other cotton should be put two or three times through the carding machines, thin and well spread. Owen had prevailed on the Dale Trustees for £1,000 to see Craig through his difficulties. (Atholl Mss., 25, XI, 3, fos. 100–102)

A note of exasperation began to enter Owen's letters. On 8 March 1808, he expressed surprise at Craig's letter—after the late large supply of funds, he did not expect that he would be in need of more so soon. He regretted that Craig had not informed the Trustees of his actions in running up more bills; in future, he should always inform Owen and More. Either loose or West Indian cotton would suit the Stanley machinery and in view of the quality required, it would be best to mix it with waste to spin into 20 water twist. Later that month, the Trustees agreed to discount Craig's bills at six months, providing he drew them in small amounts of, say £200 to £500. However, Owen was still supplying him with raw cotton. By now, Craig was drinking in the last chance saloon and in May 1808 Owen told him that his bill, falling due on the 17th, would be discounted by the New Lanark Twist Company but this would be the last time. Cotton prices were very high and he was not buying himself but would get some for Craig, if absolutely necessary. (Atholl Mss., 25, XI, 3, fos. 102–8)

The cotton industry was entering hard times. The Napoleonic Wars had disrupted trade and France's military success allowed Napoleon to impose the Continental System, which aimed to cut off British trade with Europe altogether. The American trade embargo of 22 December 1807 was in retaliation for the British government's Orders in Council, restricting trade with France and much of the rest of Europe. This hit the Scottish cotton industry particularly hard, as it was dependent on fine Sea Island cotton from Georgia and South Carolina. Owen described how 'the prices of all kinds of cotton goods advanced so rapidly and so high that the manufacturers of the article were placed in a dilemma'. His solution was to close the mills at New Lanark but pay full wages for four months, which was what David Dale had done when a fire destroyed Mill No 1 at New Lanark in 1788. (Donnachie, 2000, 100) From 1808, the French blockade began to bite. Scottish weavers held a meeting in Glasgow on 25 June 1808 to protest at falling earnings and in August 1808 a meeting was held of 'the active committee' of the weavers' union at Deanston in Perthshire. (Fraser, 1988b, 87)

Craig was desperately trying to raise money and cope with the American embargo. Owen thought Craig had done well, in August 1808, in disposing of the bleachfield. Raw cotton had maintained its high price and yarn prices should go up. In November, Owen had been away for a month but had written to Mr. More, of the Royal Bank, regarding Craig's London transaction. Craig should not dispose of his shares in the Perth Banking Company at the moment. Owen was glad to hear what the Duke had to say about waste ground—'Upon what terms has he given you the ground for a Church yard?' It was extremely hazardous to hold stocks of either cotton or yarn; the price of cotton was so high, it was better to pay the hands full wages than spin using such expensive cotton, which was Owen's solution at New Lanark. Eight days later, Craig was advised to keep as small stocks of cotton as possible, until the embargo was either lifted or confirmed. (Atholl Mss., 25, XI, 3, fos. 108–112)

Craig wanted to see (Kirkman) Finlay's looms and Owen agreed to arrange this, in December 1808 but said that at present Finlay was too cautious to agree. Craig's survival strategy included a (second) attempt at the South American market and a printfield project. Owen felt 'quite incompetent to judge the propriety of sending fancy goods to Spanish America'. Some days later, it emerged that Craig planned to let out some of the Stanley land and water-power for a printfield. Owen thought this was very desirable but did not want to become involved, nor did the Dale Trustees, who wanted to 'curtail rather than enlarge, this part of the Trust'. He urged Craig to find out what the outside parties' offer was for facilities 'with and without the first floor of the New Mill'. Owen did not know whether the power required to turn printing machinery was uniform or irregular; if the latter, it would destroy Craig's spinning operations and he could only engage to give them his surplus power in the former case. A printfield would also increase the fire risk at Stanley. Craig could more easily see Finlay's looms if he went with Owen and he should therefore come to Glasgow. (Atholl Mss., 25, XI, 3, fos. 90–92 & 113–6)

A letter headed simply 'Glasgow, Friday noon', informed Craig that Owen was coming to Stanley and mentioned an earlier visit. By February 1809, Craig was negotiating with Messrs. Marshall, Buist and Borland, who had a cotton spinning and bleaching business at Stormontfield, on the other side of the Tay from Stanley. Owen advised that cotton and yarn markets were heavy and Craig should keep light stocks. He believed all that Craig said to him about the advantages of the London market for cotton. The Trustees were worried about their liabilities for any additional advance into the Stanley concern and Craig should only enter into a conditional agreement with the Duke, subject to the agreement of the trustees. (Atholl Mss., 25, XI, 3, fos. 117–119, & Penny, 1836, 255))

A flurry of letters from Owen in March 1809 asked Craig for information about his negotiations with the Duke of Atholl for land and with Buist for workers. Raw cotton prices were falling and the embargo would soon be lifted. Raw Pernambuco cotton could be bought in London or Liverpool at 2/6d (12.5p). Cotton manufacturers in Scotland clearly had to keep an eye on European and global politics and their effects on supplies of raw cotton, and overseas markets. On 21 March 1809, Owen wrote from Glasgow to report that continental politics remained in a very uncertain state, though it was generally expected that Austria would declare war against France and that Russia and Prussia would join her.

Ten days later, Owen was glad Craig was keeping his stocks low. The Dale Trustees would not object to Mr. Borland's offer for Stanley, if a fair price was given, as Craig could sell the mills and ground for a printfield and still have some ground left. If Borland offered £24,000, Owen would recommend the Trustees accept and give a reasonable time for payment, although he had not yet mentioned it to them until a firm offer was made. He would recommend a 21 year lease but would expect a rent of £2,000 per annum. Four days later, there was advice on negotiations with the Duke of Atholl. Instead of four seven year periods, Craig should try and get four periods of twelve years. Owen and More (from the Royal Bank) hoped to visit Stanley. (Atholl Mss., 25, XI, 3, fos. 122–8)

By 18 April 1809, the negotiations with Marshall and Buist had collapsed and they were setting up works elsewhere. Ten days later, Owen thought 'a respectable printing business will add to the value of the property' but could interfere too much with the rest of the mills' operations. The London market was likely to be most favourable for cotton purchases and Craig planned to send fancy goods to Lima via his contacts, Messrs. Hunter, Rainey and Co. In August, Owen again advised Craig to keep his cotton stocks low and on 9 September despaired, 'You will never do any good with your present water twist spinning' and disagreed with Craig about looms, except his man clearly understood them. In November, Owen advised Craig to insure the New Mills with Albion at 21 shillings (£1.05), with a 1/8th and 5 per cent deduction to the amount of £5,000—'It is as low as any office will do it'. He hoped Craig's man fully understood the dressing machine 'otherwise you will expend a large sum to little purpose'. (Atholl Mss., 25, XI, 3, fos. 129–139)

On New Year's Day 1810, Owen wrote from New Lanark that the Duke was driving a hard bargain over the Stanley feu, by expecting payment in grain or in kind. He hoped that Craig's new looms and picking machines were suitable. The price of cotton was up by 2d (1p) a pound. A fortnight later, Owen said he would send the drawing head of Lanark's carding machines but doubted whether the modifications would suit the Stanley machinery. He was glad to hear that the looms were doing well. In March, he wrote that the drawing heads would be sent by cart to Mr. More in Glasgow and on to Stanley. The throstles at Lanark could not spin under 20 count— 'all our worn counts are spun upon water frames', which were better for waste on account of it breaking more in the spinning. Waste could be worked up with cotton in a second quality mule, for which there was demand and none for water twist counts of second quality.

Trade was generally good and the price of cotton was expected to fall. Owen wanted Craig to make a simple but accurate monthly report of the whole establishment and send it to him. At Lanark, they balanced every four weeks, as most people did annually. He understood that the dressing and weaving operations at Deanston and Catrine were almost complete. As regards Stanley, it was better to feu than to lease—the 40 village acres Craig should receive by all means and encourage feuing 'always securing the Manure from the houses where there is little or no land to be attached to them'. (Atholl Mss., 25, XI, 3, fos. 140–149)

The saga of the Stanley feuing continued. Owen wrote on 9 February 1810 that he had sent Craig's letter regarding the Duke's offer to the Trustees, giving his opinion that feus and lease should be accepted on the best terms Craig could obtain. In May, he was pleased that Craig was doing well with the looms; at Deanston and Down, they averaged 6 pieces per loom weekly, about 1,800 pieces weekly in total. He hoped Wright (Owen's book keeper) would have the accounts made up to the end of the month. The Stanley spinning should be doing well, as all spinners were making money. Owen would renew Craig's bill, due on the 19th but 'in consequence of new arrangements forming between the partners at the New Lanark Twist Company, none of your bills can be renewed'. (Atholl Mss., 25, XI, 3, fos. 143–144, 150–152) A new contract of co-partnery, purchasing the assets of the New Lanark Company for £80,000, was signed on 5 October 1810. (Donnachie, 2000, 102) Owen would visit Stanley again on his return from England.

Robert Owen not only had to deal with Craig's limitations but with difficult trading conditions in the cotton industry in general. There was a speculation boom in 1810, which ended in numerous bankruptcies in Scotland in the later months of the year. (Lee, 1972, 24 & 36) In Lancashire: 'The year 1810 was one of exceptionally good trade until its close when the boom collapsed and the cotton industry was plunged into a period of depression which lasted until the later months of 1813'. (Collier, 1964, 22) Perth was badly affected by this speculation boom and it had its own particular disaster. The London branch of the Cromwellpark Cotton Company, on the River Almond, had a fire on a ship in Cadiz, in 1810, which destroyed stock to the value of £100,000. This led to a series of knock-on bankruptcies throughout Perth and some sixty small companies failed, leaving only about eight firms remaining in business. (Penny, 1836, 256–7) The cotton industry in Perth never fully recovered from this disaster.

On 27 September 1810, Owen received Craig's letters regarding the project of heating and lighting the mills by gas. He was planning to visit Stanley that week and see Mr. Maikin, whose ideas 'if all prove true' might be used at New Lanark. The next month, Owen wrote: 'I fear almost everything that has been done within the Mill for a long time past must be materially changed, or in ordinary times they must ruin any company, the present period is a most extraordinary one for spinning profits and cannot be expected to last long'. He believed 'that this establishment would be making very large profit when the Stanley Mills would be losing a very large sum daily'. However, he hoped that the mills might be put on as good a footing as the land. Owen had spoken to Mr. Hawksworth in Glasgow about Mr. Maikin's gas lighting but feared that Maikin was ignorant of what Mr. Murdoch of Boulton and Watt had accomplished. (Atholl Mss. 25, XI, 3, fos. 152–157)

Between 26 October 1810 and 6 February 1811, James Craig bought raw cotton to the value of £4,938 13s. 11d., mostly from Robert Owen through the Lanark Twist Company and the New Lanark Company but also from James Finlay at a cost of £1,723, and from Colin Arnot to the value of £519. (NAS, GD, 64, 1, 247, 60) At the end of December 1810, Robert Humphreys, the under manager at New Lanark, returned from Stanley and told Owen of Craig's wishes regarding a new water wheel. Craig had claimed that Messrs. White had funds of his in their hands but would not pay him. Owen promised to investigate. On 8 January 1811, Owen wrote that, since Humphrey's return, he had been trying to arrange to cast and fit up a new water wheel for Stanley. He emphasised: 'The first moving power is of so much importance in a Cotton Mill that no pains should be spared to have it in all respects perfect and compleat. It would be the greatest folly imaginable to erect a wheel twelve feet diameter where there is a fall of 18 feet—you may preserve the light by placing the water wheel at somewhat greater distance from the Mill.' He would send the wheel to 'Lieth', then ship it to Perth and a man from Lanark would fit it together. (Atholl Mss, 25, XI, 3, 160–2)

There was general distress in the Scottish cotton industry and early in 1811 the Glasgow, Perth and Edinburgh weavers petitioned the Board of Trade against the export of cotton yarn and steam looms, which, it was complained, were being introduced into Glasgow in large numbers. (Fraser, 1988b, 86–8, 90) Eventually, Owen and the Dale Trustees became impatient with the amount of money that Craig was losing and called a halt. On 1 February 1811, he wrote that Craig must stop water spinning, the sooner the better 'but you cannot discharge any of the workpeople without giving them due notice'. Indeed, Craig should not part with any workers until Owen had visited Stanley, although he was sorry to say that several Glasgow mills were going to discharge hands as soon as their stock ran down. In the meantime, he would send Craig 20 bags of best New Orleans cotton, which could be mixed with one third or one fourth part waste and produce excellent 22 water twist, if properly prepared. He would also order 12 bags of best New Island, which with Demerara and water (twist) should keep Craig going for some time. He would visit Craig as soon as possible to determine future proceedings. (Atholl Mss., 25, XI, 3, fos. 162–5)

On 11 March 1811, Owen complained that Craig had drawn a draft on him for

SUMMONS,
The ROYAL BANK of SCOTLAND,
Against
The STANLEY COMPANY, &c.

James Dundas, C. S. Agent.

S U M M O N S,

The ROYAL BANK of SCOTLAND,

AGAINST

The STANLEY COMPANY, &c.

GEORGE, &c.   WHEREAS it is humbly complained and
shewn to Us, by our Lovite, The ROYAL BANK of SCOT-
LAND, THAT the deceafed David Dale, merchant in Glafgow,
was, at the time of his death, a partner of a company, along with
James Craig, refiding at Stanley, near Perth, which carried on the
bufinefs of fpinning and manufacturing cotton at Stanley afore-
faid; which company or concern was fometimes known by and
paffed under the defignation of the *Stanley Company*: AND THAT
the faid David Dale, by his truft-difpofition, dated the 10th November 1804, and regiftered in the books of Council and Seffion
the 27th March 1806, for fettling, during his life, the fucceffion
to his effects and fubjects after his deceafe, and for other caufes
and confiderations therein mentioned, difponed and made over to
Archibald Campbell, Efq; of Jura, John Campbell, Efq; writer
to our fignet, Robert Gray, jeweller in Glafgow, John More,
banker in Glafgow, and Robert Owen of the Lanark Cotton
Works, and to the deceafed Claud Alexander of Ballamyle, Walter Ewing Maclae of Cathkin, Robert Scott Moncrieff of Newhalls,
and Brigadier-General Colin Campbell, and to the furvivors and
acceptors, and the furvivor and acceptor of them, as truftees and
fiduciaries, or truftee and fiduciary, for the ends, ufes, and pur-
- pofes

Summons, Royal Bank of Scotland against the Stanley Company, 1816
(National Archives of Scotland GD 64/1/247)

£1,108, in spite of the Trustees' decision that business at Stanley, exclusive of the farm, was to be carried out wholly in the name of the heirs of Mr Dale. Craig was still trying to get new partners but Owen told him: 'I must candidly tell you I think you will never make a penny by cotton spinning—it is not your forte'. As soon as Mrs. Owen was confined, which Owen 'daily looked for', he would be at Stanley. (Atholl Mss. 25, XI (3), fos. 172–3) Two days later, Owen, writing from Glasgow, said he had 'taken up a place on the Perth coach tomorrow morning'. A meeting of the Trustees had decided, in view of the immense losses, that the mills should be stopped as soon as possible. Owen wished to have a full meeting to decide on details and he would write to Mr Campbell, 'the uncle of the young ladies'. Craig should stand by to attend at a day's notice. (Atholl Mss., 25, XI, 3, fos. 168–170)

Owen grew increasingly exasperated with Craig, who was very good at ignoring instructions. Stanley Mills were supervised by Owen from March to November 1811, when they were let to Stewart Douglas, a Glasgow merchant. On 2 May 1811, Owen was going to see whether Armistead was competent to carry on the business profitably, to try to recover some of the money lost. He had written to Armistead, by More's direction, informing him how to draw money for wages. He would also write to Stewart and MacNaughton to tell them to remit the amount of sales to More, so that he could pay some of the money drafts accepted by Owen. (Atholl Mss., 25, XI, 3, fos. 177–8) A set of basic accounts survive for Stanley from 12 February 1811 to 1 March 1814. They record Armistead's drafts for wages, drawn on Robert Wright, Owen's Glasgow book keeper. From 12 February to 2 April 1811, the wages bill amounted to £120 per fortnight. From 18 June 1811 to 1 March 1814, the bill fluctuated between £220 and £260 per fortnight, although there is a gap in the accounts from 11 November 1811, when Douglas's lease began, to 17 August 1813. The accounts also recorded Craig's payments of feu duties to the Duke of Atholl, amounting to £500 11s. 9d. in February 1811, £224 9s. 0d. in November 1813, £621 in April 1814, and £800 for feu and rents in May 1815. (NAS, GD 64, 1, 247b)

By the end of May 1811, Owen insisted: 'It becomes absolutely necessary that you cease all connection with the Mills'. The Dale Trustees had already suffered from Craig's management to the tune of £40,000—'The trustees would be worse than Madmen not to put a stop to such proceedings' as they would be liable for acting improperly otherwise. Owen accused Craig of withholding balances and foolishly squandering large sums of money 'for worse than no object'. They had only shown amity towards Craig because they believed his actions stemmed from ignorance. 'You may truly believe me when I tell you that were you to continue to manage the Stanley Mills you would ruin the richest Man in the Kingdom if they were connected with it.' Owen and More (from the Royal Bank of Scotland) would no longer honour Craig's drafts on them, although he was still to be given funds for the farm. (Atholl Mss., 25, XI, 3, fos. 174–176, underlining in the original)

Craig was a difficult character to deal with. In August 1811, Owen strongly objected to the farming and mill operatives at Stanley being intermixed. It was likely that the Trustees would soon stop Stanley altogether, as the cotton trade was in a bad way. In

September 1811, Owen wrote that it would be of no consequence how Mr. A. (Armistead) managed the mills, as Mr Douglas would soon make alterations. 'Our interest is to give the New Partners every facility in Management to get good rent from them.' (Atholl Mss., 25, XI, 3, fos. 179–181)

Even then, Craig did not give up and he complained to the Duke of Atholl, on 26 August 1812, about the Dale Trustees who had 'refused to advance another shilling'. This would cramp Craig's operation and render a settlement about Mills Farm between him and the Duke much more difficult, although 'it is probable Mills farm will remain with me at the Conclusion'. The Duke had asked if he was 'Pinched in my operations for money' in September 1812 and Craig told him he wanted £1,000 to complete his operations that season. He calculated that the 1813 crop would pay £2,000, which would enable him to pay the loan and have enough to complete his operations. He asked the Duke for a loan at 5 per cent or permission to subset and assign on the lease, with a complaint about 'these overbearing trustees' thrown in for good measure. (Atholl Mss, 68, 2, 338 & 368)

These were difficult economic times, with food prices rising, and challenging years for the British textile industry. Glasgow weavers protested against falling earnings in February 1812 by submitting a table of prices for weaving to the Glasgow magistrates and the Sheriff of Lanarkshire. Weavers in Perth, Edinburgh, Stirling and Renfrewshire followed their example, although the Perth magistrates refused to intervene. Food prices were rising and there were food riots in Edinburgh in August 1812. (Fraser, 1988b, 93)

Robert Owen had taken over Archibald Campbell of Jura's investments shortly before David Dale's death. Campbell claimed that his understanding was that this money would be transferred to the New Lanark Company. However, Owen failed to do this and held it in his own partnership account. By 1812, Owen owed Campbell over £25,000, which worried Campbell, particularly when the cotton industry went into depression. In July 1812, he tried to recover £6,000 from Owen and to get a guarantee about the rest of the money, assisted by his two sons-in-law. A legal battle took place over the next year, with Owen being saved from bankruptcy by the intervention of the Dale sisters, led by Jane Maxwell Dale. Settlement was reached on 15 July 1813, whereby it was agreed that the sum owed to Campbell would be repaid from November 1818 in five equal instalments of £4,000, with the Misses Dale (Owen's sisters-in-law) as guarantors. (Robertson, 1969, Cooke, 1979b, and Donnachie, 2000, 103)

Stanley Mills were advertised in June 1813 'with the whole Machinery and Utensils therein, together with the Manager's House, Outhouses and Gardens'. There was a labour supply from the village and a good source of power from the Tay. 'There are 60 Power Looms ready to be put up and the two Mills at present contain about 16,000 Mule and Water spindles in excellent condition and now going'. The proprietors would not object to a sale of the premises and could accommodate the purchaser by taking the sale in easy instalments. Mr. Craig of Stanley would show buyers round and further particulars could be obtained from him, from Messrs. Graham and Mitchell, or Mr Robert Walkinshaw, Writers in Glasgow. (*Perthshire Courier*, 10 June 1813) There were no takers and the mills closed in February 1814. The Perth textile industry went through difficult times, during the depression that followed the end of the Napoleonic Wars. Cotton weavers' earnings in Perth fell from 3.25d per ell for pullicates in January 1816, to 1.75d in March and an all time low of 1.25d in November 1816. (Murray, 1978, 51–52)

The Stanley affair became tied up with the financial problems of the Glasgow branch of the Royal Bank of Scotland under the management of John More and ended in an acrimonious court case, with the Royal Bank pursuing the Stanley Company for debts of over £40,000. More, who had been the Royal Bank's agent in Glasgow since 1806 and acted as clerk to the Dale Trustees, was said to have 'enjoyed a flamboyant and expensive lifestyle'. (Checkland, 1975, 297–298) In September 1816, investigations began into his financial affairs. These revealed that the Trustees owed the Royal Bank over £33,000, plus interest; the bills concerned related to Stanley Mills between 1806 and 1813 and Owen was deeply involved.

Craig wrote to the Duke of Atholl on 2 October 1816 giving his side of the story. He enclosed a copy of the account for the Stanley concern taken from the books and interest calculated down to 15 October 1812, having sent a copy to John More. This had been done at More's request and he had promised to give Craig an account of all advances that Dale and the Dale Trustees had made to Stanley, which More had never done in spite of repeated requests. (Atholl Mss., 68, 6, 215)

Craig claimed that there was no contract in the Stanley concern, everything was done in his name. Owen had told him that Dale would like a note in writing, stating that as Dale had advanced more money than Craig, they should share in proportion to their advances. Craig enclosed a copy of a letter he had written to Dale on 22 January 1806, just before Dale's death, which promised a complete valuation of all the property in June. Craig gave Dale the option of taking a share to the amount of money he had advanced or half as he thought fit. The last time Craig saw Dale, he was very ill and wanted a contract between them, as the Dale Trustees might take advantage of Craig. Craig had said that Owen was a good man and would protect him from the Trustees. On being told this, Owen had said he would help Craig but he now denied this. Craig ended his letter by appealing to the Duke for support against the Trustees, particularly the Campbells. He hoped to come to a settlement soon and 'have the Mills set to work'. (Atholl Mss., 68, 6, 215)

On 10 October 1816, Archibald Campbell of Jura wrote to his son, John Campbell in Edinburgh:

> It having lately come to my knowledge that the affairs of Mr. More of the Royal Bank are in a deranged state, and that it is given out, that the Trustees appointed by the late David Dale owe a good deal of money to the Royal Bank, I desire therefore that you will lose no time in enquiring into this matter, as I am at a loss to conceive how it can be, and I hereby authorise you to act for me in this business.
>
> (NAS, GD, 64, 1, 247, 35)

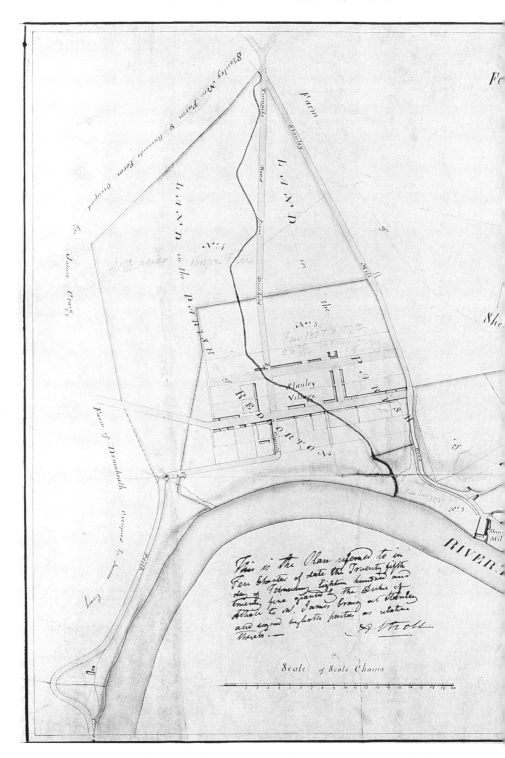

Patrick MacNaughton's Plan of the Lands of Stanley, 1823 (Atholl Mss.)

A meeting of the Dale Trustees was held in Glasgow on 25 October 1816. Those present were Robert Owen, John Campbell, Robert Gray and John More, trustees and John Archibald Campbell, agent. John More, as clerk to the Trustees, reported that bills lying over in the Royal Bank, but not retired, amounted to £33,186 8s. 10d. plus interest of £8,096 12s. 9d. The Trustees claimed total ignorance of these bills, which can hardly have been true in Owen's case. More said that at the time of Mr. Stewart's marriage, a jotting had been sent to Campbell stating that £5,000 to £6,000 was due on Stanley. When Craig was relieved of the management, a statement was produced for the Trustees that the remaining sum came to £27,000. This latter sum had, 'entirely escaped recollection' when More delivered the jotting to Campbell. (NAS, GD., 64, 1, 247, 54) David Dale had bankrolled Stanley to the tune of £24,270 2s. 10d. including interest down to his death. Advances by the Trustees after Dale's death came to £27,476 12s. 9d. (NAS, GD., 64, 1, 247, 43)

A murky tale of financial mismanagement gradually unfolded, with the Trustees falling over themselves to deny responsibility. The principal victims were Dale's daughters, whose affairs had been (mis)managed by John More since their father's death, when it was decided to carry on the management of Stanley for the benefit of the trustees. Archibald Campbell claimed, on 28 December 1816, to have been the sole dissenter to this decision, although unfortunately for him this was not recorded in the minutes. Stanley was managed by Craig and Owen, who signed bills on behalf of the Trustees. The management of the Trust had been left to John More, who had the 'complete confidence' of the Dale family. Lately, More had fallen in arrears to the Royal Bank, rumoured to be up to nearly £90,000 and the Trustees were astonished to hear that he had given up, as part of the funds of the Bank, nearly £40,000 of bills discounted by him for Stanley Mills. The Bank had recently brought an action against Archibald Campbell, the other Dale Trustees and the Misses Dale for payment of these bills. Mr. Stewart, Dale's son-in-law, had said that the Trustees were not entitled to carry on Stanley Mills after Dale's death and 'he will hold them personally liable for the share of any loss'. (NAS, GD, 64, 1, 247, 36) More's total debts amounted to £94,267, the Royal Bank seized the title deeds of Stanley Mills and he was made bankrupt. (Checkland, 1975, 297–298) He moved to Liverpool and in 1820 was described as an 'accountant' there. (NAS, SC49, 59, 149)

James Craig refused to lie down and on 13 May 1817 wrote a letter to the Duke of Atholl asking for financial support to induce new partners to join him and set the mills going again. Craig cited the annual sum of £5,000 in labour laid out on the Atholl Estates and his agricultural improvements. The dissolution of the Company had appeared in the Gazette last November but Dale's heirs and Trustees had denied having anything to do with the feus and lease and would make no offer. The Trustees owed the Royal Bank about £36,000 and if the Bank should call in that sum suddenly, the consequences might be serious even for them. (Atholl Mss., 68, 7, 176) On 8 August 1817, John Archibald Campbell wrote to Craig from Edinburgh approving the arrangements to give back part of the feus and the farm to the Duke prior to disposing of the remainder. Both the Royal Bank and the Trustees were likely to approve. On the back of this letter, Craig agreed to advertise Stanley Mills in the Perth paper and in Edinburgh. (Atholl Mss., 68, 7, 245)

Recriminations carried on for a long time. On 10 March 1819, the Duke wrote to Craig acknowledging his letter of 2 March, in which Craig described a recent visit to Stanley by Robert Owen and Campbell. Craig claimed they had offered to discharge him on receiving £3,000 and Craig paying arrears to the Duke on the feu and the leases. Atholl had seen Owen in Edinburgh and when Owen complained about Craig, he had defended him and accused the Trustees of harming the village—'the stopping of the Mills by him and Mr Dale's trustees and the carrying off nearly all the industrious part of the Villagers and the consequent leaving of a Host of Beggars had done infinite mischief'. The Duke complained that on Craig's entry Atholl had spent £1,000 on Stanley House, which was now in a dreadful condition. (Atholl Mss. 25, X, 1)

By September 1819, the Perth weavers were in great difficulties:

> The harvest is drawing to a close and the weavers who were employed in cutting it down are returning to their looms—no work, many destitute. All ranks must feel themselves called upon to come forward and mitigate the suffering of their fellow citizens whose uniformly sober, quiet and patient conduct in this country presents the strongest claim to general commiseration and assistance. We are persuaded that the landed proprietors of Perthshire only require to have the situation of the manufacturers laid before them to come instantly forward to their relief.
> (*Perthshire Courier*, 16 September 1819)

George Penny described how he chaired a meeting of Perth weavers, in 1819, 'on the express condition that no politics were to be introduced'. Perth's period of radical activism seemed to be over; 'a respectful memorial was drawn up' asking for financial support from the Lord Provost of Perth and the Lord Lieutenant of Perthshire. There was a good response, with the Duke of Atholl, the Earl of Kinnoull, the City of Perth and many others contributing £2,000 to an outdoor relief fund for the weavers. Penny reported: 'Whilst other towns were running riot, with insurrectionary movements, all was quiet and orderly here'. (Penny, 1836, 147–148) He was contrasting the quiet of Perth with a town like Paisley where: 'A meeting in Paisley in 1819 to condemn the 'butchers' of Peterloo led to five days of conflict between workers and the troops of the 80th Regiment and the 7th and the 10th Hussars'. (Knox, 1999, 59)

James Craig wrote to Frederick Graham on 21 December 1819 with an account of the distress and unemployment at Stanley. The Duke had given Craig £40 to employ men in trenching but he asked for more, as the distress was now even more severe. Craig listed fourteen men who had been employed in trenching, which was nearly finished and in future work was to be confined to Perth weavers and those who had houses from the Guildry. The list of those employed included: Nick and James McLeod, Alex Ferguson, James Campbell, John McGregor, Alex Stewart, John Crockert, Andrew Grant, Alex and Joseph Miller, John Edam, William McLeod, John Crockert (again) and William Taylor, which suggested a good many of the Stanley workforce had Highland origins. As the Duke had subscribed £105 to the Perth meeting it seemed strange that men off the Atholl estates should be denied work, as long as funds were not exhausted. Craig was in Edinburgh and expected a clear account from the Royal Bank and the Dale Trustees, when he would immediately pay the Duke's arrears. (Atholl Mss., 68, 9, 356)

Eventually, the Trustees settled with James Craig for a miserly £1,500 'which is all he is able to pay', on 28 April 1820. The Trustees at this time were—Archibald Campbell of Jura, John Campbell, Writer to the Signet, John More, 'accountant in Liverpool' and Robert Owen of Lanark Cotton Mills. Craig also agreed to pay arrears of rent and feu duty to the Duke of Atholl in consideration of his discharge. (NAS, SC49, 59, 149) Owen's debt to Campbell of Jura was paid off in November 1822, although his biographer believed he could have paid these debts earlier, without much financial difficulty. (Donnachie, 2000, 104)

5.

The Spirited Proprietors

The Buchanans of Glasgow, 1823–1852

Denniston, Buchanan and Co bought the Mills in 1823 and the Mills, Stanley House, offices and gardens, with 65½ acres of ground became jointly owned by James Buchanan, David Laird and Alex Stevenson. Alex Stevenson was 'acting resident partner' in 1833, when he gave evidence to the Factory Commission, although in 1836 James Buchanan became sole owner. (Stanley Mills, Instrument of Sasine, 19 July 1823)

The Buchanans were a Glasgow cotton dynasty, although they had their share of bankruptcies in the late 1780s and early 1790s. James Buchanan, a farmer of Carston, Stirlingshire, had five sons, all of whom became active in the cotton industry. In their early years, the Buchanan companies were 'much interwoven' and had an unenviable record of failure. Three of the brothers, John, Walter and George, entered manufacturing in 1776, when they became partners 'for the purpose of carrying on cotton spinning in Glasgow'. Their business went bankrupt in 1788, George claimed 'owing solely to the failure of other houses'. James and Archibald Buchanan's company failed in 1793 and their estates were sequestered in the same year. In 1794, George Buchanan petitioned from a Scottish prison for a warrant of Liberation having 'dissipated near £50,000 Sterling'. His brother John had already spent a year in the Fleet prison in London, where: 'he sleeps in the London Coffee-house, which is within the limits of that prison, and pays eighteen pence a-night for his lodgings. Double that sum will not keep him in eating and drinking and shows he has plenty of money'. (Fitton, 1989, 78–9)

John Buchanan was Arkwright's first agent in Scotland and his brother, Archibald, was sent to Cromford to be trained. On Archibald's return to Scotland, he and his brothers, James and George, set themselves up as 'English merchants and dealers in cotton yarn' in Glasgow, where they imported fine yarns from England and put them out to be woven. In 1787, at the age of 18, Archibald Buchanan became the manager of his father's Deanston mills, which were managed first by him, then for over thirty years by James Smith, a nephew of the Buchanans. (Finlay, 1951, 67, & Fitton, 1989, 79–80) In 1801, Archibald was appointed manager of Catrine mills in Ayrshire by Kirkman Finlay, another Buchanan relative, and served there for almost forty years. (Hamilton, 1966, 127, and Fitton, 1989, 78–9)

The Buchanans were said to have invested over £160,000 in Stanley mills and village, a huge sum for the time, which can be compared with the £60,000 Robert Owen and his partners paid for New Lanark in 1799 (Donnachie, 2000, 76) Investment on this scale suggests that the original Stanley enterprise was not big enough to give the economies of scale enjoyed by large mills, such as New Lanark or Catrine. Although £160,000 may be an exaggeration, the bulk of the present day mill buildings date from this period. In 1833, the Stanley manager reported 'the Brick Mill was erected about fifty years ago and part of the East Mill about thirty three years ago; the other part of the East Mill and all the other buildings were erected by the present proprietors'. (*Parliamentary Papers*, 1834, XX, A1, 160) A plan of 1823 showed the Old Mill and a mill on the site of the East Mill but nothing on the site of the present-day Mid Mill (Atholl Mss. D3.16)

At the end of the French Wars 'Stanley fell from a state of great prosperity to almost devastation and ruin'. Since the Buchanans took over: 'Two new Mills larger than the old ones have been finished and a third one is in progress'. The mills formed a square 'in the centre of which an extensive Gas works has been constructed for the purpose of lighting them, the vent of which is upwards of one hundred feet in height'. (*Scots Magazine*, 14 September 1825, 496) By 1831, the population was over 2,000 of whom 1,000 were employed at the mill. (*NSA*, X, 436 & 440)

The Buchanans built a new lade to give a fall of 16 feet and generate 200 h.p. from seven water wheels. The lade was carried under a 150 foot high hill, by means of a

Store Street, Stanley, 1968 (NMRS)

'mine' 800 feet long, 8 feet high and 10 feet wide, arched and paved throughout. Two other tunnels had been built through the same hill; one by John Lord Nairne in 1729 for a corn mill, the second by Dempster and Co. in 1785. (*NSA*, X, 440) A plan of 1823 showed three tunnels emerging from the hillside to run parallel to the Tay, before dividing at right angles into two channels, one running underneath a building on the site of the present day East Mill, the other running to the East of the Bell Mill. (Atholl Mss D3/18) In 1835, the seven water wheels at Stanley generated 200 h.p., compared to the 300 h.p. generated by water power at both New Lanark and Deanston cotton mills. (Baines 1835, 390) Three years later, it was reported that the water supply never failed 'though sometimes it is in such superabundance as to stop the wheels'. (*NSA*, X, 440)

In 1825, the *Scots Magazine* reported 'a new Street has been laid out, to run parallel with the South Street, in which houses, two stories high with attics are already finished, sufficient for the accommodation of one hundred and twenty families'. This was the Brick Tenement on Store Street, which survives in a much altered form. Two other streets were laid out and 'the spirited Proprietors are building a large Store-House from which the workpeople are to be supplied with all kinds of provisions and merchandise to be purchased by the Company from the best markets and sold at merely a saving profit'. (*Scots Magazine*, 14 September 1825)

Store Street is a (heavily modernised) two storey brick row with attics at the rear of the building. The size of brick is 9.75 inches x 5 inches x 3 inches and there is a Doric pilaster doorway at No 10, with a pend at No 14. There is a pepperpot stairtower at the rear of the building, the remainder of the stairs being open. The block bears a strong resemblance to workers' housing at Deanston, Perthshire, although that is stone built. The Deanston housing was extended in 1811 to the west of the village and again in 1820, when the company acquired part of the Drummond estate. (Finlay, 1951, 67–74, and Fitton, 1989, 80). None of the Stanley housing bears any resemblance to the four and five storey tenement housing of New Lanark, as it is all two storey. This may reflect the less cramped sites at Stanley and Deanston, the determination of the Atholl Estates to control development or more likely, the strong Buchanan links between Stanley and Deanston.

In the early 1830s, Alexander Stevenson, acting resident partner at Stanley, described how:

> Most (of the workers) live in the houses of their employers; the houses are occasionally whitewashed at the expense of the proprietors, who use every means in their power to enforce cleanliness; and employ servants to sweep the streets of the village. The proprietors have erected at their own expence and endowed a chapel of ease, in connexion with the Church of Scotland, where the young people under fifteen years of age are accommodated gratis; the grown up people pay 5s a year seat rent. They provide also a school house, allow the teacher a yearly salary and a free house, restricting him to a low rate of fees. There is a day school and a night school for the young people employed during the day in the works. There is also a Sunday-

evening school directed and superintended by the minister of the chapel, and usually attended by between three and four hundred young people.
(*Parliamentary Papers*, 1834, XX, A1, 162)

Sanitation in the mills consisted of water closets in each flat, separate for the sexes, with 'drainage into moveable boxes, removed daily at six a.m'. There were no washing, dressing or eating rooms but 'buckets of fresh water' were provided for washing in each room, the women changing in the rooms where they worked. The throstle flats were washed once a week with lime water, because more oil was thrown out by throstle spinning and there were more children employed, so more care was required. The preparation rooms were washed once a fortnight with hot water and wood ashes and the spinning rooms once a month. There had been no improvements in health since 1797. (*Parliamentary Papers*, 1833, XX, A2, 44)

Work rooms were 10 feet high and were kept between 55–65 °F. The 'temperature desired' in the spinning rooms was 65 °F, whereas the temperature on the day of the inspection was 74 °F. James Sharp, the manager, explained that the yarn spun at Stanley was not fine, so higher temperatures were not required. The exception was the room where webs for looms were dressed with gum or sour flour (which smelled), where a temperature of 75–80 °F was required. Twenty people were employed in web dressing, including 8 children. John Scott, a twenty seven year old dresser, described how he prepared yarn for the looms in conditions of great heat, which affected the health of the young people working in his flat. There were five fanners in this room for removing dust but the general atmosphere in the mills was described as 'rather close'. Heating was by coal-fired central heating towers, which delivered hot air to each floor, as happened at other Scottish cotton mills including Spinningdale in Sutherland. (*Parliamentary Papers*, 1833, XXI, A3, 36, 1833, XX, A1, 62, and 1834, XX, A1, 161–162) George Dempster, a partner at Stanley and Spinningdale, used this system to heat his house at Dunnichen in Angus as early as 1794. (Cooke, 1995, 91) At New Lanark, the resourceful William Kelly had devised a stove with a series of hot air ducts by March 1796 which 'was sufficient to warm a mill of 150 feet by 30 or upwards'. (Donnachie & Hewitt, 1993, 54)

Plants and flowers decorated the windowsills at Stanley mills. Gas lighting was used for six months in the year, the gas being manufactured at the mill. The health of the cotton workers was generally good, although their appearance was 'more sickly than flax or wool workers'. Illnesses included phthisis (tuberculosis), haemoptysis (which could have been either tuberculosis, or cancer of the lung), cholera, rheumatism and deafness, caused by the noise of the machinery. Twenty-seven villagers died in the cholera epidemic, which swept the country in 1832 and three mill workers died of phthisis and haemoptysis. James Sharp, the manager, said there had been no serious accidents in the mills since he came. He had 'observed cases of swelled feet and ancles among the workers, but he does not know that this was owing to the work, as they move about, and it might have happened at any rate'. Most of the hands wore mantles on going out, the men resuming coats and shoes. (*Parliamentary Papers*, 1833, XXI, A3, 36, & 1833, XX, A1, 62)

Sharp reported 'porridge is common for the young workers and tea or coffee for the old ones for breakfast, and potatoes, broth, and sometimes a bit of meat for dinner'. Breakfast was at 9.00 am, dinner at 2.00 pm, forty five minutes being allowed off, and the works were regulated by 'Perth time'. A medical report on Stanley described how 'the food of the operatives consists of porridge, potatoes, kale or broth, and oat cake, which with fish or fat, constitutes the universal food of the working classes in Scotland'. (*Parliamentary Papers*, 1833, XXI, A3, 36, & 1834, XX, A1, 162) At New Lanark, the typical diet was 'porridge for breakfast, potatoes with herring for dinner, and again porridge or potatoes for supper. Meat remained something of a luxury, and tea, according to the parish minister, might also be taken 'whenever it can be afforded'' (Donnachie & Hewitt, 1993, 153) In 1834, in Perth 'there are plenty of weavers who do not taste animal food in a month; they just have potatoes and a little milk; but I am saying barely what a man would absolutely need'. Ten years later, it was claimed that the number of Perth weavers 'who depreciate their own condition and neglect that of their families by an over addiction to Scotland's skaith' was small. Instead, they were distinguished by 'sobriety, frugality and decency of deportment'. (Murray, 1979, 124–128)

Cotton yarn was produced at Stanley for the Indian market under the brand label 'Golden Elephant'. This reflected the general pattern of the British cotton industry, which was shifting its exports from the 'old markets' of Europe, North America and the West Indies to the 'new markets' of Latin America and Asia, with India taking the largest share. (*Perthshire Advertiser*, 12 August 1929, 102, & Chapman 1987, 42–44)

A letter, dated 23 February 1834, from John Fleming at Stanley to his brother-in-law, Alexander Stewart, of Prince Edward Island, Canada, described how he had 'a good business established on such a basis that it is likely to increase. I employ from 5 to 7 hands'. After bringing Stewart up to date on family news, Fleming wrote that he had sent him 'an account of the great Political Changes which have and are taking place in our country by the passing of the Reform Act extending the representation to £10 voters, the abolition of all the close burgh corporations. I think that a separation of Kirk and State will soon take place. Also that the corn trade will be freed from the shackles of a corn law.' Stewart's mother 'lives in a house by herself beside David Ritchie at Cromwell and amuses herself by doing what she is able at winding yarn for Mr. Reid's power loom. There has been considerable improvement in that quarter. Several have been built both for spinning and power looms. Weaving in fact from present appearances it is likely that the linen manufacture of Scotland by machinery will be carried on to a greater extent than in any other country.' David Ritchie, who was married to a relative, was 'a millwright with Mr. Reid Cromwell Park . . . . He is a first rate tradesman and had his wages advanced 2 shillings a week unasked.' (Letter courtesy of Miss S. Patton, Calvine)

Stanley Benevolent Society was established in 1831 to assist the poor, supported by voluntary contributions. The total disbursement started at £40 a year but by 1838 it was exceeding £60, averaging 1 shilling (5p) per week for each beneficiary. Coal, clothing, food and medicines were also given to the needy. Stanley Funeral Society was founded in 1831 and had a membership in 1838 of about 1,200. Every member paid an entry fee of 1 shilling (5p) and thereafter 1d. (0.5p) for every funeral in the village. When the head of a family died £4 was advanced for expenses and £2 for a child '£30 was always kept in hand in case of any unusual mortality'—such as the cholera epidemic of 1833. Stanley Library contained 560 well-selected volumes. The fees were 2 shillings (10p) for entry and 9d (3.5p) per quarter. However, 'Stanley was not a reading community' and there were only 20 library members. The village had twelve public houses licensed to sell porter, ale and British spirits in contrast to Deanston and Blantyre, where public houses were banned. (NSA, X, 444–449 & Pollard, 1965, 194)

Historians such as Joyce and Knox have argued that this period saw employers moving away from confrontation with workers and aggressive accumulation of wealth in favour of 'a civic gospel . . . which stressed the virtues of philanthropy and of awarding recognition to labour'. In the West of Scotland:

> philanthropic activities and the religious conviction which underscored them were to play important parts in the evolution of a paternalistic strategy towards the labour force, particularly amongst the large thread manufacturers of Paisley.
>
> (Knox, 1995, 119)

These activities played an important part in factory villages like Stanley, New Lanark, Deanston and Catrine, which had an earlier paternalistic and landowning tradition to draw on. They depended heavily on the local landowner to feu land for mills and a village and to give water rights. Of course, there were tensions between paternalism based on the landed estate or the factory:

> Paternalism as a means of social control had developed within the relatively closed parameters of landed society and was used as a means of managing the tensions which arose from the existence of huge inequalities in the distribution of power and wealth within this mode of production.
>
> (Knox, 1995, 119–120)

Paternalism in landed society, particularly Highland society, was based on tradition, which was less easily transferred to the factory situation, where firms came and went according to the economic cycle and there was a high turnover in the workforce, at least initially. It was easier to develop in isolated, self contained factory villages like Stanley, Deanston and New Lanark in Scotland, or Cromford, Belper and Styal in England, than in the more anonymous cities of Glasgow or Manchester.

In 1842 a handsome arch was erected at the junction of the Dunkeld and Stanley roads by the mill owners, to greet Queen Victoria and Prince Albert. Just after 9.00 am a procession of over 2,000 people, led by George Buchanan, the mill owner, and two village bands arranged themselves on the side of a 'Broomie Knowe' close beside the arch and the Royal procession walked slowly past, by order of the Queen. (Ferguson, 1869) Joyce, writing about North of England mill towns, used the phrase 'the new paternalism', to describe the ways in which Victorian employers successfully invoked loyalty from their workers by sponsoring this type of communal activity, works outings and musical events. (Joyce, 1980, 134–157) Whatley described similar activities in 19th century Dundee as displaying 'orchestrated pride in workplace, locality and nation'. (Whatley, 2000, 85) The cult of Queen Victoria as Monarch (or Matriarch) was an important part of this culture:

> In small towns and isolated industrial villages, where the employer(s) had a near monopoly in the labour market, controlled housing, and through symbolic acts of public benevolence, was able to extend the workplace authority beyond the walls of the factory, paternalism was however, a realistic and indeed highly beneficial strategy. Paisley, and the industrial villages of Catrine and New Lanark were classic examples of this.
>
> (Knox, 1995, 122–3)

Stanley was another 'classic example' of industrial paternalism, where there was continuity with an earlier tradition of paternalism on the Atholl Estates. Indeed, the Atholls retained an active interest in the village into the late twentieth century.

Mill owners at Stanley were heavily influenced by these landed and aristocratic role models. James Craig, the Glasgow muslin manufacturer who mismanaged the Mills in the early 1800s, ended life as a gentleman farmer in Stanley and in 1829, at the age of 72, applied to the Highland Society for a Gold Medal for agricultural improvement. (Atholl Mss., 69, 5, 226) A later owner, Frank Stewart Sandeman, emphasised his title as Colonel of the Forfarshire Volunteers, dressed the part of the landed proprietor and boasted of his family connections with Lady Nairne, the aristocratic Jacobite poetess.

Historians such as Wiener have argued that an anti-industrial ethos lay behind Britain's long term economic decline and that second and third generation British industrialists often aspired to a landed and aristocratic lifestyle, away from the hurly burly of the market place. (Wiener, 1981) This view has been challenged by other historians, (Rubinstein, 1994) but the experience of Stanley, where industrial innovation and international competition met landed, aristocratic and Highland lifestyles, suggests the reality was more complex. The survival of Luncarty bleachfield which, like Stanley, had salmon fishing rights on the Tay, suggests that its remarkably long life may have owed as much to the attractions of salmon fishing to the senior management of Whitecroft Ltd., its Lancashire-based owners, as to any hard nosed decisions about business profitability. (Cooke, 1984, 6)

Stanley village had 55 trades people in the 1840s—shopkeepers, builders, carpenters, cabinetmakers, shoemakers, blacksmiths and a saddler. In 1841 22.5 per cent of heads of households in Stanley had been born outside Perthshire. The place of birth was given ten years later in the 1851 census, which showed that, of those born outside Perthshire, the largest groups came from Invernesshire (Lagganside), Lanarkshire and Renfrewshire. The village had a mixture of Highlanders and Lowlanders and Gaelic was widely spoken. The oldest inhabitant was Margaret Robertson, aged 90, who was born in Fortingall, Perthshire. Her family were all born in the parish and she may have been one of the original work force in the 1780s. A number of the villagers came from Ireland and one man from Kingston, Jamaica. (GROS, Census Enumerators' Returns, 1841)

George Buchanan inherited the mills from his father in 1845. He was a major partner in the Scottish Midland Junction Railway Company with a holding of 4,000 shares and became Deputy Chairman, being succeeded in 1849 by the Duke of Atholl. In 1845, when the Scottish Midland Junction (Perth–Forfar) and Scottish Central Railway Bills were before Parliament, the 'railway mania' was at its climax. Six hundred and twenty railway companies were registered, with a total capital of £563 million. (Mitchell, 1884, Vol. 2, 158) George, Thomas and John Buchanan were regular customers of the Perth Banking Company. They borrowed £25,000 from Perth Bank on bills in 1845, using their railway stock as security. (Munn, 1981, 137)

The Finance Committee meeting of the Scottish Midland Railway Company was adjourned 'sine die' on 11 November 1847, because of the illness of George Buchanan, Deputy Chairman. However, Buchanan was back chairing the meeting in February 1848, shortly before his death. (NAS, BR, SCM1, 6) By 1847, the Perth to Forfar Railway was under construction and the *Perthshire Courier* of 25 November 1847 gave an account of a fatal accident to a labourer, while working on the Stanley cutting. The railway opened on 2 August 1848 and by 1 April 1850 it reached Aberdeen. The Perth to Dunkeld Railway opened on 7 April 1856 and on 9 September 1863, it reached Inverness. (Gardner, 1934, 33)

The coming of the railway brought raw material supplies and export markets very much closer. Prior to the railways, Stanley was in weekly touch with Glasgow, carts coming all year round bringing raw cotton to Stanley and returning with spun yarn and cloth from the hand weavers—a ten day round trip. (*Perthshire Advertiser*, 12 August 1929, 102) Stanley was greatly affected by the social and economic changes which the railways brought relatively early on, because of George Buchanan's Deputy Chairmanship of the Scottish Midland Junction Railway Company. Ironically, it was at this time that the population of Stanley began to decline, from 1,973 in 1841 to 1,769 in 1851 and 1,272 ten years later. By 1871 it had fallen to 932, to recover to 1,030 by 1881. (*Ordnance Gazetteer of Scotland*, 1885, VI, 378 & Hunter, 1883, 511–6) A more drastic decline took place at New Lanark, where population fell from 1,901 in 1831 to 672 in 1891. (Donnachie & Hewitt, 1993, 144) The decline was due to a number of factors—the introduction of labour-saving machinery and the slow decline of the Scottish cotton industry, in the face of competition from Lancashire. However, a good deal of the decline at Stanley was due to the Cotton Famine, leading to mill closure from 1862 to 1867, and to the baleful influence of Samuel Howard, the new owner.

6.

The Memory of the Just is Blessed

Samuel Howard and his Trustees, 1852–1876

George Buchanan died in 1848 and his brother Thomas sold the mills to Samuel Howard of Burnley, in 1852, for under £20,000. This compared with the purchase price of £4,600, which James Craig had paid for Stanley Mills fifty years earlier. The local paper added that, although the mills had hitherto been entirely devoted to cotton, the new owner's experience had largely been in woollen manufacture and it was 'understood they will devote some of the present power to the spinning of worsted yarn'. (*Perthshire Courier*, 23 December 1852, 3) Samuel Howard (1808–1872), who had a Scottish wife, Mary Watson, was described as a 'landed proprietor, worsted spinner and wool merchant' (*Burnley Directory*, 1851).

A plan of 1855 showed substantially the present day lay-out of mill buildings, with water wheels on the courtyard side of the Bell and the East Mills. The plan showed a Bleachhouse, a circular mill lodge at the mill entrance and a grain mill to the west of the Bell Mill. Beech House to the north of the Bell Mill was marked as 'the Manager's House' and Stanley House on the peninsula to the east of the mills as 'the Mansion House'. (Perth and Kinross Archives) The grain mill survived until 1864, when it was marked on the 6 inch O.S. map but it had disappeared by the 1900 edition, which showed a gasometer in the mill courtyard. In 1857, the Stanley Mills and Lands were valued at £685 on the valuation rolls, workers houses being valued at £320 and workers' gardens at £20. (NAS, VR, 113, 3) In January 1857, a number of villagers set up the Stanley Provision Company to provide and make provisions and articles of general merchandise for sale to its shareholders and others. The Company had capital of £630 in 420 shares at £1 10s. (£1.50) each. It finally wound up in May 1882, liquidators being appointed. (NAS, BT2, 9)

The Cotton Famine of 1861 saw the disruption of raw cotton supplies, as a result of the American Civil War. The Famine 'burnt itself into the history of Lancashire' and marked 'the loss of national pre-eminence'. (Farnie, 1979, 135) In Lancashire, out of a total of 500,000 cotton workers, Boards of Guardians were paying poor relief to over 250,000 in November 1862 and the system was stretched to breaking point. (Henderson, 2nd edition, 1969, 53) In Scotland, imports of raw cotton fell from 172,055 cwt in 1861 to 7,216 cwt in 1864 and exports of cotton cloth fell from 150 to 94 million yards. (Bremner, 1869, 288) Samuel Howard became notorious in Stanley, when he stockpiled supplies of raw cotton to sell on to Lancashire at a profit, closing down the mills for five years from 1862–67. The village's population fell from 1,272 in 1861 to 932 in 1871.

At Catrine and Deanston, the Finlays closed the mills but paid the workers half wages and extended school hours, involving themselves in outlay of £13,000 a year in wages. (Anon, 1951, 45) At Stanley, a graphic account of the state of the village survived in a poem by John Campbell. Campbell, (alias Will Harrow), was born at Charleston Farm, near Stanley, in 1808 and died in the Perth workhouse in 1892. He had been active in Chartist politics in Dundee and was known as 'Chartist John'. His poem 'A Voice from Stanley Mills' is dated 1863:

> The traffic in our grass-grown streets are thinning,
> (A donkey on the verdure fondly browses),
> And none are left, alas! to do the spinning
> Except the spiders in the empty houses.
> Here merry maids the smooth footpaths have trod.
> Like blooming rose-buds linked by twos and threes,
> With swift feet tripping o'er the sylvan road—
> Their snowy kirtles waving in the breeze.
>
> 'It was a merry place in days of yore,
> But something ails it now—the place is curst',
> For long the wolf's been howling at the door
> And now into our midst the brute has burst,
> And from its hungry glare the fleet did flee,
> Some to St Mungo—others hied to Blair—
> But most have winged their flight to sweet Dundee,
> Hoping to get a crust and welcome, there.
>   (Fergusson, 1897, 139–140)

The 1850s and 1860s was a period of general economic prosperity. Whatley noted 'the absence of significant class conflict' in Scotland in the twenty years after 1850 and remarked about Dundee 'That the civic mood in should have been so harmonious, is at first sight, surprising.' (Whatley, 2000b, 71 & 81) However, not all industrial relations in Scotland in this period were 'harmonious'. Knox noted, 'Between 1850 and 1914, the Scottish cotton industry was characterised by weak trade unionism and strong and determined employer organisation'. (Knox, 1995, 164) The fact that Scottish cotton workers received less favourable treatment from the Scottish Poor Law Commissioners than their Lancashire counterparts during the Cotton Famine suggested that hard line attitudes, with sectarian and racist overtones, were still common amongst Scottish employers. These attitudes had surfaced earlier in Paisley, in 1829, when a proposal to establish a soup kitchen for the relief of the unemployed was met with the claim that no one 'but the low Irish and other dregs of society would take relief in this manner'. (Murray, 1978, 136)

Samuel Howard owned the church, which became the property of his wife when he died in 1872. (Stanley Mills, Extract Registered Trust, Disposition and Settlement by Samuel Howard, 22 December 1871) In 1876 she sold it to the Presbytery of Perth. (*Perthshire Courier*, 22 August, 1876) In the church tower there is a pendulum clock, built by Richard Roberts of Manchester for the Great Exhibition of 1851 and gifted by the Howards. There is an elaborate memorial to the Howards and members of the Watson family in the vestibule. The inscription to Samuel Howard reads:

Samuel Howard who died at Stanley House 3rd Feb. 1872 aged 64 years.
'The memory of the just is blessed'

The mill was carried on by his trustees, Mrs Mary Howard, John Howard (nephew), James Folds of Brunshaw, Burnley, Lancashire and John Miller, solicitor in Perth, until 1876, when it was bought by Sir Archibald Douglas Stewart of Grantully.

7.

The Secret Room

The Sandemans and Diversification, 1876–1921

Sir Archibald Stewart of Grandtully bought the mills in 1876 but they were run by Colonel Frank Stewart Sandeman (1838–1898) who became the owner in 1880. Sandeman was the youngest son of Glas Sandeman, of Bonskeid, Pitlochry and Sandilands, Perth. He was educated at Perth Academy and Edinburgh University, then moved to Lancashire to receive a practical training in engineering. He became a partner of Hardcastle and Co., calico printers and bleachers near Bolton, then moved back to Scotland to take up a partnership at Luncarty bleachfield. He entered a partnership in a Dundee jute spinning firm then, in 1874, built the Manhattan Jute

Colonel Frank Stewart Sandeman, mill owner,
outside Beech House, Stanley, c.1890 (Mrs. Amess, Perth)

Works in Dundee, where he was senior partner, with George Keiller as junior partner. Sandeman was a staunch Conservative but a fishing companion of the radical MP, John Bright, who came up to Stanley every year for the salmon fishing. He was Colonel Commandant of the 1st Forfarshire Volunteer Artillery and a great advocate of scientific and technical education. Manhattan Works was known for its state of the art machinery, his house in Stanley was lit by gas and electricity and he also experimented with acetylene lighting. (DPL, Lamb Collection, 196, 14 & *Dundee Advertiser*, 8 November 1898)

Sandeman had family links with William Sandeman of Luncarty, one of the original Stanley partners, and with the Jacobite poetess, Lady Nairne, whose family had owned Nairne estates (and built Stanley House) before the Atholls. Stanley House was destroyed by fire in 1887 and the Sandeman family moved into Beech House, nearer the Mills. Frank Sandeman clearly liked to play the country gentleman and a photograph showed him outside Beech House, dressed in tweed plus fours, with his dogs. He had a magnificent mastiff, called Wallace and was described as 'the very ideal of the Scottish gentleman'. Sandeman's connections with the Forfarshire Volunteers and his Perthshire upbringing gave him links with local landowners. At the opening of Manhattan Works in 1874, Sheriff Cheyne proposed a toast to 'The Landed Proprietors of this County'. The reply was by Colonel Erskine of Linlathen, who 'said he hoped the friendly feeling between the landed proprietors and the town of Dundee would long continue'. (*Dundee Advertiser*, 8 November 1898)

Sandeman's religious background was Free Church, which presumably was a relic of the family's earlier involvement in the Glasite Church. The Glasites were founded by John Glas of Tealing, who seceded from the Church of Scotland in 1730. (Cooke, 1984, 2) Many Scottish industrialists were members of religious groups other than the established Church of Scotland. David Dale founded his own church, the Independent Congregation in Glasgow, and Robert Owen experimented with Methodism and Unitarianism before turning against organised religion altogether. (Donnachie, 2000) In the West of Scotland 'One social characteristic of these entrepreneurs which stands out is the membership of the non-established churches of Scotland.' Of the Paisley thread dynasties, Thomas Coats was a Baptist, whilst Archibald Coats and John Clark were members of the United Presbyterian Church. Henry Birkmyre, of the Gourock Ropeworks, and New Lanark, was also a member of the UPC. (Knox, 1995, 118) An analysis of 30 Dundee industrialists between 1820 and 1870 revealed that only 7 (23 per cent) were members of the Church of Scotland, with 6 (20 per cent) being Congregationalists. (Miskell, 2000, 60)

Frank Sandeman clearly had a social conscience. The local paper reported, on 12 December 1876, that a spelling bee had been held in Stanley Combination Schoolroom in aid of a Free Library, with Colonel Sandeman in the Chair. He was thanked for lobbying for a new school at Stanley and replied that he would like to see a YMCA in the village and offered the use of the Drill Hall for public meetings. (*Perthshire Courier*, 12 December 1876)

A change of ownership at Stanley was often followed by changes to the power system. In 1879, the seven water wheels were replaced by Jilkes turbines, which meant that the mills could now run with a seven foot flood on the River Tay, whereas previously the water wheels came to a standstill with a flood of only three feet. Some forty to fifty working days a year had been lost in this way. Stanley Mills adopted a system of parallel flow developed by Thomson and Co. of Dundee, as opposed to the alternative systems of inflow or outflow. In 1878, a 200 h.p. turbine was installed, which proved so successful that another of 400 h.p. was ordered. The system was tested during a twelve foot flood, when it proved impossible to open the sluice gates which regulated the flow of water and the turbine wheel revolved one third slower in consequence. Divers were sent down, who opened the sixteen sluice gates, which delivered six tons of water a minute causing the wheel to revolve at its calculated speed of 70 revolutions a minute. (*Perthshire Courier*, 18 March 1879)

The Mill buildings were valued at £8,000 in 1879 (by a female valuer, Mrs G. Thomson) and the machinery, gearing and piping at a further £5,000. The clear rental on the village, deducting insurance and taxes, was estimated at £600 per annum. This compared with £250 estimated annual rent on the Mansion House (Stanley House) and Beech House and their policies and a rental of £250 per annum for the fishing rights on the Tay. The water-power generated at this period was given as 400 hp. (Stanley Mill Archives, Valuation of Stanley, 1879, now missing) The spinning of selvedge cotton and sewing twines for the Dundee and Fife jute and linen trades was the major activity, helped by the Sandeman's links with the industry through Manhattan Works, Dundee. (Cooke, 1977, 37)

William Fenton (1827–1898) leased part of Stanley Mills in 1881 to manufacture Scandinavian cotton belting using yarn produced at the Mills. Fenton was born in Burrelton, Perthshire, where he started life as a handloom weaver. He moved to Baxter Brothers in Dundee, then managed Birkmyre Brothers in Greenock. He spent eighteen years in Sweden managing the weaving department of William Gibson in Jonsorod. In 1880, he left Sweden and the following year began the manufacture of cotton machine belting at Stanley with W. Cobbett of London. Scandinavian cotton belting became established in the market and the firm, known as William Fenton, was managed by Fenton's son, David. Two other sons, John and James Fenton, worked at New Lanark, presumably through their father's Birkmyre connections. (A.K. Bell Library, Perth, Stanley Cuttings File, 48)

This belt weaving concern, which was sold to the Sandemans, became a staple of production at Stanley and more looms were installed, so that belting from 1 inch to 36 inches wide could be woven. A belt dressing plant was built to impregnate the product with bitumen solution and 'Stanley Solid Woven Cotton Belting' was sold all over the world. (*Perthshire Advertiser*, 12 August 1929) A separate sales subsidiary was formed called the Sandeman Stanley Cotton Belting Co. Ltd. with its head office in London and branches in all the large cities. (Cooke, 1977, 38 and oral evidence from the late John Culbert)

A variety of trades and occupations were carried on in Stanley in the late 1880s. Frank Stewart Sandeman Ltd were described as cotton-spinners, bleachers and finishers and William Fenton & Co., as belting manufacturers. Brick-making was still carried on in the area by William Watson, brick and tile-makers of Marlehall, Redgorton. There were only three spirit dealers and public houses listed, compared with twelve in 1838. There were seven grocers and general dealers, as well as a coffee-house. Other occupations were: engineer, millwright, tobacconist, stationer, nurseryman, salmon-fisher, coal and wood merchant (2), blacksmith, baker (3), boot and shoe maker (3), cattle dealer (2), flesher (2), joiner and wright (4), draper (4), surgeon (3) and tailor (4). (*Perth and Perthshire Directory*, 1889–90)

As working hours shortened, leisure time activities and sports began to develop. The traditional holiday on Handsel Monday, the first Monday in January, when a flute band paraded through the streets and shopkeepers gave prizes for races, had disappeared by 1890, to be replaced by New Year's Day. The Queen's Birthday on 24 May was another holiday, celebrated by bonfires and dancing. Towards the end of the nineteenth century, curling became popular, using a pond made to supply water to the mill. (Fergusson, 1893, 154) In 1895 and again in 1897, the River Tay froze over at both Perth and Stanley and a photograph showed two rinks of curlers on the frozen river by Stanley Mills. There was a fire in the Brick Buildings (Store Street), 'the property of F. S. Sandeman' on 19 September 1897, when 'Jeek' Gunn, a Glaswegian who acted as village bellman, was burnt to death. The fire was attended by the fire engine from Stanley Mills then by Perth City Fire Brigade, who reached Stanley 'in less than one hour'. (A. K. Bell Library, Perth, Stanley News Cuttings, 17)

'Jeek' Gunn, village bellman, Stanley, c.1890 (Perth Museum)

Frank Sandeman died in 1898 and the firm passed first to trustees and then to his sons—Douglas being in charge of Stanley and Fred in charge of Manhattan Works, Dundee. In 1911, the mills were valued by Alan Mellor and Co. of Oldham at a total of nearly £50,000, of which buildings amounted to £23,000, machinery, steam and water piping, power installations etc, being valued at nearly £27,000. There was a stone built bleaching croft, a brick built chlorine house and a stone and brick drying house on the site at Stanley. The Mid Mill contained a Blowing Room, a Willow Shed, two Loom Rooms, two Card Rooms and a Twisting Room. The West or Brick Mill contained a Stretching Room on the ground floor with a Dynamo House, a Loom Room with 44 looms, a Spooling Room on the third floor and Store Rooms on the two top floors. The East Mill had ring-spinning rooms on the third and fourth floors, a Twisting and Winding Room on the second and a gearing room on the ground. (Sidlaw Industries Archives, Valuation of Stanley 1911, now missing)

The First World War brought great activity to Stanley. Huge stocks of American cotton were purchased and stored in mill premises and in sheds at Stanley Railway Station. The Mills manufactured equipment webbings for the Armed Forces from one particular yarn, namely 9½ss/5 fold cotton. This yarn was reeled into hanks and sent to

Insurance Plan of Stanley Mills by Allen Mellor, Valuers, Oldham, June 1911
(NMRS)

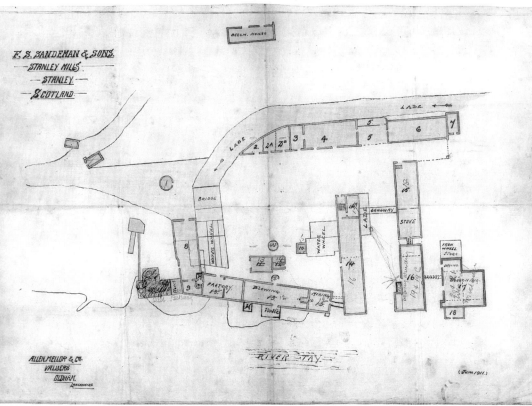

Francis Stevenson of Dundee to be dyed khaki, before being woven into various widths. A large number of light looms were set up to do the weaving. At the same time, the mills continued to produce cotton belting, which was used on the main drives of power-operated machinery. (Cooke, 1977, 39, and oral evidence from the late John Culbert)

The labour force for the spinning mill came mainly from the village, because they had the necessary skills for preparing, spinning, winding and doubling. However, the mill had to look further afield for weavers and these were recruited in large numbers, mainly from Fife, where there was a long tradition of weaving. Accommodation for these weavers, all female, was found by requisitioning hotels and large houses in the village. White's Hotel (now Tayside Hotel) became a hostel for 70 women. Hobart House and Findynate were also used as hostels and local householders were persuaded to fill their spare rooms with lodgers.

Frank Stewart Sandeman and Sons Ltd became a limited liability company on 6 April 1915, running Manhattan Works, Dundee and Stanley Mills. The partners leased the mills from the trustees of the late Mrs. Laura Stewart Sandeman in July 1912. Sandeman and Co. bought the mills in April 1915 for £120,223, of which £34,150 was for Manhattan Works, £1,363 for machinery at Stanley and £84,710 for stock in trade. The partners were Frederick David Stewart Sandeman, Douglas Charles Stewart Sandeman and Alexander Nairne Stewart Sandeman. Each of the three partners held 1,000 Ordinary shares but Frederick held the whip hand financially with 4,000 Preference shares out of a total of 5,600. Frederick and Alexander Sandeman were based at Manhattan Works, Dundee, Douglas at Stanley. The net profit for Manhattan and Stanley for the year ending 30 September 1915 was £53,106. (Perth and Kinross Archives, F. S. Sandeman Minute Books, 1915–1933, fos. 1–26)

In 1916, Douglas Sandeman began experimenting with a light loom, which wove an endless tape for use in cigarette manufacture. He treated this venture as highly confidential and any worker involved was sworn to secrecy. The place where this activity was going on became known as the Secret Room. He employed his own pattern maker for the loom parts and ordered the castings from various foundries, taking care not to indicate their ultimate use. This was the beginning of another highly successful item of manufacture at Stanley Mills. (Cooke, 1977, 39 and oral evidence from the late John Culbert)

The share capital was increased to £200,000 in April 1919 and the innovative nature of the firm was shown by the issue of 20,000 shares of £1 each to employees. These paid dividends but did not confer the right to vote at the AGM. Employees included managers, departmental managers, foremen, clerks and workmen but excluded the majority of the workforce, who were women. (Perth and Kinross Archives, F. S. Sandeman Minute Books, 1915–1933, fos. 59–60) This early example of profit sharing must have owed something to the impact of the First World War, when many Stanley workers were killed or injured in the trenches and many others, having experienced life outside the village, left the mill and the village for good.

8.

Stanley Mills has a Way With Women

From Jute Industries to Stanley Mills (Scotland) and Closure, 1921–1989

In the difficult conditions after the First World War, textile firms throughout the UK began to band together for protection against international competition. The East of Scotland was no exception and a number of Dundee-based jute and flax firms came together as Jute Industries in 1921. F.S. Sandeman and Company, who owned Manhattan Works in Dundee as well as Stanley, joined Jute Industries, who paid £550,000 for the firm.

A new hydro-electric system was installed in 1921. The existing lade was widened and extended towards the river. Concrete was used extensively in the tunnel, lade and power station and Swedish Boving turbines were installed. The new system generated 1100 h.p. and electricity was generated for the mills, streets and many of the Stanley houses. (*Perthshire Advertiser*, 12 August 1929, 102) A series of photographs, taken by an uncle of the late John Culbert, a former Chief Engineer at Stanley Mills and member of the Stanley Extra-Mural class in the mid 1970s, showed the construction work on the turbines.

The old flooring consisted of pitch pine and this wood was still in remarkable condition when taken out. The contractor for the lade work and the building of the concrete power station was Duncan of Murthly. The whole of the excavation work for the lade and power station was done by pick and shovel and employed a large number of men from Stanley and the surrounding area. Several years later, a high walled tailrace was built in the river bed to control the water level during floods. The hecks (gratings), which were placed immediately in front of the turbines, required regular clearing and this was done by long shafted rakes. This was not an easy task, especially during a flood, when the water was full of debris. In the autumn, when leaves were falling or when ice was breaking up after a severe frost, the hecks had to be manned 24 hours a day. (Cooke, 1977, 39 and oral evidence from the late John Culbert)

F. S. Sandeman and Sons made a loss of £31,069 in the year ending 30 September 1921. The following year, the firm produced cotton yarns and goods, bindings, loop bindings, tapes, webbings and girthings in all fibres, conveyors and Stanley cotton belting. They guaranteed delivery 'under exception of fires, breakages of machinery, strikes, lockouts and other unforeseen circumstances'. (Perth and Kinross Archives, F. S. Sandeman Minute Book 1915–1933) The inter-war years were difficult ones for the British textile industry and Stanley was no exception. In 1925, the Mills made a half year profit of £13,928 on a turnover of £16,000, of which webbing made £6,457, spinning £5,042, cotton belting £2,506 and tapes £1,184. The half year profits for Manhattan Works, Dundee were £10,434. (Dundee University Archives, Sidlaw Archives, VII, 4/2)

In 1928, on the retiral of Fred Sandeman, the management at Stanley was restructured and divided into Engineering, Technical and Sales. Mr. Robertson took charge of Engineering, T. H. Dick, was in charge of Technical, and Sales were divided between Mr. Dick (Dundee buyers of selvage yarns) and Col. Skene (No 11 Department). The salary of T.H. Dick, the Technical Manager, was increased from £1,200 to £1,500 and that of Col. Skene, the Sales Director, from £850 to £1,000 rising to £1,200 in 1930. Alexander Sandeman was asked to retire from the Board to make way for a new director.

There were 'urgent questions' to be sorted out at Stanley, including the management of the works and the factoring of the village. It was proposed to wind up F. S. Sandeman and Company in voluntary liquidation. The final meeting of the Company was held on 21 March 1933, when Sandemans were absorbed into Jute Industries. (Dundee University Archives, Sidlaw Industries Archives, VII, 4/3, & Perth and Kinross Archives, F. S. Sandeman Minute Books, 1915–1933)

Construction of Turbine House at Stanley Mills, 1921 (the late John Culbert, Stanley)

The Depression of the 1930s saw a decline in production and wage rates were reduced but although there was short time working at Stanley, there were no long periods of total unemployment. Between 1933 and 1936, the workforce fluctuated between a low of 291 and a high of 327. (Stanley Mills, Numbers Employed, Jan. 1933 to Jan. 1936) During this time, recruitment of labour was mainly from Stanley village plus a small number from Perth. Tayside Hostel remained open, the 50 to 60 female residents coming chiefly from Fife. In April 1934, the Stanley manager was Mr. Hutton, who stayed in post until well after the Second World War. The local paper reported that 'cotton belting is a feature of the work undertaken' and contrasted the current workforce of 300 with the 1,500 formerly employed. (*Perthshire Advertiser*, 4 April 1934)

Business began to improve from the mid 1930s and the spinning mill, as well as supplying yarn to the Dundee jute trade and to Fife weaving firms, had to meet increasing demand from Stanley's own weaving departments—belt weaving, Northrop weaving (sailcloth), Hattersley weaving (Narrow Webbings), as well as the weaving of other webbings such as spindle driving tape, Ford brake lining for motor cars, hose pipes, bookbinder webbing and chair webbings for upholstery. The mills also won a contract to supply yarn to the carpet weavers, Blackwood, Morton of Kilmarnock. The Tape Department was flourishing and supplying cigarette machine tapes to leading cigarette manufacturers. (Cooke, 1977, 40, and oral evidence from the late John Culbert)

When the Second World War came, the bulk of the machinery at Stanley was turned over to the manufacture of equipment webbings for the Armed Forces. There was a shortage of labour, as many of the men left to join the Forces but many jobs were classified as a 'reserved occupation' so key workers were retained. The end of the Second World War and Indian Independence in 1947 brought large-scale changes. The new Indian government introduced import licences for belting and spindle tapes, which led to the loss of a major export market. At the same time, the domestic market was changing, as the introduction of individual electric motors on machines meant that heavy cotton drive belting was becoming obsolete. This led to a steady decline in the demand for woven cotton products, so that by the 1960s the only cotton weaving left at Stanley was the cigarette machine tape section. (Cooke, 1977, 41 and oral evidence from the late John Culbert)

The hydro-electric system at Stanley, installed in 1921, was abandoned in 1965, because of the rising costs of maintenance for the tunnel and lade system and the mills and village went onto mains electricity. Two years later, the Six Day War broke out in the Middle East and energy prices soared. In October 1967, the local paper ran a feature entitled 'Changed Days in the Mills' extolling the virtues of Stanley. Whereas cotton mills had formerly been regarded as 'symbols of poverty, of the struggle of the lower classes, of pure old fashionedness' workers had now entered an era of modern, clean, hygienic conditions, unrivalled in the working world. A campaign to recruit 80 female workers was launched under the slogan, 'Stanley Mills has a way with women.' The firm offered 'excellent working conditions, clean secure employment, transport to and from work, and a sick pay scheme'. (*Perthshire Advertiser*, 28 October 1967, 13)

In November 1967, Ian McArthur, the MP for Perth and East Perthshire, visited Stanley and was shown around by Mr. H. F. Stott, general manager and Mr. J. Shaw, assistant manager. The Mills employed 170 people making cigarette tape, yarn for carpet and industrial sewing yarn for use in the bagging industry. It was planned to expand the manufacture of man-made fibres. (*Perthshire Advertiser*, 18 November 1967, 30) A week later, Mr. Stott, general manager, announced at a meeting in the canteen that the company was handing over, free of charge, a hundred houses in Store Street, Charlotte Street, Mill Street and King Street to the Tay Valley Housing Association for modernisation. (*Perthshire Advertiser*, 25 November 1967, 1) Bert Stott's appointment as general manager was obviously behind the flurry of announcements about Stanley in the *Perthshire Advertiser*.

The miners' strike of 1973–4 saw short time working at the mills because of power cuts and the introduction of a three day week. As a result of the activities of OPEC, the price of a barrel of oil increased from $2.46 in 1972 to $9.76 in 1974 and electricity prices soared. (More, 1997, 226) The price of raw cotton began to increase substantially and there was a gradual change to spinning man-made fibres. The market was now the knitwear trade, mainly in Leicester, Nottingham and Yorkshire. The parent company had diversified so greatly that the name 'Jute Industries Ltd.' was altered to 'Sidlaw Industries Ltd.' Part of the premises, formerly occupied by the Tape Department, was let to an outside knitwear firm to make up knitted garments and this provided work for some local women. The end of weaving at Stanley came in 1976, when the cigarette machine tape section closed. The declining labour force at the mills gradually brought about a change in the character of the village. By 1977, only 83 people were employed at the mills, of whom 58 lived locally and 25 came from outwith the village. (Cooke, 1977, 42 and oral evidence from the late Bert Stott)

In 1979, the mills were taken over by Stanley Mills (Scotland) Ltd., a management buy-out by Bert Stott, who had managed Stanley for Jute Industries, and Colin Dracup, who had strong links with the English knitwear trade. Production was entirely concentrated on acrylic fibres and 10–12 tons of acrylic yarn were produced weekly, building up to a weekly peak of 24 tons. The main customer was the sock industry in the English Midlands. In the mid 1980s, following demand from British chain stores, English sock manufacturers moved back to cotton yarn and this, combined with the strength of the pound, rising prices for acrylics and a 50 per cent fall in the price of cotton, spelt the death knell for Stanley Mills. The firm tried to diversify by producing heavy count acrylic yarn for fleece fabrics, such as dressing gowns and invested £500,000 in rotor spinning equipment. This was described as 'a capital intensive' situation in which the Mills could be operated by around 30 people and 26 of the current staff of 54 were already working their notice. Production finally ceased in March 1989, by which time the workforce had shrunk to a mere 28 people. David Crawford, the Managing Director at Stanley, announced that the last kilo of yarn would leave in early April. (*Perthshire Advertiser*, 3 February 1989, 5)

9.

Sober, Virtuous and Industrious

The Stanley Workforce

Stanley was a greenfield site, with little population in the immediate area. It was chosen for access to water-power resources, rather than labour, and workers had to be recruited, trained and housed by the Company. However, the village was only seven miles from Perth, which was an active centre of textile manufacture, with a population of 19,877 in 1790.

The skills of the Perth workforce were a key factor in persuading Richard Arkwright to become involved at Stanley. George Penny recalled that when Arkwright visited Perth, he met William Sandeman of Luncarty bleachfield, the 4th Duke of Atholl and Penny's father in the King's Arms Inn, Perth to discuss Stanley. Arkwright was 'highly delighted' with the quality of the muslin produced by Penny and asked if Penny, 'could weave them himself and teach others'. On being told yes, Arkwright said 'the erection of the Mills might be immediately proceeded with; there could be no fear of success'. Building began and 'a number of boys and girls were sent up to Manchester to learn the spinning trade'. (Penny, 1836, 251)

The original Contract of Co-partnership for Stanley in 1785 referred to: 'Sundry Indentures with different persons to be sent to the said Richard Arkwright at Cromford aforesaid to be taught the constructing and making of the Machinery used by him in preparing and Spining of the said (cotton) wool itself'. (NAS SC 49, 48, 104, fos. 1–5) According to George Dempster, writing in 1800, 'Sir Richard instructed Mr. Dale's artisans and young people gratis as he also did those sent from Stanley'. (Cooke, 1979a, 196) In the isolated Peak District community of Cromford, the new arrivals clearly made an impact. The *Derby Mercury* reported on 12 May 1785:

> A few days since, between forty and fifty North Britons with bagpipes and other music playing, arrived at Cromford near Matlock-Bath, from Perth in Scotland. These industrious Fellows left that place on account of the scarcity of work, were taken into the service of Richard Arkwright Esq. in his cotton mills and other extensive works, entered into present pay and provided with good quarters. They appeared highly pleased with the

reception they met with and had a dance in the evening to congratulate each other on the performance of so long a journey.

(Fitton and Wadsworth, 1958, 105)

This was similar to New Lanark, where 11 men and 15 boys dressed in 'complete dresses of brown cloth, with red collars to their coats' were sent to Cromford in 1785 to learn cotton spinning. (Donnachie and Hewitt, 1993, 35) Indeed, Arkwright was almost overwhelmed by people looking for work and training at his mills. In 1783, two Scots came looking for work in his Manchester mill but 'Arkwright had so many applications from people anxious to enter his employment that he could do nothing for the Scotch emigrants'. (Pollard, 1965, 178)

There was considerable resistance to working in a cotton mill from workers who were 'averse to indoor labour' and factory discipline. Millowners had to resort to paying high wages or recruiting vulnerable groups like orphans, widows with large families, or Highland or Irish workers, who were moving, or being moved, off the land. All of these groups were recruited at Stanley, except for Irish workers, who were always in a small minority in the village. George Dempster, a partner at Stanley, wrote to George Thorkelin, the Icelandic antiquary on 21 August 1788 '80 people came to us from the Highlands (80 families) which have all proved sober, virtuous and industrious'. Dempster added significantly 'by their means we lower our wages to the current price of cotton yarn and suffer less by its fall than most other cotton spinners'. (Laing Mss. III, 379, 217)

This paralleled experience at other Scottish mills such as New Lanark, where 'the Highlands became the main recruiting ground'. David Dale advertised in Highland newspapers and built Caithness Row to house the newcomers. A letter by Dale, published in the *Scots Magazine* in October 1791, gave his apologia for Highland recruitment. 'Could the people find employment in the Highlands it would be much better for them to remain there; but as this is not the case the best thing that can be done for them and this country is to invite all that cannot find employment to come here and they will be provided for.' (Donnachie and Hewitt, 1993, 37–39) At Deanston in Perthshire, the supply of labour 'was chiefly from the Highlands, where, from the introduction of sheep, the farmers and small cotters were forced away to seek employment in such establishments'. (Fitton 1989, 205) However, it was said that 'the Highlander never sits at ease at the loom; it is like putting a deer at the plough'. (Pollard, 1965, 161)

Married couples or widows with large families were a favourite target for cotton mills, north and south of the Border. David McVicar, the Stanley manager, wrote to Graham of Fintry on 17 October 1789 that the tailor Graham had mentioned would have to rely on 'his own exertions' as far as earning a livelihood in the village. There were already one or two tailors, who McVicar believed did very well. He wrote:

if he is married with children who will work at the Mill their wages will be a great assistance or if he has a wife who will be at the trouble of learning to

pick cotton I could give her constant employment and our women earn and
have employment for 3 to 6s a week.

I would be happy the Duke of Atholl would give his houses to such
people as have Familys who would send their children to the Mill and in
that case would chearfully retain a part of their wages for payment of their
rents as we do our own.

(NAS, GD 151, 11, 24)

Another source of labour was orphans from the workhouses. At New Lanark, John
Marshall, the Leeds flax spinner, reported in 1800 '400 to 500 apprentices are lodged
in a half of one of the mills, which has not yet been worked. They give them 1½ hours
schooling each night after the usual mill hours 7 o'clock. The present proprietors it is
said wished to give that up, but could not because it was contracted for in the indentures.'
(Donnachie, 2000, 80) There is no evidence of pauper children being employed in the
early days at Stanley but in the 1830s orphans 'were sent to the works by the kirk
session of Perth, and are looked after by their overseers'. (*Parliamentary Papers*, 1834,
XX, A1, 161) At New Lanark, poor-house apprentices were being phased out as
early as 1807, when Marshall reported: 'They have built more houses and are nearly
giving up the plan of having parish apprentices . . . . Mr Owen is said to be very strict
and is not popular in the neighbourhood'. (Donnachie, 2000, 96) In Scotland, factories
were referred to as 'public works', showing the link in the popular mind with workhouses.

Women and children made up the major part of the workforce at Stanley, as in other
cotton mills. Rev. William Chalmers, minister of Auchtergaven parish, reported in
1795:

Near an hundred families now reside in the village of Stanley. Above 350
persons are employed about the cotton mills—of this number 300 are
women or children under 16 years of age. The boys and girls, although
confined at work in the mill for many hours of the day, and at times during
the night, are in general very healthy.

(OSA, XII, 34)

If this is matched with Dempster's account, it appears that the bulk of the population
were Highlanders. The workforce of 350 in 1795 was much smaller than the estimated
1,334 employed by David Dale at New Lanark in 1793 (Donnachie and Hewitt,
1993, 35)

On 7 January 1808, when James Craig was struggling to keep Stanley going, Robert
Owen wrote to him from New Lanark to enquire 'have you any steady valuable mecanics
leaving you at the time you mention either millwrights clockmakers or other' as Owen
would be glad to offer them employment. (Cooke, 1979b, 108) This reflected the
perennial search for skilled labour that cotton manufacturers faced, particularly for workers
who could build and maintain machinery. For example, Richard Arkwright advertised
on 10 December 1771 in the *Derby Mercury* from the 'Cotton Mill, Cromford' for:

two Journeymen Clock-Makers, or others that understands Tooth and Pinion well; Also a Smith that can forge and file—Likewise two Wood turners that have been accustomed to Wheel-making, Spole-turning, &c. Weavers residing in this Neighbourhood, by applying at the Mill, may have good Work. There is employment at the above Place, for Women, Children &c. and good Wages.

(Fitton, 1989, 30)

It was important to locate cotton mills close to an area with existing skills in textile manufacture or machine making. Just as Perth had a reputation for muslin manufacture, 'Lanark . . . did have some sort of reputation for its clockmaking skills as well as certain linen-weaving and building skills'. (Donnnachie and Hewitt, 1993, 35)

Labour mobility and high labour turnover was a feature of all cotton mills in this period. An extreme example of this occurred at Stanley in 1814, when the Auchtergaven Kirk Session considered the case of Janet Bisset, a cotton spinner, whose husband was serving in the 42nd regiment with Wellington. She had had a child by a cotton spinner from Blantyre, who had spent only one day in Stanley, as he had come looking for work. The session clerk had written to the man and his brother, a teacher in Glasgow, but had had no reply. (NAS, Auchtergaven Kirk Session Minutes, 15 May, 1814)

In 1818, women and girls made up 61 per cent of the workforce in the Scottish cotton industry, compared to 50 per cent in Lancashire. Outside Glasgow, women were more prominent, as they were employed on spinning throstles and short mules. (Berg, 1994, 140) At Stanley in 1833, women made up 61 per cent of the workforce— 540 out of 885. Young people under 18 comprised 56 per cent (497) of the workforce. A higher proportion of males than females were under 18—64 per cent of males (222), compared to 51 per cent of females (275). Working hours were 5.30 am to 7.00 pm, with three quarters of an hour for breakfast at 9.00 am and the same for dinner at 2.00 pm. Work on Saturday stopped at 3.15 pm. Children worked from 9.45 am to 3.15 pm and then attended the Company School. There were two unpaid holidays per year—Handsel Monday (the first Monday in January) and the Queen's Birthday on 24 May. (*Parliamentary Papers*, 1833, XXI, A3, 36 and XX, A1, 62) The wage scale was:

Male Spinners	13/- to 16/-	(65–80p) per week
Female Spinners	9/- to 11/-	(45–55p) per week
Reelers	6/- to 9/-	(30–45p) per week
Young Children	2/-	(10p) per week

Female spinners under 16 years seldom had full wages, spinners being paid by the 'piece'. Piecers, their assistants, were paid by the day or week. Spinners had to work regular hours, so no married women of childbearing age were employed as spinners, as in all large factories. Married women could, however, work as reelers, as this could be done at home if necessary. (*Parliamentary Papers*, 1834, XX, A1, 161) In 1929, it was claimed that, in Buchanan's time, an old inhabitant of Stanley, now dead, had worked in the mills as a child from 5.30am to 7.00pm daily for 2/6d (12p) a week. Adult wages, at this time, were 6 to 7 shillings (30–35p) for women, 16 shillings (80p) for men, 'gaffers' (foremen) having a shilling or two more. (*Perthshire Advertiser*, 12 August 1929)

Although wages for adult workers were relatively high, a large proportion of the workforce were under 18 and on lower wages. In 1835, out of a total Stanley workforce of 850, 436 (51 per cent) were under 18 and 161 (19 per cent) were under 13. This explained the hostility of James Craig, the former owner of Stanley, to factory reform, particularly any reform that tampered with the sacred cow of cheap child labour. In 1833, he claimed that children under thirteen or fourteen were the most contented workers at Stanley. Craig believed that rivals would 'chuckle' at any attempt to do away with child labour, 'the Pillars of the Cotton manufacture'. By forcing the employment of older workers at double the wages, legislation would 'destroy the exertions of the most enterprising men in the British Empire'. (Whatley, 2000, 228) James Craig, 'formerly proprietor of Stanley Mills' died on 15 December 1839 at the ripe old age of 82. His personal estate came to £1049. (*Perthshire Advertiser*, 26 December 1839, 2, & NAS, SC.49, 44, 30)

Evidence given to the Factory Commission, in 1833, revealed working conditions at Stanley and how they affected individuals. Mary Macgregor, aged 12, had worked at Stanley for three years. She had been unwell at first and continued hoarse but was otherwise well. She reported that she liked the work and had no complaints, also that she couldn't write. An older worker, Janet Scott, aged 31, said she had been employed at Stanley for over two years and before that was in 'genteel' places but her mother got ill and she had to work in the mill. She liked the liberty of the mill, preferred the higher wages and didn't mind the long hours and the standing. (*Parliamentary Papers*, 1833, XX, A1, 63 and A2, 43–4)

Other workers told a different story. John Scott, a twenty seven year old yarn dresser, thought the heat in his factory flat harmed the health of the young people who worked there. The workers were anxious for shorter hours and willing to take lower wages but were scared of talking. A petition had been presented from the workers for shorter hours, the only source of discontent. James Stewart, aged 36, had worked at Stanley for three years and was now in the dressing-web department. He had lost his appetite, was sickly and his bones were sore from going from hot to cold. He also complained of the long working hours.

The official line at Stanley was that there was no corporal punishment in the mill, except for a small strap, which the overseer used when the young workers misbehaved, misdemeanours of the older workers being punished by sackings. (*NSA*, X) David Hunter, a thirty three year old overseer, claimed that although working hours were from 5.30 am to 7.00 pm, he could see no signs of exhaustion in the children working under him 'they have too much to do to fall asleep'. Any accidents that had occurred were 'just through mere carelessness'. Parents had complained against Hunter for strapping their children but his response was that three was the largest number of straps he had given—'bairns like those must be corrected or you could not keep them down at all'. Hunter had worked for eight years at Stanley and before that for fourteen years at New Lanark. (*Parliamentary Papers*, 1833, XX, A1, 63 & A2, 43–4)

David Hunter's robust attitude to factory discipline was echoed by a sinister comment from the manager at Catrine, who admitted 'the children were all newcomers, and were very much beat at first before they could be taught their business'. An analysis of the methods used by British firms to discipline factory children, gleaned from the Factory Commission Reports, showed that negative methods outnumbered positive ones by 575 to 34. Dismissal was mentioned 353 times, fines and deductions 101 times and corporal punishment 55 times. By contrast, kindness was mentioned only twice, promotion or higher wages 9 times and reward or premium 23 times. (Pollard, 1965, 161 & 189)

The age structure of the workforce in the Scottish cotton industry began to change, as the number of young children employed began to fall dramatically. In 1836, children under 13 accounted for 13.3 per cent of the total Scottish workforce, compared to 18.9 per cent at Stanley, 25 per cent at Deanston but only 4 per cent at New Lanark in 1835. By 1847, the total Scottish figure for under thirteens employed in the industry was a mere 2.1 per cent, compared to 13.3 per cent in 1836. (Baines, 1835, 390 & Knox, 1995, 46)

The Stanley workforce was largely Scottish–born, unlike Glasgow, where Henry Houldsworth reported in 1833 'our mills are almost full of Irish'. (Knox, 1995, 147) Stanley had more similarities to Deanston, where many workers came from the Highlands, and New Lanark where, apart from orphans from the urban workhouses, 'the Highlands became the main recruiting ground'. (Fitton, 1989, 205 & Donnachie and Hewitt, 1993, 37)

An age analysis of the 1841 workforce at Stanley is given below:

Age	Under 10	10–15	16–19	20–29	30–39	40–49	50–59	60–69	70 plus
Female	6	185	92	165	74	37	23	8	4
Male	10	148	52	113	101	78	55	17	17
Total	16	333	144	278	175	115	78	25	21

Certain occupations had a particularly high proportion of young people. For example, out of 280 cotton-spinners in the village, 165 (59 per cent) were below the age of sixteen. (GROS, Census Enumerators' Returns, 1841)

The 1841 census showed that, out of a total Stanley population of 1,973, 1,185 (60 per cent) were in employment, of whom 582 (49 per cent) were female, 516 employed in the mill and 66 elsewhere. The 603 men in employment constituted 51 per cent of the working population and included a much larger number working for other employers—348 in the mills and 255 self-employed or employed by others. The mill workforce was heavily feminised with 60 per cent of the workers female. No less than 864 people (72 per cent of the working population) worked in the mills and many more must have been indirectly dependent on them. By comparison, at Catrine Mills, Ayrshire, in 1832, out of a population of 2,716, 853 worked in the mills (53 per cent of the working population) and of the 759 who worked elsewhere, 194 were in ancillary textile occupations. (Pollard, 1965, 206)

The most prevalent surnames in Stanley in 1838 were Paton, Crichton, Duff, Chalmers and Dow. Many Highlanders had moved to the parish in the last twenty years. During the last three years, there had been 9 illegitimate births in Stanley and 5 in other parts of the parish. 'The discipline of Stanley is quite distinct from that of Auchtergaven.' (*NSA*, X, 436)

The degree of control that the Company exercised in Stanley might be expected to have inhibited trade union organisation but, even in Stanley, there were limits to paternalism. A Savings Bank was founded by a few individuals connected with the Mills in 1831 but: 'The baleful influence of the Cotton Spinners Combination has prevented this institution from producing the benefits which it is fitted to yield to the inhabitants of such a village as Stanley'. The workers believed that, if they put their wages into a savings bank, 'it would be the signal for their employers to reduce their wages; and prefer spending them as they are won, to laying aside what might be spared against sickness or old age'. In four years, only 27 depositors had entered the Bank,

All-female trade union committee, Stanley Mills, 1915 (Anthony Cooke)

deposits being a mere £214. No Benefit or Friendly Society existed in Stanley, although several people in the parish belonged to ones in Dunkeld and Perth. (NSA, X, 447–448) This may have been simply an example of an idea before its time. In Paisley, it was not until 1883 that Coats established a Friendly Benefit Society and encouraged their workers to deposit some of their earnings in the local Savings Bank. (Knox, 1995, 134)

The strength of the Cotton Spinners' Union in Stanley is surprising, considering the extent of tied housing and tight company control of the village. This may reflect close social and economic links with Glasgow, where in 1837, out of 1,000 cotton spinners in the city, some 850–900 were members of the Spinners' Union. There was a virtual (male) closed shop in spinning in Glasgow but the failure of the Spinners' Strike in 1837 and the violence associated with it led to a steep decline in the union's influence. (Fraser, 1988b, 152–5 & Knox, 1999, 55) This was a period of severe trade depression and in 1837 the Stanley Company gave notice of the possibility of half time working. Some handlooom weavers in the village were thrown out of work but most were employed outdoors. (*Perthshire Courier*, 15 June 1837, 3) In Perth, a reduction of 15 per cent took place in the output of its principal fabrics. (Murray, 1979, 57)

In 1852, when the Buchanans sold the mills to Samuel Howard of Burnley, nearly 1000 people in the village were 'entirely dependent on the works'. (*Perthshire Courier*, 23 December 1852, 3) The Cotton Famine during the American Civil War brought great hardship to Stanley, as it did to the British cotton industry in general. Stanley Mills were closed from 1862 to 1867 and workers had to leave Stanley to find work. The population of the village fell from a peak of 1,973 in 1841 to a low of 932 in 1871, to recover to 1,030 in 1881.

A boom period came with the First World War, when the mills were manufacturing webbings for the armed forces. Women workers were recruited from Fife, a hostel for 70 women was established at White's Hotel and workers were housed in other buildings such as Hobart House. A photograph, dated 1915, showed an all-female trade union committee and there is oral evidence from the 1960s that women were transferred to 'men's work' during the First World War. (*Perthshire Advertiser*, 8 July 1964, 8)

Paisley thread manufacturers provided welfare schemes and community facilities for their workers, including canteens from 1884, a girls' hostel in 1901, a convalescent home in 1911 and baths in 1913. Most striking of all was the company pension scheme provided by Coats for employees who had served the Company for over twenty years. The pensions were discretionary but paid to both men and women. In the early 20th century, women received 8s 0d (40p) a week, men 10s 0d (50p) and foremen 20s. 0d. (£1), although this was reduced with the introduction of state old age pensions in 1908. (Knox, 1995, 128–129) Nothing so elaborate happened in Stanley, perhaps because it was protected from competition for workers by its isolation. However, an innovative profit sharing scheme was introduced in 1919, possibly in response to labour turnover and unrest in the wake of the First World War.

The end of the 1st World War meant reduced business for Stanley mills and numbers employed declined, particularly in weaving. In 1920, the mill employed 470 workers, with a total annual wages bill of £46,380. By 1921 this had fallen to 372 workers, with an annual wages bill of £35,551. The numbers employed in weaving fell from 240 in 1920 to 165 in 1921, with a reduction in the annual wages bill from £25,245 to £16,524. Average wages at Stanley fell from £1.94 a week in 1920 to £1.86 a week in 1921. Mill workers earned less than weavers—their average weekly earnings in 1920 were £1.89, compared to £2.02 for weavers. By 1921, average weekly earnings for mill workers had fallen to £1.85, compared to the weavers' £1.92 weekly average. The working week at the mill was 55 hours—ten hours a day from Monday to Friday and five hours on Saturday. (Stanley Mills, Wages Declaration for Employers Liability Insurance, 1921)

There was a trade depression at the end of the 1st World War and difficult labour relations, with strikes to protest at wage cuts and short time working. This was the era of 'Red Clydeside', when tanks were deployed in George Square, Glasgow and socialist leaders such as John Maclean were imprisoned for 'anti-war' activities. (Foster, 1998, 224–7) There was a strike at Stanley in January 1919 and strikes in the nearby bleachfields of Luncarty and Pitcairnfield in 1920. (Cooke, 1984) The (largely female) Jute and Flax Workers' Union in Dundee went on strike in 1923 at Camperdown Works in Lochee for 27 weeks, with two periods of lock out throughout Dundee, one for a month, the second for a week. (Walker, 1979, 486, and Gordon, 1991)

Wages at Stanley were low, because most of the workers lived in low-cost company housing and there were few alternative sources of employment. A comparison of wages for higher-paid workers in Stanley and Oldham in 1921 showed that wage rates in Oldham for comparable jobs were over £1 a week higher than at Stanley. A card room slubber earned £2 9s. 0d. (£2.45) a week at Stanley in 1921, compared with £1 3s. 8d. (£1.18) in 1913, but the same worker in Oldham earned £3 15s. 10d. (£3.78) a week in 1921. Similar differentials existed for other workers. (Stanley Mills, Wages at Stanley compared with Oldham, 1921) Oldham was a traditionally high wage area compared to other cotton manufacturing areas. In 1906, it topped a table of average weekly earnings in the British cotton industry, with earnings of 21s. 0d. (£1.05) a week compared to 20s. 8d. (£1.04) in Blackburn, 18s. 6d. (92p) in Preston, 16s. 3d. (81p) in Manchester, and 14s. 9d. (78p) in Scotland. (Knox, 1995, 88) The Stanley/ Oldham comparison was probably connected with the Stanley strike of 1921. Despite short time working, the workforce stayed relatively stable during the Depression of the 1930s, fluctuating between a low of 291 and a high of 327 in the period 1933–36. Workers were mainly recruited from the village plus a small number from Perth. Tayside Hostel remained open, housing some 50 to 60 women from Fife.

The Second World War brought a boom in production, as demand soared, and a labour shortage, as young men left for the army. At the end of the War, there was an acute labour shortage, as many of the men who had joined the Forces did not return to Stanley. Jute Industries had to search much further afield for workers and a temporary solution was to bring in displaced persons (D.P.s), and European Voluntary Workers (E.V.W.s), both male and female. They were mainly married couples and were given housing in the village but soon began to drift away, some emigrating to the USA.

Again, there was a labour shortage and to fill the gap large numbers of women were brought over from Germany and Italy. Stanley Hotel, (renamed Millbank Hostel), was converted to a Hostel to house them. Some of the German women married local men and eventually, due to falling numbers, Millbank Hostel closed down, followed several years later by Tayside Hostel, which was sold and converted to a hotel. (Cooke, 1977, 41, and oral evidence from the late John Culbert)

In the mid 1960s, the local paper recorded the retiral of Agnes McIntosh of South Street, Stanley, after 52 years continuous employment at Stanley Mills. She had started her working life at 13 and a half, as a doffer in the spinning section and was allowed six months exemption from school. When World War One broke out she was 'transferred to a man's job as a rove and bobbin carrier and had been doing the same type of work ever since'. Her mother had been employed at Stanley as a weaver in the 1890s, her sister was still working after 30 years service and her brother after 44 years. (*Perthshire Advertiser*, 8 July 1964, 8) This type of family continuity was common in the cotton industry and in British industry in general, from the second half of the nineteenth century down to the 1980s. Long service awards and the presentation of gold watches on retirement were some of the ways in which British firms rewarded loyalty and built up a spirit of camaradie amongst the workforce.

In the boom of the late 1960s, the mills ran a recruitment campaign under the slogan 'Stanley Mills has a way with women' designed to recruit 80 women to its tape department, where they would earn an average of over £11 for a forty hour week. The mills offered a ten week training course, a modern canteen, 'excellent working conditions, clean secure employment, transport to and from work and a sick pay scheme'. (*Perthshire Advertiser*, 28 October 1967, 7 & 13) By 1977, only 83 people were employed at the mills, of whom 58 lived locally and 25 came from outside the village. (Cooke, 1977, 42) When the mills closed in March 1989, there were only 54 staff left and the production side could be operated by a mere 30 people. (*Perthshire Advertiser*, 3 February 1989, 5)

10.

Rational and Praiseworthy Amusements

Education, Religion and Social History

When Stanley began to be laid out as a village there was no school or church in the immediate area. One problem was that the village straddled three parishes—Auchtergaven, Kinclaven and Redgorton, although the bulk of the population lived in Auchtergaven. A private school, supported by school fees, was set up around 1786 'to meet the wants of an increasing population' and some form of schooling was provided in the village from that time onwards. (*Parliamentary Papers*, 1826, Vol. 18, 768, & 1837, Vol. 47, 571) For children working in the mills, any education had to be fitted around long working hours, although it was reported rather optimistically in 1795 that 'the boys and girls, though confined at work in the mill for many hours of the day and at times during the night, are in general, very healthy'. (OSA, XII, 34) In 1825, the school had about 70 pupils, who were charged fees of 3s 0d, 3s 6d, and 4s 0d (15p, 17p and 20p) a quarter, although the fees were paid very irregularly. The schoolmaster, James Scott, reported that the branches of education taught were reading, writing and arithmetic. The school rooms were provided free, as with a similar school at Bankfoot. The Auchtergaven school also taught Latin, had similar fees and had 50 to 60 pupils. (*Parliamentary Papers*, 1826, Vol. 18, 768–9)

The provision of a church took longer. Soon after the mills were built, the Company employed a preacher to minister on Sundays in a schoolhouse. (NSA, X, 444) In August 1802, James Craig, the mill owner, wrote to the Duke of Atholl about finishing a house at the end of the church in Stanley village, though this may have actually been the schoolhouse. (Atholl Mss. 48, 3, 115) Craig complained on 11 June 1810 that he had to find security for a stipend of £100–£150 and build a church, which might cost £1,000. The 'Burgher Seceders' had offered to build a house and supply an able preacher of their persuasion without any obligation on Craig's part, except to join their society. He asked the Duke to bring before the government the need to make some provision or stipend for new villages of 1,000 inhabitants over three miles from the nearest church. (Atholl Mss. 48, 11, 144)

A new church had to wait until the arrival of the Buchanan Company. In 1828, they petitioned the Presbytery of Dunkeld for permission to build a Chapel of Ease at their own expense. The church cost over £3,000 to build and could hold 1,150 people. Mr Johnstone, who was ordained as its first minister in 1829, was given a house and garden, 1 Mill Brae, and £150 per year by the Company. The church was in Redgorton parish but over 65 per cent of the hearers were from Auchtergaven. The average number of communicants at Stanley from Auchtergaven parish was 600. The mill workers were not obliged to attend but all those under 15 had free seats. (NSA, X, 440–445, & 1135–6) A list of 185 male heads of households who were communicants at Stanley in July 1834 revealed that the major occupations amongst adult men in the village were labourer (22), weaver (12), wright (12), tenter (11), carder (10), mason (9), pensioner (9), spinner (8), feuer (8), farmer (6), and shoemaker (6). Other occupations included 3 fishers, 2 ferrymen, a bellman, a drover, a cattle dealer, a beadle and a greaser. (Stanley Kirk Session Records)

In 1834, a private school at Stanley was attended by 136 children of both sexes, The Stanley Company provided a large schoolhouse and paid the teacher £20 a year. The master at the parish school got £34 a year plus irregularly paid school fees which amounted to about £12 a year. Another school at Stanley was said to have 60 pupils. It was claimed that few children in the parish went to school until they were five but all could read long before they were fifteen. (*Parliamentary Papers*, 1837, Vol. 47, 571) In 1838, there was a day school and a Sunday school in Stanley; the schoolmaster got an annual salary of £20, plus a house and garden from the Company. Boys outnumbered girls at the day school, although not in the Sunday School. The average number of pupils in 1836 was 144 (86 boys, 58 girls), in 1837 it was 163, (94 boys and 69 girls). Children attended school without reference to their parents' religion, although the doctrines of the Church of Scotland were taught. They attended between the ages of 4 and 16, most staying for seven years. (Parliamentary Papers, 1841, Vol. XIX, 613)

The teacher, John McLiesh, was educated at Dollar Academy, was a member of the Church of Scotland and had no outside employment. He was qualified to teach 'the common branches', Latin and mathematics. Fees varied from 1s 6d to 5s 0d (7.5p to 25p). General instruction was chiefly English reading, writing and arithmetic. The schoolmaster also taught Greek, Latin, Modern Languages, Mathematics, Geography, History, Religion and Catechism but not Drawing or Singing. School hours were 9.30 am—1.00 pm, 2.30 pm–5.00 pm and 7.30 pm–10.00 pm and holidays were four weeks in September. The system of instruction was the Intellectual. The children were taught in classes, beginners separately, and monitors were employed, although under no particular system. There was no instruction in gardening, agriculture or mechanical occupation. Rewards took the form of prizes and punishment was 'chiefly corporal'. (*Parliamentary Papers*, 1841, Vol. XIX, 613)

The Company were clearly supportive of education and their school was far from being a token provision, with a large schoolhouse and a well qualified schoolmaster. In this, they were following the example of most Scottish mills, which provided schools as standard practice, unlike England, where schools were largely confined to factory villages. Stanley people were 'abundantly alive to the benefits resulting from education', their only fault being 'a capricious desire of novelty leading them perpetually to change their teachers'. There was such a demand for education that adventurers had opened schools in both Stanley and Bankfoot, which initially met support 'but both these teachers and their employers soon became mutually tired of each other'. However, the high school fees for the Company school, which varied from 1s 6d to 5s 0d (7.5p to 25p) a quarter, financial pressures on parents to send children to work in the mills and long working hours must have put full-time schooling beyond the means of most working class children. An attempt was made in 1838 to solve this problem by founding an Educational Society in Stanley to assist the poor to pay for the education of their children. (NSA, X, 445–447)

The 1833 Factory Act banned the employment of children under nine in textile mills and restricted working hours for those aged 9 to 13 to nine hours a day, provided they attended school two hours a day. However, it was possible to grant exemption certificates and 589 were granted in Stanley in 1834. (Cooke, 1977, 52) John Scott, a yarn dresser, testified that although the Company provided a school, the children preferred 'to run about' when the mill finished, because of the long hours they worked. Mary Macgregor, aged twelve, the only young Stanley worker to give evidence to the Commission, could not read although she had worked at the mills for three years. A greater impact on the education of young mill workers must have been made by the Sunday School, which was attended by 400 young people—150 males, 250 females. (Parliamentary Papers, 1833, XX, A2, 43–44 & 1841, XIX, 613)

Both religion and education promoted by the early companies at Stanley as a form of social control. Employers were interested in developing the 'sober, virtuous and industrious' workforce that George Dempster wrote about in the 1780s. (Laing Mss. III, 379, 217) This formed part of a campaign by employers to promote habits of discipline, as against traditional working practices and holidays. Foremost amongst the traditional holidays was Handsel Monday, the first Monday in January, when the ploughmen left the fields and paraded through Stanley village to a flute band. Another holiday was the Queen's Birthday on 24 May, which was marked by bonfires and dancing. (Fergusson, 1893, 84 &154) Millowners worried about losing control on these occasions. At New Lanark, an 1820 directive requested village boys to 'give up play at the shinty or clubs and throwing stones, as they are by the first practice destroying the woods and by the latter breaking windows and sometimes hurting people'. (Donnachie & Hewitt, 1993, 90)

In 1836, a group of workers formed a Singing Club and with the Stanley Instrumental Band gave a concert on Handsel Monday for the benefit of the poor, with an audience of 400–500. Whereas Handsel Monday had 'commonly been set apart for the degrading purpose of intoxication', it was hoped 'the day is not far distant when people generally instead of spending their holidays in riotous drinking and other bacchanalian festivities, will employ them in rational and praiseworthy amusements'. (Perthshire Courier, 28 January 1836, 3)

This proved a vain hope, as the minister reported in 1838 that there were twelve public houses in Stanley village alone, one for every thirty one families. He complained 'at least three-fourths of these are public nuisances, and most hurtful to the morals of the inhabitants, as it is by them chiefly that they are maintained'. (NSA, X, 449) Some factory villages went further than simply fulminating against alcohol and banned it altogether. Neither Deanston nor Blantyre allowed any public house in their village and at Deanston 'no drunkard is permitted about the establishment'. (Pollard, 1965, 194 & Fitton, 1989, 206)

The first crack in Company control came with the Disruption in 1843. Most of the congregation left the Church of Scotland with their minister and established Stanley Free Church at the north end of the village. A Free Church School, established three years later, attracted the bulk of village children. By 1854, numbers at Stanley School had fallen so low, that the General Assembly were asked if they would take it over. (Cooke, 1977, 45, 52) The Disruption led to a long-running split in the village between the 'up-byes' or the Free Church end and the 'doon-byes' or the Church of Scotland end. The children from the two schools fought at regular intervals, although by the 1890s the antagonism between the two parts of the village had 'almost died down'. (Fergusson, 1893, 66)

The 1860s saw a number of short-lived attempts at self-improvement. A Mutual Improvement Society was formed in 1862, with a membership of 23, based in the Free Church Hall but lasted less than a year. A Literary Society was formed two years later but again lasted under a year. (Perth Art Gallery, doc. 226) This was a period of great hardship when Samuel Howard closed the mills from 1862 to 1867 during the Cotton Famine of the American Civil War. A longer lasting activity was that of a group of men known as 'the scientifics', who took a strong interest in natural history and organised night expeditions to catch moths and butterflies. By the 1890s, these activities had died out, to be replaced by football and cricket. Curling also appeared on the scene, which had a wide appeal across the social spectrum—'the laird and the tenant, the baker and the mason, the grocer and the smith, enjoyed the free intercourse of the brethren of the ice'. (Fergusson, 1893, 159) Photographs from the late 1890s showed an all-male group curling on a pond behind the mills and two mixed groups curling on the Tay in front of the Mills during the great freeze of either 1895 or 1897.

The Education (Scotland) Act of 1872 set up elected School Boards to replace the burgh and parish school system. The new School Boards of Auchtergaven, Kinclaven and Redgorton met in Stanley, in December 1873, to discuss the establishment of a Combined School for the village and to transfer the Free Church School to the Auchtergaven Board, with a Board of Management drawn from the three parishes. The school had a roll of 180, whereas the building was adequate for only 120. A new school on the west side of Duke Square was opened in June 1878 and the old school on Russell Street was converted into a house for the headmaster. (Cooke, 1977, 54)

By 1890, there were only three public houses in Stanley compared to the twelve listed fifty years earlier. Seven grocers and general dealers were listed, as well as a coffee house. Other occupations were: tobacconist, stationer, coal and wood merchant (2), blacksmith, baker (3), boot and shoemaker (3), flesher (2), draper (4), tailor (4), surgeon (3), joiner and wright (4) and cattle dealer (2). (Leslie's *Perth and Perthshire Directory* 1889–90) In 1921, the same directory showed that Stanley Coffee House was still in business, the number of tobacconists had risen to five and new trades such as cycle agents (3), motor hirers and carriage hirers (2) had appeared. Other trades included a painter, a plumber, a fruiterer and a confectioner. (*Leslie's Directory* 1921–2)

In 1929 the national reunion of the Established Church and the United Free Church took place. The Free Church at Stanley approved the national decision by the narrowest of margins but the two churches remained separate—the Free Church taking the name Stanley St. James, the Established Church being called Stanley Tower. It was only in 1959 that the two churches finally merged with a single minister and the sale of the St. James Church and Manse. (Cooke, 1977, 46–9)

At the end of the Second World War, the school leaving age was raised to fifteen and in 1947 Stanley Junior Secondary School came into being, with a roll of 185. The school numbers rose steadily till they reached 336 by 1955, putting a severe strain on the old school buildings. At this time there were 18 teaching staff—5 full-time primary and 6 full-time secondary, plus a headmaster and 6 visiting secondary staff. A new extension was added in 1958 to cope with the pressure of numbers. A major change took place in 1972, when the Secondary Department transferred to Perth Grammar School. The school roll fell from over 300 to under 200 pupils and the number of teachers from 20 to 8. (Cooke, 1977, 57) In 2003, there were 190 pupils and 8 teachers at Stanley Primary School, including a nursery class.

Curling on the frozen Tay, Stanley, 1895 or 1897 (Mrs. Sim, Stanley)

11.

Postscript

Commuter Suburb and Heritage Site—Stanley Today

Community building is the most important aspect of history, but as it is also
the most difficult aspect, it is the one that has been least studied.
(George Unwin, *Samuel Oldknow and the Arkwrights*, 1924, 157)

the key to the Industrial Revolution was to be found in the dynamics of
technological creativity and the structures of industrial communities
(Maxine Berg, *The Age of Manufactures 1700–1820*, 1994 edition, 4)

Stanley Mills provide an outstanding example of industrial survival. Textile production
was carried out at the mills from 1787 until closure in 1989, although there were
periods of closure from 1811 until 1823 and again from 1862 until 1867. This
remarkable survival record was due to a number of factors. An obvious one was the
lavish resources of water power available from the River Tay, which Dempster and Co.
harnessed initially by water wheels in the 1780s and Sandeman and Co. adapted for
turbines to generate electricity in 1878. Sidlaw Industries rather shot themselves in the
foot, when they blew up the hydro-electric system on the grounds of high maintenance
costs in 1965, just before the Six Day War sent energy prices soaring.

A key factor behind the success of Stanley in surviving and prospering for so long
was the ingenuity and skills of the management and workforce. The Mills lay at a
considerable distance from both raw material supplies and markets. In the late eighteenth
century, the important London market was accessible through the port of Perth. However,
Glasgow, which was the main source of raw cotton, was a long overland return journey
of ten days from the Mills. A major break through was the arrival of the railway in
1848, facilitated by George Buchanan's position as owner of Stanley Mills and Deputy
Chairman of the Scottish Midland Junction Railway Company.

Stanley Mills survived by adapting their products and switching markets with
remarkable skill. They found 'niche markets', such as their Elephant brand of yarn for
the Indian market in the Buchanan era or selvedge cotton and sewing twine for the
Dundee and Fife jute and linen industry, which was developed by the Sandeman

management. In 1881, another 'niche market' was developed, when part of the mills were leased to William Fenton to produce Scandinavian cotton belting, using yarn produced at the mills. This belting was sold all over the world through the Sandeman Cotton Belting Company to drive steam powered machinery.

This impressive spirit of innovation and adaptability continued into the twentieth century. During the First World War, the mills were largely turned over to the production of equipment webbing for the armed forces, although the manufacture of cotton belting continued. In 1916, Douglas Sandeman began experimenting (in a Secret Room) with a light loom to weave an endless tape for use in cigarette production. This became a staple of production, only closing down in 1976, which marked the end of weaving at Stanley. The Inter-War years were difficult times at Stanley, as they were in the rest of the British cotton industry. Another boom period came during the Second World War, when the mills were again largely turned over to the manufacture of equipment webbings for the armed forces.

The end of the Second World War saw an acute shortage of labour at Stanley, as elsewhere in British industry. Jute Industries responded by importing workers from Germany and Italy and housing them in hostels in the village. Indian Independence in 1947 meant the loss of a major export market, as the new Indian government introduced import licences for cotton belting and spindle tapes. At the same time, steam powered machinery, which required heavy cotton belting, was being replaced by machinery driven by individual electric motors, so that cotton belting became obsolete. By the late 1960s, the mills were beginning to spin man made fibres and this became the main product in

East Mill, Stanley during renovation by Phoenix Trust, 2000 (Anthony Cooke)

the 1970s. In 1979, when there was a management buyout from Sidlaw Industries, Stanley Mills (Scotland) concentrated on spinning acrylic yarn for the sock trade in the English Midlands. Another change in fashion, this time ironically from man made fibres back to cotton, spelled the death knell for the Company and it closed the mills in 1989, ending a remarkable two hundred year history of textile production.

Nowadays, British industry in general, and Scottish manufacturing in particular, faces criticism for its conservatism and inability to adapt to change. There were periods of poor management at Stanley, resulting in stagnation or closure, during James Craig's ownership from 1800 to 1811 and again during the ownership of Samuel Howard and his trustees from 1852 to 1876. However, these coincided with difficult external trading conditions for the industry as a whole, such as the Napoleonic Wars in the case of James Craig or the American Civil War in Samuel Howard's case. In general, Stanley provides an impressive example of the skills, adaptability and innovative ability of Scottish management and workers in surviving and prospering, often against heavy odds, over two hundred years. In many ways, it was an exceptional survivor in the Scottish cotton industry, which had all but disappeared by the 1960s, except for specialised cotton thread firms like Coats and Clarks in Paisley. Knox divided Scottish cotton firms into 'three distinct groups: losers, hangers-on and winners'. (Knox, 1995, 79 & 173) If the Perth cotton industry was an early loser, Stanley was a survivor for an astonishing 200 years.

Shrinking employment at the mills and their eventual closure brought a change to the character of Stanley. From a rather isolated mill village with the overwhelming majority of its population dependent on the mills for employment, either directly or indirectly, it has become an expanding commuter settlement for Perth with rapid access via the improved A9. This mirrors experience elsewhere in the UK and in the advanced Western economies generally, where economies based on manufacturing have changed into ones based on service industries. Between 1973 and 1990, British manufacturing's share of gross domestic product fell from 30 per cent to 20 per cent and has carried on falling ever since. (Berg, 1994 edition, 2) This trend was particularly marked in Perthshire where, by 1991, only 11 per cent of the working population were engaged in manufacturing, as compared to 24 per cent in distribution and catering, and 30 per cent in other services. (Cooke, 1999, 188) This is the hallmark of the post-industrial society.

At Stanley, there was a happier postscript. The closure of the mills in 1989 led to an alarming deterioration in the condition of the historic mill buildings. The site was bought by Historic Scotland in December 1995, helped by a grant of £1.4 million from the Heritage Lottery Fund. In May 1998 Historic Scotland and its partner, the Phoenix Trust, were awarded grants totalling £7.4 million by the Heritage Lottery Fund for conservation work at Stanley. The first stage of the work involved recording, historical investigation and external conservation of the Old Mill, North Range and Lodges. The second stage involved the conversion of the East Mill and part of the Mid Mill, for 39 houses and apartments by the Phoenix Trust. This consisted of 30 flats in the East Mill and 5 four storey terrace houses and 4 maisonettes in the Mid Mill. Two large wheel pits were uncovered alongside the Old Mill and evidence was found of turbines installed by the Sandeman management in 1878. The Boving Turbine House installed by Jute Industries in 1921, which housed Swedish turbines, is being restored by Innogy PLC and will generate electricity to be fed into the National Grid. Historic Scotland plan to develop interpretation and visitor facilities at the Old Mill, which will focus on the history of the Tay, including salmon fishing, ferries and the history of the textile industry. Plans are also afoot for further development on the site including business or other uses.

Stanley is a site of great historical importance, in an area of outstanding natural beauty. The Old Mill is probably the finest surviving example of an early Arkwright mill anywhere in the world and its situation on the Tay is exceptional. The Phoenix Trust have done an excellent job in conserving two out of the three mill buildings and Historic Scotland are to be commended for their initiative in securing Heritage Lottery funding, buying the mills and securing them for the future. Stanley Mills offer an outstanding opportunity to illustrate not only the history of cotton manufacture but of water power and the many and varied uses of a great river like the Tay. They boast well documented links with historically significant figures like Richard Arkwright, David Dale and Robert Owen and illustrate more general historical themes such as population movement, aristocratic patronage, community building and the globalised nature of the Scottish cotton industry. For all these reasons, the Old Mill at Stanley is a prime site for imaginative conservation.

Water Wheel Pits by Old Mill, Stanley, 2002 (Anthony Cooke)

Appendix 1

Valuations of Stanley Mills

A. Valuation of Cotton Mills at Stanley 1796 :
(Sun Fire Office Policy 640186 : Guildhall Library, London).

George Dempster and Company of Stanley near Perth Cotton
  Manufacturer on their Cotton Mill situated as
  aforesaid warranted to be conformable to the Rules
  of the first class of Cotton Rates not exceeding
  two thousand five hundred pounds.   2,500
Millwrights work including all the going gears therein only
  not exceeding two thousand five hundred pounds   2,500
Clockmakers Work Carding and Breaking Engines
  and all moveable utensils therein only
  not exceeding two thousand pounds   2,000
New Cotton and Flax Mill near unfinished
  not exceeding two thousand pounds   2,000
Millwrights work including all the going gears therein only
  not exceeding seven hundred and fifty pounds   750
Clockmakers Work Carding and Breaking Engines
  all moveable utensils therein only
  not exceeding two hundred and fifty pounds   250
Stock including Flax therein not exceeding five hundred pounds   500
                                                               £10.500

All Stone and Slated This Policy is declared void in case the
  above New Cotton and Flax Mill is used for any manufactory.

B. Valuation of Stanley by Mrs G. Thomson 1879 :
(formerly at Stanley Mills, Perthshire, notes in possession of A.J. Cooke).

Water-power £2 per annum per HP = £800			
which at 14 years purchase is equal to	£11,200		
Total Buildings connected with trade purposes	8,000		
Motors, Gearing and Piping	5,000		
Clear rental of village and deducting insurance and taxes			
say £600 at 10 years' purchase	6,000		
Clear rental of Mansion House, Beech House policies			
and land say £250 at 20 years purchase	5,000		
Fishing £250 at 10 years' purchase	2,500		
	£37,700	0s.	0d.
Less: fue duty £507 16s. 6d. at twenty years	10,156	10	0
TOTAL	£27,543	10s.	0d.

C. Valuation of Stanley Mills Buildings and Machinery by Allan Mellor and Co., Oldham—September 1911 :
(formerly at Sidlaw Industries, Dundee, notes in possession of A. J. Cooke)

Fast and Loose Machinery and Utensils	£20,624	0s.	4d.
Millwright's Work	2,179	0	5
Steam and Water Piping	317	13	1
Sprinkler Installation	605	7	0
Turbines, Steam Boilers and Pumps	3,130	0	0
Mill buildings and hoists	£22,880	12s.	0d.
	£49,736	12s.	10d.

Bibliography

MANUSCRIPT SOURCES

DUNDEE PUBLIC LIBRARY
Lamb Collection

DUNDEE UNIVERSITY LIBRARY
Sidlaw Industries, (some of F.S. Sandeman papers now missing)

EDINBURGH UNIVERSITY LIBRARY
Laing Papers

GENERAL REGISTER OFFICE FOR SCOTLAND
Census Enumerators' Returns 1841 and 1851

GUILDHALL LIBRARY, LONDON
Sun Fire Office Policies

NATIONAL ARCHIVES OF SCOTLAND
Auchtergaven Kirk Session Minutes
Campbell of Jura Muniments
Graham of Fintry Papers
Scottish Midland Junction Railway Company Papers
Sheriff Court of Perthshire Register of Deeds
Sinclair of Ulbster Muniments, (microfilm)
Stanley Provision Company Records
Stanley Free Kirk Session Minutes
Stanley Kirk Session Minutes

A.K. BELL LIBRARY, PERTH
Perth-Dunkeld Turnpike Trust Minute Books 1811–1879
F.S. Sandeman Papers
Stanley Combination School Minute Book 1874–1919

MANUSCRIPT SOURCES

PRIVATE MUNIMENTS
Atholl Papers, Blair Castle
Stanley Mills (Scotland) Ltd. (now missing)

PRINTED SOURCES

BOOKS AND ARTICLES

Adams, I. H., (1998), 'The Agricultural Revolution in Scotland: Contributions to the Debate,' in Cooke, A. J., Donnachie, I., MacSween, A. and Whatley, C. A., (eds.), *Modern Scottish History 1707 to the Present. Volume 3: Readings, 1707–1850*, East Linton, Tuckwell Press

Anon, (1951), *James Finlay and Company Ltd., 1750–1950*, Glasgow, privately printed

Anon, (1878), *The Old County Houses of the Old Glasgow Gentry*, Glasgow,

Atholl, John, 7th Duke of, (1908), *Chronicles of the Atholl and Tullibardine Families*, 5 Vols., Edinburgh, Ballantyne Press

Baines, E., (1835), *History of the Cotton Manufacture*, (reprinted 1966), London, Frank Cass

Berg, M., (2nd edition 1994), *The Age of Manufactures 1700–1820: Industry, Innovation and Work in Britain*, London and New York, Routledge

Boase, C. W., (1867), *A Century of Banking in Dundee, 1764–1864*, Edinburgh, 2nd edition

Bolin-Hort, P. (1994), 'Managerial Strategies and Worker Responses: A New Perspective on the Decline of the Scottish Cotton Industry,' *Journal of the Scottish Labour History Society*, 29

Brown, P. Hume, (ed.), (1891), *Early Travellers in Scotland*, Edinburgh

Bremner, D., (1869), *The Industries of Scotland. Their Rise, Progress and Present Condition*, reprinted 1969, Newton Abbot, David and Charles

Butt, J., (1967), *The Industrial Archaeology of Scotland*, Newton Abbot, David and Charles

Butt, J., (ed), (1971), *Robert Owen, Prince of Cotton-Spinners*, Newton Abbot, David and Charles

Butt, J., (1977), 'The Scottish Cotton Industry during the Industrial Revolution 1780–1840,' in Cullen, L.M., and Smout, T.C., (eds.) *Comparative Aspects of Scottish and Irish Social and Economic History 1600–1900*, Edinburgh

Butt, J., (1987), 'Labour and Industrial Relations in the Scottish Cotton Industry during the Industrial Revolution', in Butt, J. and Ponting, K., (eds.), *Textile History*, Aberdeen, Aberdeen University Press

Bythell, D., (1969), *The Handloom Weavers*, Cambridge, Cambridge University Press

Campbell, A., (1811), *A Journey from Edinburgh through parts of North Britain*, 2 vols, Edinburgh, A. Constable

Campbell, R.H., (1965), *Scotland since 1707: The Rise of an Industrial Society*, Oxford, Blackwell (reprinted 1971)

Campbell, R. H., (1995), 'The Making of the Industrial City', in Devine, T. M. and Jackson, G., (eds.), *Glasgow. Volume 1; Beginnings to 1830*, Manchester, Manchester University Press

Cant, J., (1806), *Memorabilia of the City of Perth*, Perth, William Morrison

Chaloner, W. H., (1954), 'Robert Owen, Peter Drinkwater and the Early Factory System in Manchester, 1788–1800, *Bulletin of the John Rylands Library*, Vol. 37

Chapman, S. D., (1967), *The Early Factory Masters*, Newton Abbot, David and Charles

Chapman, S. D., (1970), 'Fixed Capital Formation in the British Cotton Industry, 1770–1815,' *Economic History Review*, 2nd Series, XXIII

Chapman, S.D., (1987), *The Cotton Industry in the Industrial Revolution* (2nd edition), London, Macmillan

Chapman, S. D. and Butt, J., (1988), 'The Cotton Industry 1775–1880,' in Feinstein, C. H. and Pollard, S. (eds.), *Studies in Capital Formation in the United Kingdom 1750–1920*, Oxford, Oxford University Press

Checkland, S. G., (1975), *Scottish Banking. A History 1695–1973*, Glasgow

Checkland, O., and S. G., (1989, 2nd edition), *Industry and Ethos. Scotland 1832–1914*, Edinburgh, Edinburgh University Press

Clarkson. L. A. (1990), 'Proto-Industrialisation: The First Phase of Industrialisation?' in Clarkson, L.A. (ed.), *The Industrial Revolution: A Compendium*, London, MacMillan

Clow, A. and N., (1952), *The Chemical Revolution: A Contribution to Social Technology*, London

Collier, F., (1964), *The Family Economy of the Working Classes in the Cotton Industry 1784–1833*, Manchester, Manchester University Press

Cooke, A. J., (ed.) (1977), *Stanley, Its History and Development* Dundee, University of Dundee

Cooke, A. J. (1979a), 'Richard Arkwright and the Scottish Cotton Industry', *Textile History*, Vol. 10

Cooke A. J., (1979b), 'Robert Owen and the Stanley Mills, 1802–1811,' *Business History*, Vol. XXI, No. 1

Cooke, A. J., (1980), *Baxters of Dundee*, Dundee, University of Dundee

Cooke, A. J., (ed.), (1984), *A History of Redgorton Parish*, Dundee, University of Dundee

Cooke, A. J., (1995), 'Cotton and the Scottish Highland Clearances—Spinningdale 1791–1806', *Textile History*, Vol. 26, (1)

Cooke, A.J. (1998a), 'Industry and Commerce', in Omand, D. (ed.), *The Perthshire Book*, Edinburgh, Birlinn Press

Cooke, A.J., Donnachie, I., MacSween, A. and Whatley, C. A. (eds.), *(1998b)*, *Modern Scottish History 1707 to the Present*, 5 Volumes, East Linton, Tuckwell Press

Cooke, A. J. and Donnachie, I. (1998c), 'Industrialisation in Scotland 1707–1850' in Cooke, Donnachie, MacSween, and Whatley, *op. cit.*, Volume 1: *The Transformation of Scotland, 1707–1850*

Cowan, S., (1909), *Three Celtic Earldoms*, Edinburgh, Norman MacLeod

Crafts, N. F. R., (1985), *British Economic Growth during the Industrial Revolution*, Oxford, Clarendon Press

Crafts, N. F. R., (1989), 'British Industrialisation in an International Context', *Journal of Interdisciplinary History*, XIX

Crafts, N. F. R., (1994), 'The Industrial Revolution', in Floud, R. and McCloskey, D., (eds.), *The Economic History of Britain since 1700*, Vol. 1, 2nd edition, Cambridge, Cambridge University Press

Daniels, G. W., (1920), *The Early English Cotton Industry with Some Unpublished Letters of Samuel Crompton*, Manchester, Manchester University Press

Dawson, J. H. (1862), *Abridged Statistical History of the Scottish Counties*, Edinburgh

Deane, P., (2nd edition 1979), *The First Industrial Revolution*, Cambridge, Cambridge University Press

Defoe, D., (1724–6), *A Tour Through the Whole Island of Great Britain*, London, Penguin (reprinted 1971)

Devine, T. M., (1976), 'The Colonial Trades and Industrial Investment in Scotland c.1700–1815', *Economic History Review*, 2nd series, XXIX

Devine, T. M. and Mitchison, R., (eds.), (1988), *People and Society in Scotland. Vol.1, 1760–1830*, Edinburgh, John Donald.

Devine, T. M., (1990 edition), *The Tobacco Lords. A Study of the Tobacco Merchants of Glasgow and their Trading Activities c.1740–1790*, Edinburgh, Edinburgh University Press

Devine, T. M. and Jackson, G., (eds.), (1995), *Glasgow. Volume 1: Beginnings to 1830*, Manchester, Manchester University Press

Devine, T. M., *The Scottish Nation*, (1999), London, Penguin

Dickson, A. and Treble, J. H., (1992), *People and Society in Scotland, Vol. III, 1914–1990*, Edinburgh, John Donald

Dingwall, C., (1987), *The Falls of Bruar. A Garden in the Wild*, Dundee, Christopher Dingwall

Donnachie, I. and Hewitt, G., (1993), *Historic New Lanark. The Dale and Owen Industrial Community since 1785*, Edinburgh, Edinburgh University Press.

Donnachie, I., (1994), 'A Tour of the Works: Early Scottish Industry Observed, 1790–1825', in Cummings, A. J. G. and Devine, T., (eds.), *Industry, Business and Society in Scotland since 1700. Essays Presented to John Butt*, Edinburgh, John Donald

Donnachie, I., (1995), ''The Darker Side': A Speculative Survey of Scottish Crime during the first half of the Nineteenth Century,' *Scottish Economic and Social History*, 15

Donnachie, I., (2000), *Robert Owen. Owen of New Lanark and Harmony*, East Linton, Tuckwell Press

Dunn, M. (1994), 'Housing in Cotton Factory and Iron Works Villages of the late 18th and 19th Centuries'. *Vernacular Building*, 18, Edinburgh, Scottish Vernacular Buildings Working Group.

Durie, A. J. (1979), *The Scottish Linen Industry in the Eighteenth Century*, Edinburgh, John Donald.

Durie, A. J., (ed.), (1996), *The British Linen Company 1745–1775*, Edinburgh, Scottish History Society

Edwards, M. M., (1967), *The Growth of the British Cotton Trade 1780–1815*, Manchester, Manchester University Press

Encyclopaedia Perthensis, (1815), Perth

Eyre-Todd, G., (1934), *History of Glasgow. Volume III, From the Reformation to the Passing of the Reform Acts 1832–33*, Glasgow, Jackson Wylie

Farnie, D. A., (1979), *The English Cotton Industry and the World Market 1815–1896*, Oxford, Clarendon Press

Ferguson, R. M., (ed.), (1897), *A Village Poet*

Ferguson, R. M., (1893), *My Village*, London, Digby Long

Ferguson, S. (1869), *The Queen's Visit and Other Poems*

Fergusson, J. (ed.), (1934), *Letters of George Dempster to Sir Adam Fergusson, 1756–1813*, London

Fitton, R. S., and Wadsworth, A. P., (1958), *The Strutts and the Arkwrights 1758–1830*, Manchester, Manchester University Press

Fitton, R. S., (1989), *The Arkwrights, Spinners of Fortune*, Manchester, Manchester University Press

Foster, J., (1882), *Members of Parliament. Scotland 1357–1882*, London

Foster, J., (1998), 'Class', in Cooke, A. J., Donnachie, I., MacSween, A. and Whatley, C. A., *Modern Scottish History 1707 to the Present, Volume 2, The Modernisation of Scotland 1850 to the Present*, East Linton, Tuckwell Press

Fraser, W. H., (1976), 'The Glasgow Cotton Spinners 1837' in Butt, J. and Ward, J. T. (eds.), *Scottish Themes*, Edinburgh

Fraser, W.H., (1988a), 'Patterns of Protest', in Devine, T.M. and Mitchison, R. (eds.), *People and Society in Scotland, Vol. 1 1760–1830*, Edinburgh, John Donald

Fraser, W. H., (1988b), *Conflict and Class*, Edinburgh

Fraser, W. H., and Morris, R. J., (eds.), (1990), *People and Society in Scotland, Vol. 2 1830–1914*, Edinburgh, John Donald.

Galt, J. (1919 edition), *Annals of the Parish*, London and Edinburgh, T.N. Foulis

Gardner, J. W. F., (1934), *London, Midland and Scottish Railway*, Edinburgh

Gillies, W. A., (1938), *In Famed Breadalbane*, Perth, Munro Press

Gordon, E., (1991), *Women and the Labour Movement in Scotland 1850–1914*, Oxford

Hamilton, H., (1932, reprinted 1966), *The Industrial Revolution in Scotland*, London, Frank Cass

Hamilton, H., (1963), *An Economic History of Scotland in the Eighteenth Century*, Oxford, Clarendon Press

Harding, A. W., (1991), *Pullars of Perth*, Perth, Perth and Kinross District Libraries

Hay, G. D., and Stell, G. P., (1986), *Monuments of Industry*, Glasgow, Royal Commission on the Ancient and Historical Monuments of Scotland

Haynes, N., (2000), *Perth and Kinross, An Illustrated Architectural Guide*, Edinburgh, Rutland Press

Henderson, W. O., (2nd edition, 1969), *The Lancashire Cotton Famine 1861–1865*, Manchester, Manchester University Press

Heron, R., (1799), *Scotland Delineated*, Edinburgh (facsimile by James Thin, Edinburgh, 1975)

Hobsbawm, E. J., (1969), *Industry and Empire. From 1750 to the Present Day*, London, Penguin

Hooker, Sir W. J., (1844), *Perthshire Illustrated*, London, A. Fullarton

Hudson, P., (ed.), (1989), *Regions and Industries: A Perspective on the Industrial Revolution in Britain*, Cambridge, Cambridge University Press

Hudson, P., (1992), *The Industrial Revolution* London, Edward Arnold

Hume, J., (1971), 'The Industrial Archaeology of New Lanark,' in Butt, J., *Robert Owen, Prince of Cotton Spinners*, David and Charles, Newton Abbot.

Hume, J., (1976, 1977), *The Industrial Archaeology of Scotland* Vols. 1 and 2, London, Batsford

Hume, J. (ed.), (1980), *Early Days in a Dundee Mill 1819–1823. Extracts from the Diary of William Brown, an early Dundee Spinner*, Dundee, Abertay Historical Society, No. 20

Hunter, T., (1883), *Woods, Forests and Estates of Perthshire*, Perth, Henderson, Robertson and Hunter

Joyce, P., (1980), *Work, Society and Politics. The Culture of the Factory in later Victorian England*, London, Methuen

Knox, W. W., (1995), *Hanging by a Thread: The Scottish Cotton Industry, c.1850–1914*, Preston, Carnegie Publishing

Knox, W. W., (1999), *Industrial Nation: Work, Culture and Society in Scotland 1800–Present*, Edinburgh, Edinburgh University Press

Lee, C. H. (1972), *A Cotton Enterprise, 1795–1840: A History of M'Connel and Kennedy, fine cotton spinners*, Manchester, Manchester University Press

Leneman, L., (1986), *Living in Atholl: A Social History of the estates 1685–1785*, Edinburgh

Lenman, B., Lythe, C. and Gauldie, E., (1969), *Dundee and its Textile Industry 1850–1914*, Dundee, Abertay Historical Society, No 14

Leslie's Perth and Perthshire Directory, 1889–90, Perth

Leslie's Perth and Perthshire Directory, 1921–2, Perth

Leyden, J., (1903), *Journal of a Tour in the Highlands and Western Islands of Scotland in 1800*, Edinburgh

Loch, D., (1778), *A Tour Through Most of the Trading Towns and Villages of Scotland*, Edinburgh

Lockhart, D. G., (1983), 'Planned Village Development in Scotland and Ireland', in Devine, T. M. and Dickson, D. (eds.), *Ireland and Scotland 1600–1850: Parallels and Contrasts in Economic and Social Development*, Edinburgh

Lowson, A., (1893), *Portrait Gallery of Forfar Notables*, Aberdeen

Lythe, S. G. E., Ward, J. T. and Southgate, D. G., (1968), *Three Dundonians: James Carmichael, Charles William Boase and Edwin Scrymgeour*, Dundee, Abertay Historical Society, No 13

Lythe, S.G.E. and Butt, J., (1975), *An Economic History of Scotland 1100–1939*, Glasgow and London, Blackie

Macinnes, A. I., (1996), *Clanship, Commerce and the House of Stuart, 1603–1788*, East Linton, Tuckwell Press

Macinnes, A. I., (1998), 'Highland Society in the Era of 'Improvement'', in Cooke, A. J., Donnachie, I., Macsween, A. and Whatley, C. A., *Modern Scottish History 1707 to the Present. Volume 1: The Transformation of Scotland*, East Linton, Tuckwell Press

MacKenzie, A., (1883, 2nd edition, 1946), *The History of the Highland Clearances*, Glasgow, Alex Maclaren

McLain, N. E., (1970), 'Scottish Lintmills, 1729–1770,' *Textile History*, 1

McLean, A., (ed.), (1901), *Handbook on the Industries of Glasgow and the West of Scotland*, Glasgow, British Association for the Advancement of Science

MacPherson, D., (1805), *Annals of Commerce, Manufactures, Fisheries and Navigation*, Edinburgh

Mantoux, P., (1928), *The Industrial Revolution in the Eighteenth Century*, London, Methuen (revised edition 1964)

Marwick, W. H., (1924), 'The Cotton Industry and the Industrial Revolution in Scotland', *Scottish Historical Review*, XXI

Mathias, P., (1959), *The Brewing Industry in England 1700–1830*, Cambridge

Mathias, P. (2nd edition, 1983), *The First Industrial Nation. An Economic History of Britain 1700–1914*, London, Methuen

Maver, I., (2000), *Glasgow*, Edinburgh, Edinburgh University Press

Meikle, H. W., (1912), *Scotland and the French Revolution*, Glasgow, James Maclehose

Miskell, L., (2000), 'Civic Leadership and the Manufacturing Elite: Dundee, 1820–1870', in Miskell, L., Whatley, C. A. and Harris, B., *Victorian Dundee, Image and Realities*, East Linton, Tuckwell Press

Mitchell, G. M., (1925), 'The English and Scottish Cotton Industries', *Scottish Historical Review* XXII

Mitchell, J., (1884), *Reminiscences of My Life in the Highlands*, 2 Vols., reprinted 1971, Newton Abbot, David and Charles

Mitchell, J. O., (1903), *Old Glasgow Essays*, Glasgow

Mitchison, R., (1962), *Agricultural Sir John. The Life of Sir John Sinclair of Ulbster 1754–1835*, London, Geoffrey Bles

More, C., (1977), *The Industrial Age. Economy and Society in Britain 1750–1995*, London and New York, Longman

Morris, R. J., (1976), *Cholera 1832: The Social Response to an Epidemic*, London, Croom Helm

Mudie, Sir F. and Walker, D. M., (1964), *Mains Castle and the Grahams of Fintry*, Dundee, Abertay Historical Society, No. 9

Munn, C., (1981), *The Scottish Provincial Banking Companies 1747–1864*, Edinburgh, John Donald

Murray, N. (1978), *The Scottish Handloom Weavers 1790–1850*, Edinburgh

Murray, N. (1994), 'The Regional Structure of Textile Employment in Scotland in the Nineteenth Century: East of Scotland Textile Weavers in the 1830s,' in Cummings, A. J. G. and Devine, T. M., (eds.), *Industry, Business and Society in Scotland since 1700. Essays presented to John Butt*, Edinburgh, John Donald

New Statistical Account of Scotland, (1845), Vol. X, (Perthshire), Edinburgh

O'Brien P. K., and Quinault, R., (eds.), (1993), *The Industrial Revolution and British Society*, Cambridge, Cambridge University Press.

Ordnance Gazetteer of Scotland, (1885), Edinburgh

Owen, R., (1857), *The Life of Robert Owen, written by himself*, London and Philadelphia

Owen, R. D., (1874), *Threading my Way*, London

Payne, P. L., (ed.), (1967), *Studies in Scottish Business History*, London

Payne, P. L., (1998), 'Industrialisation and Industrial Decline,' in Cooke, A. J., Donnachie, I., MacSween, A. and Whatley, C. A., (eds.), *Modern Scottish History 1707 to the Present. Volume 2:The Modernisation of Scotland, 1850 to the Present*, East Linton, Tuckwell Press

Peacock, D., (1849), *Perth, Its Annals and Archives*, Perth, Thomas Richardson

Pennant, T., (1769), *A Tour in Scotland*, Warrington (reprinted Perth, 1979)

Penny, G., (1836), *Traditions of Perth*, Perth (reprinted with an introduction by A. J. Cooke, Coupar Angus, 1986)

Phillipson, N., and Mitchison, R., (1970), *Scotland in the Age of Improvement*, Edinburgh, Edinburgh University Press

Pollard, S., (1965), *The Genesis of Modern Management*, London

Rees, A., (1819), *The Cyclopedia of Arts, Sciences and Literature*, London

Reid, R., (1884), *Glasgow Past and Present*, Glasgow

Richards, E., (1982 & 1985*), A History of the Highland Clearances*, 2 Volumes, London, Croom Helm

Richards, E. (1993), 'Margins of the Industrial Revolution', in O'Brien, P. and Quinault, R., (eds.), *The Industrial Revolution and British Society*, Cambridge, Cambridge University Press

Richards, E., (2000), The Highland Clearances, Edinburgh, Birlinn

Robertson A. J., (1969), 'Robert Owen and the Campbell Debt 1810–1822,' *Business History*, XI

Robertson, A. J. (1970), 'The Decline of the Scottish Cotton Industry, 1860–1914', *Business History, XII*

Robertson R., (1799), *General View of the Agriculture in the County of Perth*, Edinburgh

Rodgers, R., (1988), 'Concentration and Fragmentation: Capital, Labour and the Stucture of Mid-Victorian Scottish Industry', *Journal of Urban History*, 14, ii, reprinted in Cooke, A. J., Donnachie, I., MacSween, A. and Whatley, C. A., *Modern Scottish History 1707 to the Present, Volume 4: Readings 1850 to the Present*, East Linton, Tuckwell Press

Rogers, C., (1886), *Life and Songs of the Baroness Nairne*, Edinburgh, John Grant

Rostow, W. W., (1960), *The Stages of Economic Growth*, Cambridge, Cambridge University Press

Rubinstein, W. D., (1994 edition), *Capitalism, Culture and Decline in Britain 1750–1990*, London and New York, Routledge

Saint Fond, Faujas de, (1907), *A Journey through England and Scotland to the Hebrides in 1784* (revised edition of English translation by Sir Archibald Geikie), Glasgow, 2 Volumes

Sandeman, J. G. (1895), *The Sandeman Genealogy*

Saunders, L. J., (1950), *Scottish Democracy, 1815–1840*, Edinburgh

Scarfe, N., (2001), *To the Highlands in 1786. The Inquisitive Journey of a Young French Aristocrat*, Woodbridge, Boydel Press

Shaw, J., (1984*), Water Power in Scotland 1550–1830*, Edinburgh, John Donald

Sinclair, Sir J. (1825), *Analysis of the Statistical Account of Scotland*, Edinburgh (reprinted 1970) 2 Volumes

Sinclair, Sir J., (1831), *Correspondence of Sir John Sinclair*, 2 Volumes, London

Sinclair, Sir J., (ed.), *The Statistical Account of Scotland 1791–1799*, (reissued 1977), Vol. XI, South and East Perthshire, Kinross-Shire, Vol. XII, North and West Perthshire, Vol. XIII, Angus, Wakefield, EP Publishing

Smith, A. (1776), *An Inquiry into the Nature and Causes of the Wealth of Nations*, 2 Volumes, (1976 edition, Oxford)

Smout T. C., (1964), 'Scottish Landowners and Economic Growth 1650–1850' *Scottish Journal of Political Economy*, X1

Smout T. C., (1969), *A History of the Scottish People 1560–1830*, London, Collins

Smout, T. C. (1970), 'The Landowner and the Planned Village in Scotland 1730–1830', in Phillipson, N. T. and Mitchison, R., (eds.), *Scotland in the Age of Improvement*, Edinburgh, Edinburgh University Press

Smout, T. C., (1986) *A Century of the Scottish People 1830–1950*, London, Collins

Stewart, D., (1822), *Sketches of the Character, Manners and Present State of the Highlanders of Scotland; with Details of the Military Service of the Highland Regiments*, Edinburgh, John Donald, (reprinted 1977)

Stewart, G., (1881), *Curiosities of Glasgow Citizenship*, Glasgow

Thompson, E. P., (1963), *The Making of the English Working Class*, London, Pelican (revised 1968)

Turner W.H.K., (1957), 'The Textile Industry of Perth and District', *The Institute of British Geographers' Transactions and Papers*, No. 23

Turner W.H.K., (1958), 'The Significance of Water Power in Industrial Location. Some Perthshire Examples', *Scottish Geographical Magazine*, 74

Unwin, G., (1923), *Samuel Oldknow and the Arkwrights. The Industrial Revolution at Stockport and Marple*, Manchester, Manchester University Press

Wadsworth, A. P. and Mann, J. de Lacy, (1931), *The Cotton Trade and Industrial Lancashire, 1600–1780*, Manchester, Manchester University Press

Walker, W. M. (1979), *Juteopolis: Dundee and its Textile Workers, 1885–1923*, Edinburgh, Edinburgh University Press

Warden, A., (1864), *The Linen Trade, Ancient and Modern*, Dundee

Warner, R., (1802), *A Tour through the Northern counties of England and the Borders of Scotland, I*, Bath

Watson, M., (1990), *Jute and Flax Mills in Dundee*, Hutton Press, Tayport

Whatley, C.A. (1988), 'The Experience of Work' in Devine, T.M. and Mitchison, R., *People and Society in Scotland, Vol. 1, 1760–1830*, Edinburgh, John Donald

Whatley, C. A., (1995), 'Labour in the Industrialising City', in Devine, T. M. and Jackson, G., *Glasgow. Volume 1: Beginnings to 1830*, Manchester, Manchester University Press

Whatley, C. A. (ed.), (1996), *The Diary of John Sturrock, Millwright, Dundee 1864–65*, East Linton, Tuckwell Press

Whatley C. A., (1997), *The Industrial Revolution in Scotland*, Cambridge, Cambridge University Press.

Whatley, C. A. (2000), *Scottish Society 1707–1830: Beyond Jacobitism, towards industrialisation*, Manchester, Manchester University Press

Whatley, C. A., (2000b), 'Altering images of the industrial city: the case of James Myles, the 'Factory Boy', and mid-Victorian Dundee,' in Miskell, L., Whatley, C. A. and Harris, B., (eds.), *Victorian Dundee: Image and Realities*, East Linton, Tuckwell Press

Whyte, I. D., (1989), 'Proto-industrialisation in Scotland,' in Hudson, P. (ed.), *Regions and Industries: A Perspective on the Industrial Revolution in Britain*, Cambridge, Cambridge University Press

Whyte, I. D., (1994), *Scotland Before the Industrial Revolution c.1050 to c.1750*, London, Longman.

Whyte, I. D., (1998), 'Rural Transformation and Lowland Society', in Cooke, A. J., Donnachie, I., MacSween, A., and Whatley, C. A., *Modern Scottish History 1707 to the Present. Volume 1: The Transformation of Scotland 1707–1850*, East Linton, Tuckwell Press

Wiener, M. A., (1981), *English Culture and the Decline of the Industrial Spirit, 1850–1980*, London, Harmondsworth

Withers, C. W. J., (1986), *Highland Communities in Dundee and Perth, 1787–1891. A Study in the Social History of Migrant Highlanders*, Dundee, Abertay Historical Society

Young, J. D., (1979), *The Rousing of the Scottish Working Class*, London, Croom Helm

MAPS

Ordnance Survey, 1st Edition, 6 inch and later surveys.

Stobie J., (1783 and 1805) Map of Perth and Clackmannan

NEWSPAPERS AND MAGAZINES

Dundee Advertiser

Glasgow Mercury

Manchester Mercury

Nottingham Journal

Perthshire Advertiser

Perthshire Courier

Scots Magazine

PARLIAMENTARY PAPERS

Sheriff Returns on Parochial Schools, *Parliamentary Papers* 1826, Vol. XVIII

Factory Inquiry Commission Reports, *Parliamentary Papers* 1833, Vols. XX and XXI and 1834, Vol. XX

Abstract of Education Returns Scotland, *Parliamentary Papers* 1837, Vol. XLVII

Papers relating to Parochial Education in Scotland, *Parliamentary Papers*, 1841,Vol. XIX

B. PHIL. AND PH. D. THESES

Gauldie, E. E., (1966) *Scottish Bleachfields 1718–1862*, B.Phil. Thesis, St Andrews

Harding, A. W., (1975) *Education in Perthshire to the Act of 1872*, PhD Thesis, Dundee

Lockhart, D. G., (1974) *Planned Villages in North East Scotland*, PhD Thesis, Dundee

Index

Act of Union, 1707: 26

American Civil War: 36, 127, 133, 137

American Embargo, 1807–1808: 76, 86

American War of Independence: 22, 44

Anderston, Glasgow, weaving suburb: 27, 47

Arkwright, Sir Richard, (1732–1793) cotton manufacturer: 27–28, 30–31, 45–48, 50–54, 57–59, 62–63, 75, 99, 120–122, 138

Atholl, John Murray, 4th Duke of (1755–1830): 11, 13, 18–20, 39, 43–45, 48–50, 57–58, 62, 65, 68, 70–72, 74, 76, 78–79, 87, 91–93, 96–98, 120, 122, 130

Atholl Estates: 12, 15, 18, 20, 39, 44, 64–65, 98, 101, 105

Atholl Highlanders: 44

Auchtergaven, parish, Perthshire: 11, 12, 19–20, 70, 122–123, 126, 130–131, 133

Ballindalloch Mills, Stirlingshire: 35

Banks, Sir Joseph, botanist and President of the Royal Society: 53–54, 58

Banks, Scottish provincial : 58, 61, 77

Berg, Maxine, historian: 24, 30, 135

Bank Top Mill, Piccadilly, Manchester: 73, 75

Barr, Robert, manager, Stanley mills: 82–84

Beech House, Stanley: 107, 110–112, 141

Bisset, Janet, cotton spinner, Stanley Mills: 123

Blackburn, Lancashire: 29–30, 128

Blair Atholl, Perthshire: 16, 43

Blairingone, Clackmannanshire, coal mines: 44

Blantyre Mills, Lanarkshire: 35, 104, 123, 133

Bleachfields:

    Huntingtowerfield, Perthshire: 18–19, 65, 78

    Laurencekirk, Kincardineshire: 50

    Luncarty, Perthshire: 11–12, 18–19, 22, 59, 61, 65, 71–72, 83, 105, 110, 128

    Pitcairnfield, Perthshire: 19, 128

    Stormontfield, Perthshire: 72, 87

Tulloch, Perthshire: 59, 65
Board of Trustees for Manufactures and Fisheries: 43, 59, 72
Borland, John, Perth textile manufacturer: 72, 87
Boulton and Watt, Birmingham engineering firm: 35, 89
Brickmaking, at Stanley: 50, 62–64, 112–113
Breadalbane Estates, Perthshire: 15
Buchanan, Archibald, manager at Catrine and Deanston cotton mills: 31, 99
Buchanan, George, (died 1848) Stanley mill owner: 104, 106–107, 135
Buchanan, James, Stanley mill owner: 99, 106
Burns, Robert, (1759–1796) poet: 44, 58, 71

Campbell, Archibald of Jura, landowner and Dale trustee: 74–75, 92–93, 98
Campbell, Caroline, wife of David Dale: 74
Campbell, John, (1808–1892) Stanley poet: 108
Campbell, Roy, historian: 23, 38
Campsie Linn, Stanley (rapids): 11, 39, 71
Carron Iron Company: 63
Catrine Mills, Ayrshire: 31, 33–35, 44, 84, 88, 99, 105, 107, 125–126
Chapman, Stanley, historian: 24:
Cholera epidemic, 1832: 102
Clearances:
    Perthshire: 13–19
    Sutherland: 58 :
Cowley, Hannah, poet: 21
Cotton Famine (1861–1865): 36, 106–108, 127, 133
Cotton industry:
    Child employment: 24, 34, 46, 77, 121–125, 132
    Employers: 38, 105, 111
    Employment: 24–25, 34–38, 46, 77, 121–125, 127, 132
    Exports: 36, 86–88, 103, 108, 112, 118, 136
    Factory discipline: 33, 121, 124–125
    Female employment: 24, 34–38, 121–124, 127
    Imports of raw cotton: 22, 36, 77, 79, 80–83, 85–87, 89, 107–108
    Irish workers: 38, 109, 125
    Machinery & inventions: 24, 33–35, 46, 79, 84–88, 92
    Management methods: 31–33, 78, 80–82, 88
    Managers, remuneration: 82–83
    Mill design: 63–64
    Paternalism: 104–105, 127, 129
    Printworks: 65, 71, 86–88
    Productivity: 37–38
    Spinning: 34–38, 78–79, 84
    Wages: 20, 35–38, 46, 86, 128–129
    Weaving: 34–38, 78, 86, 92, 97, 103, 115
Cotton Mills:
    Ballindalloch, Stirlingshire: 35

Blantyre, Lanarkshire: 35, 104, 123, 133
Catrine, Ayrshire: 31, 33–35, 44, 84, 88, 99, 105, 107, 125–126
Cromford, Derbyshire: 31, 53–54, 57, 104, 120
Cromwellpark, Perthshire: 19, 64, 71, 88, 103
Deanston, Perthshire: 15, 30–35, 84, 86, 88, 99, 101, 104, 108, 121, 125, 132–133
Glasgow: : 21–22, 27, 30, 35, 38, 45, 127
New Lanark, Lanarkshire: 31–33, 35, 44–45, 48, 51–52, 54, 64, 75, 77–78, 83–89,
    99, 101–102, 104, 106, 112, 121–122, 125, 132
Newton Stewart, Dumfriesshire: 44
Paisley: 35, 38, 47, 97, 104–105, 108, 111, 127, 137
Penicuik, Midlothian: 30, 51
Rothesay, Isle of Bute: 31, 51
Spinningdale, Sutherland: 21, 58, 75, 102
Stanley, Perthshire: see entries under Stanley
Woodside, Aberdeen: 31, 35, 54
Cotton Spinners' Combination, Stanley: 126–127
Cotton Spinners' Strike, Glasgow, 1837: 30, 38, 127
Craig, James, (1757–1839) Stanley mill owner: 19–20, 73–88, 91–93, 96–98, 103, 107,
    122, 124, 130, 137
Cromford Mills, Derbyshire: 31, 53–54, 57, 104, 120
Crompton, Samuel, (1753–1827) inventor of spinning mule: 27, 33
Cromwellpark Mills, Perthshire: 19, 64, 71, 88, 103
Crop rotation: 12, 19–20
Culbert, John, chief engineer, Stanley Mills: 116
Curling, Stanley: 113, 133

Dale, Caroline, wife of Robert Owen: 77, 81, 91
Dale, David, (1739–1806) cotton manufacturer: 31, 52–54, 73–83, 86, 91–93, 96, 111,
    120–122, 138
Dale Trustees: 87, 89, 91–93, 96–98
Deanston Mills, Perthshire: 15, 30–35, 84, 86, 88, 99, 101, 104, 107, 121, 125, 132–
    133
Defoe, Daniel, (1660–1731) writer and traveller: 39–40
Dempster, George of Dunnichen, M.P., (1732–1818) landowner & Stanley partner: 21,
    45, 47–48, 50–51, 57–59, 61, 64, 66, 71, 75, 102, 120–121, 132
Dempster and Co., Stanley Company: 49, 66, 84, 135
Devine, Tom, historian: 26
Disruption, 1843: 133
Donnachie, Ian, historian: 26
Douglas, Stewart, Glasgow merchant: 91–92
Dracup, Colin, Stanley mill owner: 119
Drinkwater, Peter, Manchester mill owner: 75
Dull, parish, Perthshire: 15
Dundas, Henry, Viscount Melville (1742–1811): 61, 67–68, 70
Dundee Banking Company: 58
Dunkeld, parish, Perthshire: 12–13, 44, 78, 127

East India Company: 28, 44, 58–59
Enlightenment, Scottish: 45, 58

Factory Act, 1833: 132
Farquhar, George, W.S., Duke of Atholl's Edinburgh lawyer: 50, 66
Fenton, William, (1827–1898) cotton belting manufacturer, Stanley: 112, 136
Finlay, James and Co., cotton manufacturers: 34, 89
Finlay, Kirkman, Glasgow cotton manufacturer: 33–34, 74, 84, 86, 99
Flax, cultivation: 12, 43
Fleming, John, small businessman, Stanley: 103
Forestry: 44
Fortingall, parish, Perthshire: 15–16
Friends of the People, Perth: 30, 66–69
Fustians: 26–27

Galt, John, (1779–1839) novelist: 21
Gardenstone, Lord, judge & landowner: 50
Glasite Church: 59, 111
Glasgow:
    Chamber of Commerce: 75
    Cotton industry: 21–22, 27, 30, 35, 38, 45, 127
    Cotton Spinners' Strike, 1837: 30, 38, 127
    Irish cotton workers: 38, 109, 125
Glen Lyon, Perthshire: 15
Gow, Neil, fiddler: 44
Graham, Robert of Fintry, (1749–1815) patron of Robert Burns & Stanley partner: 45,
    50, 57, 59, 66, 121
Gunn, 'Jeek', (died 1897) village bellman, Stanley: 113

Hamilton, Gilbert, Secretary, Glasgow Chamber of Commerce & Lord Provost: 48
Hamilton, Henry, historian: 22, 36
Handsel Monday: 113, 123, 132
Hargreaves, James, inventor of spinning jenny: 30–31
Highs, Thomas, English inventor: 57
Historic Scotland: 8, 137–138
Horner, Leonard, Factory Commissioner: 35
Houldsworth, Henry, Glasgow cotton manufacturer: 38, 125
Howard, Samuel, (1808–1872) Stanley mill owner: 34, 106–109, 127, 133, 137
Humphreys, Robert, under manager at New Lanark: 75, 78, 85, 89
Hunter, David, (born 1800) overseer, Stanley Mills: 124–125
Huntingtowerfield bleachfield, Perthshire: 18, 19, 65, 78
Hutton, Mr., manager, Stanley Mills: 118

Indian Independence, 1947: 118, 136
Irish, cotton workers in West of Scotland: 38, 109, 125

Jacobite Rebellion, 1745: 11, 67
Johnstone, Rev., Stanley minister: 131
Jute Industries Ltd.: 115–117, 119, 136, 138

Kames, Lord, judge & agricultural writer: 15
Keay, Andrew, Stanley mill manager: 33, 47, 50, 54, 57, 61, 66
Keay, James, Stanley Company's lawyer: 50–51, 61, 66
Kelly, William, New Lanark mill manager: 33, 102
Killin, parish, Perthshire: 15
Kincardine, Moss of, Stirlingshire: 15:
Kinclaven, parish, Perthshire: 11, 20, 130, 133
King's Birthday: 67
Knox, W. W., historian: 26, 36, 38, 108

Lanarkshire, cotton industry: 23, 27, 34, 36
Lancashire, cotton industry: 22–23, 26, 30, 36–38, 48, 77–78, 84, 88, 106–107, 123,
    128
Laurencekirk, Kincardineshire: 50
Leneman, Leah, historian: 13–14
Letham, Angus: : 50
Lime, use of: : 12, 19, 55
Linen industry: : 22–23, 26–29, 34, 39, 43, 46, 50, 59, 74
Lint mills: : 43
Little Dunkeld, parish, Perthshire: : 19, 43
Loak, Mansion House, Perthshire: : 12
Luddism: : 29–30
Luncarty bleachfield, Perthshire: 11–12, 18–19, 22, 59, 61, 65, 71–72, 83, 105, 110,
    128

Macclesfield, Cheshire: 29
Machine breaking: : 29–30
Mair, James, partner at Stanley mills: 73–74
Manchester, cotton industry: 22, 35–36, 38, 41, 77
Manhattan Jute Works, Dundee: 110–112, 114–116
Mantoux, Paul, historian: 22
Marl, use of: : 12
Marshall, John, Leeds flaxspinner: 122
Macgregor, Mary, (born 1821) child worker, Stanley Mills: 124, 132
McIntosh, Agnes, (born 1899) rove and bobbin carrier, Stanley Mills: 129
MacLean, John, (1879–1923) Glasgow socialist: 128
McLiesh, John, Stanley schoolmaster: 131
McVicar, David, mill manager, Stanley Mills: 61, 64, 71–72, 121
Mealmaker, George, Dundee weaver and radical: 68–69
Meal mobs:
    Dundee: 58
    Perth: 30, 40

Militia Riots, 1797: 70–71
Moncrieff, Robert Scott, Glasgow agent of Royal Bank of Scotland: 74, 77
More, John, Glasgow agent, Royal Bank of Scotland, clerk to Dale Trustees: : 84, 86–88, 91, 93, 96, 98
Murdoch, William, pioneer of gas lighting: 89
Murray, Major General James: 44, 46, 48
Murray, George, Captain & Mrs.: 53
Murray, William, Lord: 11
Muslins, manufacture: of: 27–29, 59, 120, 123

Nairne Estates, Perthshire: 12, 18, 19, 111
Nairne, John, Lord: 101
Nairne, Robert, Lord: 11
New Lanark: 31–33, 35, 44–45, 48, 51–52, 54, 64, 75, 77–78, 85–89, 99, 101–102, 104, 106, 112, 121–122, 125, 132
New Lanark Twist Company: 81, 85, 88–89, 92

Oldknow, Samuel, English cotton manufacturer: 23, 27–28
Owen, Robert, (1771–1858) cotton manufacturer and social reformer: 19, 73–88, 91–93, 96–98, 111, 122, 138

Paisley, cotton industry: 35, 38, 47, 97, 104–105, 108, 111, 127, 137:
Palmer, Thomas, Unitarian minister and radical: 68–69
Penicuik Mills, Midlothian: 30, 51
Pennant, Thomas, writer and traveller: 12
Penny, George, (1771–1850?) Perth weaver and historian: 22, 30, 40, 45, 69–70, 97, 120
Perth:
    Cotton industry: 19, 22, 35, 38, 41–42, 45, 65, 71, 77, 88, 93, 97, 103, 123, 127
    Linen industry: 19, 26, 35, 39–41, 46, 65, 71
    Radical politics: 30, 66–71, 97
    Population: 67
    Salmon: 11
Perth United Bank: 57, 59, 61, 77
Perthshire Highlands:
    Clearances: 13–19
    Emigration to North America: 18, 46
    Linen industry: 39, 43, 59
Phoenix Trust: 137–138
Pitcairnfield bleachfield, Perthshire: 19, 128
Pitcairngreen, Perthshire: 13, 21, 50
Planned villages, Scotland: 50–51
Power looms: 34, 36–38, 86–89, 92, 103

Queen's Birthday: 113, 123, 132:

Radical War, 1820: 30:
Railways: 106, 135
Redgorton, parish, Perthshire: 11, 13, 20, 64, 130–131, 133
Reform Act, 1832: 103
Renfrewshire, cotton industry: 21, 27, 34
Roberts, Richard, Manchester engineer: 33, 109
Robertson, Alexander of Bohespick, Perthshire, Gaelic poet: 14
Robertson, Margaret, (born 1751) Stanley villager: 105
Rochefoucauld, Alexandre de, French writer and traveller: 41–42
Rostow, W. W., historian: 22
Rothesay Mills, Isle of Bute: 31, 51
Royal Bank of Scotland, Glasgow branch: 74, 77, 84, 86–87, 91, 93, 96, 98

Salmon, Tay: 11, 43, 78–79, 105, 113, 138, 141
Salte, Samuel, London agent: 23, 27–28
Sandeman, Douglas, Stanley cotton tape manufacturer: 115, 136
Sandeman, Frank Stewart, (1838–1898) Stanley mill owner: 105, 110–111, 114
Sandeman, Frank Stewart and Sons Ltd.: 112, 115–117, 135
Sandeman, Fred, Manhattan Works, Dundee: 117
Sandeman, William of Luncarty (1722–1790), bleachfield owner: 45, 48, 50, 54, 57, 59–
    61, 66, 111, 120
St. Fond, Faujas de, French writer and traveller: 41
Scott, James, Stanley schoolmaster: 130
Scott, Janet, (born 1802) millworker, Stanley Mills: 124
Scott, John, (born 1806) yarn dresser, Stanley Mills: 102, 124, 132
Scottish Midland Junction Railway Company: 106, 135
Sea Island Cotton: 73–74, 81, 86
Sharp, James, (born 1791) mill manager, Stanley Mills: 102–103
Shaw, John, assistant manager, Stanley Mills: 119
Sheep: 13–16, 58, 121
Sidlaw Industries: 119, 135, 137
Sinclair, Sir John of Ulbster, (1754–1835), compiler of the *Statistical Accounts*: 25, 34,
    50, 59, 71
Smout, Christopher, historian: 23, 43
Spinningdale, Sutherland, cotton mills: 21, 58, 75, 102
Spinning jennies: 29–30, 34
Spinning mules: 33–34, 46, 77, 79, 92, 123
Stanley, Perthshire:
    Brickmaking: 50, 62, 64, 112–113
    Churches: 79, 84, 86, 101, 109, 130–134
    Corn mill: 49–50, 63, 101, 107
    Cotton Mills: 11, 13, 18, 22, 31, 34–35, 38–39, 43–45, 47–66, 70–133, 135–138,
        140–141
    Curling: 113, 133
    Diet: : 79, 101, 103, 107, 113, 133–134
    Farming and farms: 12–20, 78, 80, 84, 91–92, 96, 105

Flax mill: 64–65, 71, 79, 140

Health: : 102, 104, 118, 122, 124, 129–130, 132

Housing and village: 13, 19, 49, 61–64, 73, 79–80, 84, 88, 99, 101, 104, 113, 119, 130, 132–134

Lighting of mills: 78, 89, 100, 102, 111

Population: 71, 100, 105–106, 108, 125–127, 131

Production: 65, 76–91, 102, 106–107, 112, 114–115, 117–120, 122, 124, 127–129, 135–137

Public houses: 104, 113, 133

Recruitment and training, worker: 18–19, 57–58, 118, 120–122, 127–129, 136

Schools: 64, 101, 130–134

Wages: : 91, 121–124, 128–129

Water power: 11, 39, 49, 54–55, 71–72, 85–86, 89, 92, 100–101, 111–112, 114, 116, 118, 135, 138, 140–141

Workforce and working conditions: 53, 57–58, 72, 83, 89, 97, 102–103, 108, 115, 118–125, 127–129

Stanley Societies and Organisations:

Stanley Benevolent Society: 103

Stanley Coffee House: 133–134

Stanley Educational Society: 132

Stanley Funeral Society: 103

Stanley Instrumental Band: 132

Stanley Library: 104, 111

Stanley Literary Society: 133

Stanley Mutual Improvement Society: 133

Stanley Provision Company: 107

Stanley Savings Bank: 126

Stanley House: 11, 13, 79, 97, 99, 107, 109, 111–112

Stanley Mills (Scotland) Ltd.: 119, 137

Statistical Accounts (Old): 12, 21, 25, 50

Stevenson, Alex, resident partner, Stanley Mills: 99, 101

Stewart, James, (born 1797) yarn dresser, Stanley Mills: 124

Stobie, James, of Marlehall, Perthshire (died 1804) surveyor & factor to Duke of Atholl: 13, 45, 49–50, 55, 61, 70–73, 77–78

Stormontfield, Perthshire, bleachfield: 72, 87

Stott, Bert, Stanley mill manager and owner: 119

Strikes:

Glasgow Cotton Spinners' Strike, 1837: 30, 38

Jute and Flax Workers' Strike, Dundee, 1923: 128

Perthshire bleachfield Strike, 1920: 128

Stanley Strike, 1919: 128

Tay, River: 11, 19, 39, 48–49, 55, 62–63, 71–72, 78, 87, 92, 101, 105, 112–113, 116, 133, 135, 138

Tayside Hostel, Stanley: 118, 128–129

Thistle Bridge, rock formation on River Tay: 62

Thorkelin, George, Icelandic antiquary: 58, 121
Tobacco trade, Glasgow: 22, 26
Turnpike roads: 13

United Scotsmen, Perth: 30, 69–70
Unwin, George, historian: 135

Victoria, Queen: 104

Wages:
    Agricultural labourers: 19–20
    Cotton spinners: 20, 35–38, 42, 46, 128
    Cotton weavers: 35–38, 42, 46, 86, 92–93, 128
    Flax spinners: : 42
    Linen weavers: : 35
Water frames: : 28, 57, 79, 84
Watson, Mary, wife of Samuel Howard, mill owner: 107, 109
Watt, Robert, spy: 69
Weem, parish, Perthshire: : 15
Whatley, Christopher, historian: 25–26, 29, 61, 104, 108
Whitecroft Ltd., bleachers: 105
Woodside Mills, Aberdeen: 31, 35: :
World War, First: 114–116, 127–129, 135
World War, Second: 118, 128–129, 134–135
Wright, John, bookkeeper, Lanark Twist Company: 75–76, 79, 81, 83, 88, 91